Contents

Vive la Résistance! 1

What You'll Need 5

Getting Started.................................... 7

The Basics of Play 9

Advice for Players 13

The Spark That Lights a Fire 17

Creating Your Character 18

Build la Résistance.............................. 26

Build the Government............................. 29

Fragments.................................33

AR and VR: A Crash Course...................... 51

The Fall 52

The World Beyond the Walls 55

Important Laws of Paris Nouveau 58

Strange Bedfellows..................59

La Société 60

The Cleaner...................................... 62

The Blueblood 64

The Officer...................................... 66

Les Citoyens 68

The Hacker...................................... 70

The Soldier...................................... 72

The Malcontent.................................. 74

Les Exilés....................................... 76

The Ex-Cit 80

The Naturel 82

The Armiger 84

Who You Are............................87

Aspects 88

Secrets: That Which Motivates 95

Before the Storm.................... 105

Prep Advantages 106

Equipment 108

Favors: The New Currency................... 109

In the Thick of It 119

Conflicts.. 121

Taking Your Turn 123

The Four Means 128

The Four Ends 131

Narrating Actions.............................. 133

Zones... 139

Boosts 141

Marking Conditions 142

Taking People Out.............................. 146

Death, Sacrifice, and Betrayal 147

At Mission's End.................... 149

Step 1: PC Advancement 150

Step 2: Resistance Advancement...... 151

Step 3: Government Advancement ... 151

Step 4: Accusations........................... 151

Augmentations 153

Contacts.. 158

Resistance Advances 159

Government Advances 161

Your Corporate Sponsor: A Citizen's Guide 165

Corvid Economics 168

Cryptiq, Inc. 170

InfoSec-West 170

LaFleur Digital Media 172

Paragon Gyromantics 172

Quesada Méchaniques Élite 173

Rathburn Chemical Laboratories 174

Sun Systems Biotech 174

Verdi Transportation 175

Black Bags and Jackboots 177

The Budget & the Bank 178

Blowback 180

Making and Playing NPCs 184

Acting and Opposing with NPCs 189

Bringing Missions to Life 189

Making Your Own Missions 194

Advice for GMs 195

We Shall Die with Our Arms Unbound 199

Warehouse Raid 202

Convoy Ambush 207

Corporate Espionage 210

Corporate Retaliation 216

Missing Supplies 220

Peace Offering 229

Mercy 234

Recruitment Drive 239

White Hats, Black Market 243

Black Bag 246

Raid 250

Demonstration 253

The Friend 257

Rendition 260

The Paymaster 264

The Revolution (Endgame Mission) .. 267

The Purge (Endgame Mission) 272

Appendices 276

French Terms 277

Character Sheets 278

Government Advancement Sheet 296

La Résistance Advancement Sheet .. 298

Secret Cards 300

Index 303

1 Vive la Résistance!

An Introduction to *Uprising*

Welcome to *Uprising: The Dystopian Universe Roleplaying Game*! This roleplaying game is based on the hit games *The Resistance, Coup,* and *One Night Revolution* from Indie Boards & Cards. It's a game of cunning spies and government agents, of loyalty and betrayal, of propaganda and unrest and violent revolution. To start, here are six things you should know about *Uprising*.

This Is a Cooperative Game

You and your fellow players are agents of la Résistance, an underground group of revolutionaries trying to overthrow an oppressive regime ruled by corporate oligarchs in Paris Nouveau. You cooperate during missions, each player deciding actions for their own player character (PC), their avatar within the game. One player, the game master (GM), plays your opposition—spies, agents of the government, soldiers, gendarmes—and also plays all of the supporting and incidental characters in the game. Although the GM provides opposition, they're not your opponent; in a roleplaying game, everybody's job is to create a compelling story together and to ensure that everyone else at the table has a good time.

This Is a Game of Betrayal

This game is designed to push the story toward betrayal, intrigue, and mistrust, and your fellow Resistance agents—other players at the table—will betray you from time to time. Sometimes you'll be able to reconcile this betrayal, move past it, and rebuild trust. Sometimes the betrayal will end in someone's death or defection. Even so, remember that your job is to make sure that everyone else has a good time, and that you're all cooperating to tell the same story. In short: don't take betrayal personally. However, if betrayal isn't your thing, this might not be the game for you; it's not an optional part of the experience, and while you could remove it from the game, doing so would fundamentally change the kinds of stories the game produces, and it might not be as fun.

You Tell Stories in This Game

As I've alluded to already, you're cooperating with your fellow players—the GM included—to tell a story. Players do this by describing what their characters do, reacting to the world around them, and trying to portray their characters with sincerity in a way that feels real. The GM describes setting elements, speaks for supporting characters and nameless characters alike, and ensures that the PCs are always under some sort of pressure.

Vive la Résistance!

You Roll Dice in This Game

When you tell the GM you want to do something, they'll either allow it to happen or tell you to roll the dice, though the rare action will be flatly impossible, like trying to walk up the side of a building. The dice will show whether or not you're successful, but you'll have ways to manipulate the dice rolls too. More on all this later.

Your Character Might Die

You have a lot of control over whether your character lives or dies, but they might die. If that happens, don't panic! Paris Nouveau is a violent, dangerous place, and people die and are disappeared all the time. Making a new character doesn't take long, and you'll be back in the action in no time. Just try to make your death mean something.

Have Fun

This is a game, and you'll play it with friends. There will be tension, mistrust, and betrayal, but remember that you're all doing this to have a good time. Don't be afraid to take breaks if things are getting too tense, and remember that you care about the people around the table and want them all to have a good time. Respect their boundaries, don't be a jerk, and you'll all have fun.

And, as always, be wary of gendarmes.

Brian Engard

Creative Director, *Uprising: The Dystopian Universe RPG*

I. BIENVENUE À PARIS NOUVEAU

Welcome, Citoyen, to your new life in Paris Nouveau. Though you have lived here all your life, you now have access to important services to improve your daily experience. Please read this handbook in its entirety and indicate your acceptance with the fingerprint scanner. Being a Citoyen is a great responsibility, one you have earned, and this orientation module will enlighten you to all the changes in your life.

God, I think we finally got through. We've been trying to hack the orientation module for weeks and it looks like you're seeing us now. **If so, nod your head...**

...are you surprised we can monitor that? You shouldn't be. Your government monitors it. The corporations here monitor it. They know when you eat, when you make love, when you piss. All tabulated in the metadata. But wait, I'm getting ahead of myself. It's rude not to introduce yourself to a new friend. I hope we'll be friends, oui?

Not friends in the sense of going out for a beer together. I mean, one day, knowing me might help you survive.

...I see from your elevated heart rate you're concerned about getting in trouble. Don't worry—we override the government's feed. They can't see us...yet. But sit down and read on. Don't believe everything you read; I will tell you the real story of Paris Nouveau.

And then you can decide.

What You'll Need

To play this game, you'll need to gather together some people and things.

- » **Three to five friends.** *Uprising* works best with three to five players and a GM.

- » **At least one copy of this book,** whether physical or PDF.

- » **One copy of each playsheet,** found starting on *page 279*.

- » **Printed copies of all the secret cards,** found starting on *page 300*.

- » **Pencils,** one for each player plus the GM.

- » **Index cards,** scraps of paper, post-it notes, or other small things to write on.

- » **Tokens for fate points.** You'll want about 5 per player plus the GM.

- » **Tokens for blowback.** About 8 to 10 per player is good.

- » **A few sets of Fate Dice™,** which are special six-sided dice with plus 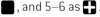, minus ⬛, and blank ⬛ faces.

You can pick up some Fate Dice™ at the Evil Hat webstore (evilhat.com/store), at your favorite local game store, or elsewhere online. If you don't have Fate Dice™, you can use regular six-siders in a pinch—just treat 1–2 as ⬛, 3–4 as ⬛, and 5–6 as ⬛.

Differences from *Fate Core*

If this is your first Fate game, don't worry about reading the following list of changes; it'll all be new to you. If you *have* played Fate games before, here's a helpful primer on how *Uprising* differs from *Fate Core*.

» *Uprising* doesn't use skills or approaches; instead, it uses four **means**. When you roll for an action, you'll add your means rating, like you would add a skill rating. The process is familiar, though *Uprising* introduces the concept of **risky** and **suited** means.

» *Uprising* doesn't use the standard four actions; instead, it uses four **ends**, which are similar, but differ in some key ways.

» Invoking and compelling aspects work the same, but pay attention to the changes to boosts; they're important to the *Uprising* fate point economy.

» Stress doesn't exist in *Uprising*. Instead, characters have **conditions**, which work like predefined consequences, but also have mechanical effects of their own.

» *Uprising* focuses on conflicts, and doesn't include rules for contests or challenges. Conflicts will be familiar, though there are some changes to how turn order and zones work.

» There are two new kinds of scenes in *Uprising*: **prep scenes** and **debriefs**. Play is organized into **missions**, with a prep scene and a debrief bracketing the action.

» Characters advance by accumulating **advancement points**, which they get by taking character-specific actions that can sometimes put them at odds with the group. Milestones still exist, but only when a PC dies or becomes an NPC.

Getting Started

Once you have everything you need, you'll want to get everyone together for the first time. During this session, the players will create their characters using the playsheets, get their secrets, and collaborate to create la Résistance and the government. This process is pretty quick, so you'll also probably get to play a mission or two before the session is over.

GM, you'll start each session off by picking a **mission** to play (*page 199*). You can collaborate with the players or simply let them pick what they want to do next, if you wish. Once you've picked a mission, the players get to have a **prep scene** (*page 106*), where they'll prepare for the coming mission and stack things in their favor as much as they can.

After finishing the prep scene, run the mission. GM, during the mission, you'll play the government and its operatives, any bystanders the PCs run into, allies, neutral parties, security systems, and so forth. Portray them with panache and sincerity, be a fan of the players, and don't be afraid to let characters die off.

Players, your job is to portray your own character with as much authenticity as you can muster. Play boldly! Don't be afraid to put your character in harm's way for the sake of their cause. The GM will present you with various obstacles, enemies, and problems to deal with, and you'll have to figure out how your character deals with them, how much they rely on their allies, and how much they trust (or mistrust) them.

Once the mission is over, run a **debrief scene** (*page 150*). During the debrief, the players get a chance to improve their characters, make accusations against one another, and recover from harm they've suffered over the course of the mission. GM, you get a chance to make the government stronger.

In most sessions, you'll run through one, two, or maybe even three missions. As the campaign progresses, la Résistance and the government will grow stronger until eventually one of them triggers the **endgame mission** (*page 201*). During the endgame mission, the group gets to find out if la Résistance overthrows the government once and for all, or if the government crushes them into the forgotten recesses of history.

SHADOWED

Marya: CLARE

Clare: Marya, don't type in capital letters. Makes it sound like an emergency

At Pere with the delivery

How many guns?

3 rifles, 8 handguns, 1 RPG. Good chunk of ammo

Need more

They're really clamping down on Le Chat Noir - gendarmes on the way in and out

Dammit. Arielle and Sidenge with you?

Arielle left - think she's got a boyfriend. Always heading out to 3rd arrondissement

She's selling us out

No Clare just she's young, you know? Not much happiness in this shithole. Let her have hers

Love is not for revolutionaries

I know you weren't always this jaded Clare - give the girl a break

I'll talk to her

The Basics of Play

Players, when you create your character, you'll choose and fill out a **playsheet** (*page 279*) from nine options, and during play you'll often refer to it. In this section, we'll walk through an extended example of play with Illyana, a Malcontent, to show how the various parts of the playsheet work during a session.

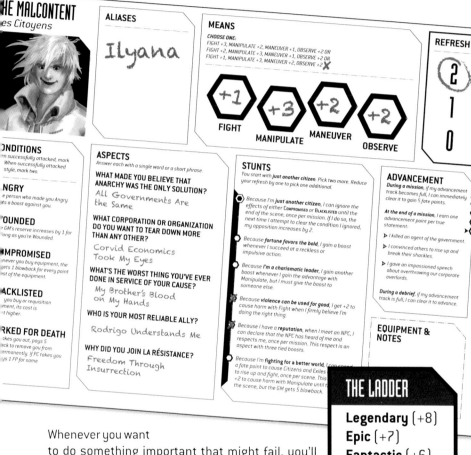

HE MALCONTENT
es Citoyens

ALIASES

Ilyana

MEANS

CHOOSE ONE:
FIGHT +3, MANIPULATE +2, MANEUVER +1, OBSERVE +2 OR
FIGHT +2, MANIPULATE +3, MANEUVER +1, OBSERVE +2 OR
FIGHT +1, MANIPULATE +3, MANEUVER +2, OBSERVE +2 ✗

+1 FIGHT
+3 MANIPULATE
+2 MANEUVER
+2 OBSERVE

REFRESH
2
1
0

ONDITIONS
en successfully attacked, mark
When successfully attacked
style, mark two.

NGRY
e person who made you Angry
s a boost against you.

OUNDED
GM's reserve increases by 1 for
ong as you're Wounded.

MPROMISED
never you buy equipment, the
ets 1 blowback for every point
st of the equipment.

ACKLISTED
you buy or requisition
ment, its cost is
t higher.

RKED FOR DEATH
akes you out, pays 5
ck to remove its mark
ermanently. If PC takes you
s 1 FP for same

ASPECTS
Answer each with a single word or a short phrase.

WHAT MADE YOU BELIEVE THAT
ANARCHY WAS THE ONLY SOLUTION?
All Governments Are
the Same

WHAT CORPORATION OR ORGANIZATION
DO YOU WANT TO TEAR DOWN MORE
THAN ANY OTHER?
Corvid Economics
Took My Eyes

WHAT'S THE WORST THING YOU'VE EVER
DONE IN SERVICE OF YOUR CAUSE?
My Brother's Blood
on My Hands

WHO IS YOUR MOST RELIABLE ALLY?
Rodrigo Understands Me

WHY DID YOU JOIN LA RÉSISTANCE?
Freedom Through
Insurrection

STUNTS
You start with *just another citizen.* Pick two more. Reduce
your refresh by one to pick one additional.

Because I'm *just another citizen,* I can ignore the
effects of either COMPROMISED or BLACKLISTED until the
end of the scene, once per mission. If I do so, the
next time I attempt to clear the condition I ignored,
my opposition increases by 2.

Because *fortune favors the bold,* I gain a boost
whenever I succeed at a reckless or
impulsive action.

Because I'm *a charismatic leader,* I gain another
boost whenever I gain the advantage with
Manipulate, but I must give the boost to
someone else.

Because *violence can be used for good,* I get +2 to
cause harm with Fight when I firmly believe I'm
doing the right thing.

Because I have a *reputation,* when I meet an NPC, I
can declare that the NPC has heard of me and
respects me, once per mission. This respect is an
aspect with three tied boosts.

Because I'm *fighting for a better world,* I can spend
a fate point to cause Citizens and Exiles
to rise up and fight, once per scene. This
+2 to cause harm with Manipulate until t
the scene, but the GM gets 5 blowback.

ADVANCEMENT
During a mission, if my advancement
track becomes full, I can immediately
clear it to gain 5 fate points.

At the end of a mission, I earn one
advancement point per true
statement:

▶ I killed an agent of the government.

▶ I convinced others to rise up and
break their shackles.

▶ I gave an impassioned speech
about overthrowing our corporate
overlords.

During a debrief, if my advancement
track is full, I can clear it to advance.

**EQUIPMENT &
NOTES**

Whenever you want to do something important that might fail, you'll start by choosing one of your four **means** (*page 128*)—Fight, Manipulate, Maneuver, and Observe—to show how you try to accomplish your goal. Then you'll roll four fate dice.

Fate dice have three faces: ⊞ (read as +1), ⊟ (read as -1), and ■ (read as 0). Add up all the plusses, subtract all the minuses, and add the roll to your means rating to get your **effort**.

THE LADDER

Legendary (+8)
Epic (+7)
Fantastic (+6)
Superb (+5)
Great (+4)
Good (+3)
Fair (+2)
Average (+1)
Mediocre (+0)
Poor (-1)
Terrible (-2)

Vive la Résistance!

Your effort will fall somewhere on **the ladder**. Each rung of the ladder has a one-word name. These names don't affect gameplay, but they can give you an idea of how good your roll is.

Once you get your effort, you'll interpret your result by comparing your effort to the **opposition**, which is a number set or rolled, often by the GM. If your effort is higher than the opposition, you get what you want. If it's equal or lower, you don't get what you want, and something else will go awry.

> Illyana wants to shoot the gendarme, so she rolls Fight. She rolls four dice and gets ⊞⊞⊟☐ for a total of +1. She adds her roll to her Fight rating shown on her playsheet. Her Fight rating is Average (+1), so her effort is Fair (+2). Emily, the GM, rolls for the gendarme and gets an opposition of Fair (+2), so Illyana's shot misses. Unless…

Your playsheet also shows many **aspects** (*page 88*). Aspects are short, descriptive phrases that convey elements of your character. Before or after your roll, you can spend a **fate point** to **invoke** one of your aspects, which adds +2 to your roll or lets you reroll your dice. To invoke an aspect, though, you must narrate how the aspect helps you in the current situation.

> Illyana decides it's important that she take this gendarme out quickly, so she invokes an aspect. She has the aspect RODRIGO UNDERSTANDS ME, so she explains to the GM that Rodrigo, knowing that Illyana will need every edge she can get, distracts the gendarme at just the right moment. Illyana spends a fate point to invoke the aspect and chooses to add +2 to her effort, bringing it up to Great (+4). She hits the gendarme, but doesn't kill him—to do that, she'll need to succeed with style, meaning her effort is three steps higher than the opposition.

You also have a few **stunts** (*page 24*), bonuses or abilities that you can call upon in certain situations. Some stunts will require you to spend a fate point to use, others may have a limited number of uses per mission, while still others will only be useful in very specific circumstances.

> Illyana really wants this gendarme dead. Because the gendarme is standing between her and bringing medicine to the many people who need it, she explains to the GM that she believes killing the gendarme is the right thing to do in this situation. Because she's rolling Fight to cause harm, her stunt **violence can be used for good** grants her +2 to the roll, bringing her effort up to Fantastic (+6). This is enough to kill the gendarme outright.

When you take harm, you have a choice: get **taken out** of the scene (**page 146**), or mark a **condition** on your playsheet to remain in the scene (**page 142**). Marking a condition makes it an aspect on your character, and usually makes you suffer some consequence or gives your enemy an advantage.

> Another gendarme arrives on the scene and opens fire on Illyana. She rolls poorly to avoid the gunfire, and she has no fate points left to invoke aspects, so she takes harm.
>
> Illyana describes the shot grazing her shoulder; she rounds on the gendarme, fire in her eyes, but it clouds her judgment. Illyana marks her condition ANGRY. Because she marked ANGRY, the gendarme gains a boost, a resource that he can spend against her on his next turn. Thankfully, she'll be able to clear ANGRY relatively quickly—all it takes is some time to cool down.

Your playsheet also shows your **refresh**: the number of fate points you will start each session with. You can also earn fate points during play by accepting **compels** on your aspects, situations where your aspects make your life harder.

Finally, your playsheet has an **advancement track** and some ways to fill it by earning **advancement points**. If you fill your advancement track, you can clear it during your mission to get 5 fate points, or you can wait until the end of the mission and clear it to **advance**. Beyond your playsheet, you'll also have a secret, which provides you more ways to earn advancement points or an immediate advance.

Illyana's player, Amanda, looks at her playsheet and notices that she gets 1 advancement point when she kills a government agent. She asks the GM if killing the gendarme earlier counts for this, and the GM agrees that it does. Amanda marks an advancement point. This fills up her advancement track! Amanda has no fate points left, so she decides to clear her advancement track, giving her 5 fate points.

Where'd you go, girl?

Hey Sidenge, went for a walk

A walk? In this pissing rain? Marya's gonna stir it up

Cover for me, yah?

Did last week, when you disappeared

I owe you one

You owe me bunch

You know that sweet shinguard I salvaged last week? Boosts your top speed by, like, 3x

Can't keep doing this

It's yours if you tell Marya you sent me on a Resistance errand

Not lyin for you anymore Arielle

I'm not doing anything wrong

Fine, tell Clare all about it

Can't

What I thought

You know Clare, so bleeding single-minded. Tired of all these rules. What good is a resistance when you can't do anything you need to do?

I know you're Naturel, but these rules keep us safe - one misstep and the government descends

That's what Clare says, but I'm better at hiding than she thinks. Been hiding my whole life, gonna do what I need to do now

Clare's not going to like this treason-talk

Clare's not a government, can't be treason. And she doesn't own me - I'm my own person. I'll help, but not gonna hop when she says /Sautez!/

Arielle come meet me, let's talk

Can't

[User has disconnected]

Advice for Players

Players, your job is to portray your character in a way that seems real and convincing, as well as to entertain the other players at the table and the GM. To that end, here's some advice.

Respectful Play

Your first, and most important, rule is that the people at your table are more important than the game. **Uprising** is a game about betrayal, intrigue, injustice, violent revolution, interrogation, and other themes that can veer into uncomfortable territory. Discuss all of this at the beginning of the first session, and let everyone know what you don't want to see in the game. Respect their choices about what they don't want to see in the game, and trust them to respect yours.

That said, sometimes people get carried away unintentionally. If anyone, for any reason, feels uncomfortable with something happening in the game, that person can say "brake." When someone says "brake," it's everyone else's responsibility to skip past the uncomfortable scene and move on to something else. There is no judgment or pressure involved with this; it's everyone's job to respect everyone else's boundaries.

Play Hard

Go for what you want. Take risks. Make the interesting choice. Put your character in harm's way. **Uprising** works best when people have unclear motives, when they act in ways that create doubt, and when they do big, dramatic things.

Seize on opportunities that the GM gives you, and squeeze them for all they're worth. You want the other players grinning in anticipation about what you're going to do. That said, don't be selfish. Hand other players opportunities whenever you can. Let them have the spotlight, and help them shine. Even if your characters are at odds with each other, the actual people at the table are your allies and collaborators, and you're all trying to make the best game you can.

Don't Get Too Attached

Characters in this game are easy come, easy go, and sometimes sacrificing yourself in a big, spectacular way is a lot of fun. A dramatic death or capture is the stuff of stories that people tell after the game. Making a new character is quick, so losing a character only means that you're out of the action for a brief period. Playing a variety of different characters can be a lot of fun, and remember that when your character is removed from play, you get a benefit to carry forward into your next character.

Remember that you can always opt for a glorious death (*page 147*). Doing so gives you a big, dramatic spotlight moment, and can provide a lot of vital aid (or well-timed betrayal) to the other PCs.

That said, don't treat your characters as entirely disposable. Each character has an arc, a personality, goals, and motives of their own. Your character's death is entirely within your hands. The GM does not get to kill you without your permission. If you've marked the MARKED FOR DEATH condition, you've indicated that it's okay for your character to die. If you haven't, the GM can't kill you unless you choose to die. Hanging on to a character for a long time is a valid way to play the game, and has its own rewards. Conversely, playing a character hard, burning through them, and moving on to the next one can be fun too.

Collaborate

Don't get too wrapped up in what your character would do. Real people act out-of-character all the time, and your character in the game is no different. Don't do something "because it's what your character would do" if that action would make the game less fun for everyone else. Instead, look for ways to help build an interesting story and a fun play experience for everyone.

Help Your Allies Right Up Until You Betray Them

As a member of la Résistance, your job is to work as part of a team and ensure the team's success. As a person who lives in Paris Nouveau, your own motives might run counter to the team's. Betrayal is an expectation in *Uprising*, but it shouldn't become predictable. Just because your friend's last character betrayed the group doesn't mean their next one will, and that applies to everyone at the table.

In this game, you must rely upon each other, but trust is often folly. Remember that.

Ma chère E,

Meet me under the P.N. at 23h00. I know you'd rather meet virtually, but there are some things too dangerous to even type. Use Protocol 37, to ensure no one follows you. I'll be wearing the single white blouse I have left, the one my mother made me. Know that it will be dangerous. I'm turning off portable tech so the Resistance can't track me. C_ and M_ suspect us and even S_ won't help me anymore. May be time to move on. I thought la Résistance was the way and now_please come.

Toujours,

- A

2 The Spark That Lights a Fire

Creating Your Game

Before you start playing Uprising, you'll need to prepare a few things.

It can be helpful to take some time to prepare together. Some groups like to devote an entire session to this process, while others will get through it quickly and move on to playing the game; either approach is fine.

Preparing for a game of **Uprising** starts with the player characters. Each player except the GM will create a character by choosing one of the nine **playsheets** and using it to flesh out the details of their characters. Feel free to brainstorm and play off each other's ideas during this process, and if you're ever stuck for ideas, ask the GM and your other friends. Come up with cool relationships and conflicts between your characters.

You'll also take some time setting up **the Resistance (*page 26*)**. This is a communal process, involving everyone at the table, and it can help you get a sense for what the game world is like. There's plenty of setting information in this book to use for inspiration, but this is *your* game so, ultimately, what your group decides to run with is canon.

Finally, you'll go through a similar process for **the government (*page 29*)**, fleshing out what your enemy looks like. The GM has final say as far as choices for the government go, but a clever GM will listen to what her players suggest, incorporating those suggestions in ways that will help the players be more invested in the setting.

Once you're done with those three steps, you're ready to get started.

Creating Your Character

Paris Nouveau, the near-future setting of **Uprising: The Dystopian Universe RPG**, is a rigidly stratified city. Given this, you'll begin creating your character by choosing a **social class**.

Social class describes how you're perceived in Paris Nouveau, what privileges you have in society, what your responsibilities are, and who you answer to. It defines what you're allowed to do, who you're allowed to talk to, and where you're allowed to go. Are you one of the haves or the have-nots?

In *Uprising*, there are three broad social classes: la Société, les Citoyens, and les Exilés:

» **La Société** are the upper echelons of society. They are the ones who make the decisions and they receive the lion's share of the wealth, status, and privilege in Paris Nouveau.

» Below them are the **les Citoyens**, Citizens. The vast majority of officially recognized society in Paris Nouveau falls into this social class. Citizens have some rights and protections under the law, but they're often exploited and rarely appreciated. They are also under the most direct scrutiny by government and corporate surveillance.

» Not even an officially recognized social caste, **les Exilés** live outside of polite society. Many of them are in la Résistance, and even those who aren't are considered criminals and undesirables by those in charge.

One thing to note: no matter which social class you choose, you are a member of la Résistance. Think about why you joined.

Your social class determines a few things about your character:

» Your set of five **conditions**, which you can mark when you take harm in order to stay in the fight.

» Your unique **stunt**, a special ability that you can use in particular circumstances.

» Your set of three **playsheets**, which represent various character archetypes. You will choose one of these three playsheets later.

Lucy, John, and Mike are playing, with Emily as the GM. Lucy decides she wants to play Luce, a hard-boiled Exile whose specialty is scrounging up weapons and tech. John is playing Berne, a member of la Société who's feeling a lot of class guilt and has decided to join la Résistance. Mike creates Elayna, a Citoyen who is the best wearable-tech hacker in la Résistance.

Because she's an Exile, Luce gets the conditions ANGRY, WOUNDED, PERSON OF INTEREST, BLACKLISTED, and MARKED FOR DEATH, as well as the **friend of the resistance** stunt.

Because he's a member of la Société, Berne gets COMPROMISED and DEPLETED instead of PERSON OF INTEREST and BLACKLISTED, and he gets the stunt **great wealth**.

Choose Your Playsheet

Your social class gives you the option of three playsheets. Each playsheet has unique abilities, and their strengths and weaknesses differ significantly.

Choose one playsheet from your three options, and fill it out as you follow the remaining steps in this chapter. During play, you'll use your playsheet as a reference.

La Société

The Cleaner is a ranking member of the secret police, a government assassin and problem-solver. She excels at killing, subterfuge, and information-gathering.

The Blueblood is a corporate noble. He uses money, influence, and fame to get what he wants.

The Officer is a leader of soldiers, a high-ranking member of a military or para-military organization. She uses her combat training, security clearance, and subordinates to achieve her objectives.

Les Citoyens

The Hacker has learned to manipulate her neural augmentations. She can affect her perceptions and the perceptions of others, and can control machinery around her. Her very existence is illegal.

The Soldier is a rank-and-file member of a military or paramilitary organization. He has combat training, as well as physical and psychological conditioning that makes him a better killer.

The Malcontent is a rabble-rouser, an activist, and sometimes a terrorist. He uses passion, words, violence, and whatever other tools are at his disposal to wake the citizenry from their slumber.

Les Exilés

The Ex-Cit was once a Citizen, but her augmentations have been deactivated, either by choice or by force. She's used to adversity; her stolid determination is her greatest asset.

The Natural has never been part of Paris Nouveau society, and has never had augmentations. Part of a tight-knit community of other Naturels, he's learned to move unseen and to rely on his family and friends.

The Armiger is a living protest. She's replaced much of her body with big, obvious, gauche cyberware. She's an engine of destruction, but more importantly, she's a visual rebellion against everything Paris Nouveau society stands for.

Emily tells her players to choose their playsheets. For Mike and John, this is pretty obvious. Mike's character Elayna is a hacker, so the Hacker is a great fit, and John is playing a member of la Société, so he chooses the Blueblood. Lucy hesitates on what works best for Luce, but settles on the Ex-Cit, which gives her some strong ideas for her background.

On French Terms

You may have noticed some French terms already. If you don't speak French or know how to pronounce these words, don't worry! The truth is, most people in Paris Nouveau don't either; the French language died off decades ago, and most everyone in Paris Nouveau speaks English. They pepper their speech and writing with French words, but many don't spell or pronounce them correctly, or even use them correctly. Even the city's name—Paris Nouveau—is not proper French.

Members of la Résistance *do* use French, mostly as a code language. Because many Citizens don't speak the language, Resistance agents can communicate in it relatively safely, though they still must take care not to draw too much attention by speaking in a non-English language. If you want help pronouncing some of these words, there's a pronunciation guide on **page 276**.

Write Your Aspects

How do you make the world of Paris Nouveau breathe for your character and group? **Aspects**. An aspect is a descriptive word or short phrase that tells us something about who your character is, what they're good at, and why they do what they do. It can also give insight into how your character relates to the world and people around her.

Your character gets a total of seven aspects. You'll make five of these aspects by answering the questions on your playsheet in a concise, impactful way. Each playsheet has four unique questions, but the fifth question is always the same: *Why did you join la Résistance?* Your sixth aspect is your social class, and your seventh is your playsheet's name; you don't have to write down either of these—they're already on your playsheet.

> Lucy is working on Luce's aspects. Her playsheet lists five questions, and she has two left to answer.
>
> **Why were you stripped of your citizenship?**
>
> Lucy decides that Luce was the first member of her family to receive citizenship. Her family was comprised of Naturels—people with no augmentations, living outside the Wall—who were extremely proud of her achievement. Unfortunately, Luce's brother joined la Résistance and was killed. Knowing that the augmentations would allow her to be tracked by the government, Luce chose the painful path of deactivating her augmentations and joined la Résistance in her brother's memory. She writes the aspect IN MY BROTHER'S FOOTSTEPS.
>
> **Who were you in your old life?**
>
> Before she became a Citizen, Luce was a Naturel. She was a hunter in that life, but became a Citizen after something important happened; she'll figure out what that was during play. As a Citizen, Luce was a spy for a corporation. She writes the aspect EX-HUNTER, EX-SPY.

If you need to, you can just answer the first two questions on your playsheet and start playing. Once you've got a sense for who you want to play and how you want to relate to other characters, you can start answering the other questions to get the rest of your aspects.

Similarly, if after a session or two you find that one of your aspects just isn't getting used, talk to the GM about changing it. As long as doing so doesn't cause any problems in the narrative or break anyone's enjoyment of the game, changing your aspects is fine.

If you'd like more tips on writing aspects and details on using them, read *"Aspects"* (**page 88**).

Pick Your Secret

At this point, you'll pick a **secret**. Your secret is a piece of information that's true, but nobody at the table knows it but you and the GM, and it will motivate your character throughout their career. Each secret has some questions for you to think about, a couple ways to earn advancement points, and a way to reveal your secret dramatically for an immediate advance.

GM, lay all of the secret cards (**pages 300–302**) except the five Spy cards out on the table. One by one, each player chooses one secret to add to the secret deck. Once each player has done so, add a number of random *Spy* cards to the deck based on the number of players, not counting the GM:

- » **3 players:** 1 Spy card
- » **4 players:** 1 Spy card
- » **5 players:** 2 Spy cards
- » **6 players:** 2 Spy cards
- » **7–8 players:** 3 Spy cards

After adding Spy cards, shuffle the deck, and choose, as a group, a player to draw first. Each player, one by one, draws two secret cards, chooses one, and puts the other secret anywhere they like in the deck, even at the top or bottom, taking care not to look at the other cards in the deck. Keep all of these cards secret.

When the players are done choosing their secrets, shuffle all remaining secrets, including all Spy cards and unused secret cards, into the secret deck. GM, take a look at each player's secret so you can plan accordingly.

If you'd like more details on secrets, read *"Secrets: That Which Motivates"* (**page 95**).

Choose Your Means Spread

Whenever your character does something important that might fail, you will choose one of your **means** to show how you get what you want. There are four means:

- » **Fight** is your means for direct confrontation and physical violence.
- » **Manipulate** is your means for subtlety, misdirection, charm, coercion, and deceit.
- » **Maneuver** is your means for mobility, stealth, acrobatics, and social positioning.
- » **Observe** is your means for noticing things and making deductions.

Choose one means spread from the three spreads on your playsheet. Each means has a **rating**, which is how good your character is at using those means.

For all the details on how means work in play, read *"Rolling for Action"* (**page 123**).

> Lucy looks at the three options for the Ex-Cit. One favors violence, one mobility, and the third subtle deceit. Luce seems like the rough-and-ready type, so violence is a good option, but she's also had a lot of training and experience in sneaking around, working as a spy, and so forth. After careful consideration, Lucy chooses the third option, which gives her Average (+1) Fight, Good (+3) Manipulate, Fair (+2) Maneuver, and Fair (+2) Observe.

Choose Your Stunts

Stunts are abilities that bend or break the rules in small ways. Some give you a bonus in a specific situation, while others allow you to do something you otherwise wouldn't be able to do.

Your playsheet lists five stunts unique to it. Pick two of these. If you want a third stunt, you can take it by reducing your **refresh** from 2 to 1. In addition, you always get the unique stunt provided by your social class.

Refresh

Refresh is the number of fate points you'll start each session with. No matter how many fate points you have at the end of the session, you'll always start the next session with a number of fate points equal to your refresh. Use them or lose them.

You can't reduce your refresh below 1, though some things during play can.

As you advance, you may pick up more stunts from your playsheet. While you cannot take stunts from other playsheets, you can incorporate elements of other playsheets into your character by getting augmentations and contacts. You'll find more information on advancement in *"At Mission's End"* (**page 150**).

Most stunts don't cost anything to use; as long as you meet a stunt's requirements, you get its benefit. Some stunts, however, do carry a cost. Most of the time the cost is a fate point. Some stunts may require you to mark conditions or hand the GM blowback, a resource she can spend to make your life harder. Rather than a cost, you might be limited in how many times you can use the stunt per mission. If a stunt has a cost or limitation, it'll be described in the stunt itself.

Sidenge this is Clare.

hi

You've always been one of our top people, Sidenge. Your built-in armaments and tech make you simply invaluable. And because I value you, I'm going directly to you to straighten this out about Arielle.

I don't know where she is

Sidenge I know you're old friends and your loyalty is commendable, but this is a matter of Resistance security. If Arielle has gone rogue, I need to know as soon as possible to minimize damage.

Arielle's not like that

I know you don't want to believe it. Nobody wants to believe their friends can turn on them. But believe me it happens. And it's not even necessarily that Arielle's a bad person. But I know she's not had the commitment to our mission like you. We need people like you, people I can count on. If she brings the gendarmes, a lot of good Resistance people could die. We could suffer grave setbacks. Arielle knew a lot about our organization, our secrets, our stashes.

Arielle's not like that. Swear

Sidenge, I need you to face reality. She's been gone fourteen hours. She's not coming back. Even if she simply got captured, she could crush everything we've worked for simply by being unable to resist interrogation.

I've known her since she's ten, she hates the government. They've treated her family like garbage, all Naturels like they're expendable. I'd stake my life on her

You may have to.

Build la Résistance

Once all the players have finished their playsheets, it's time to fill out a play-sheet for la Résistance itself. Players, you'll fill out this playsheet together. At any time during play, anyone at the table can look at this playsheet.

First, decide on la Résistance's **manifesto**. This is la Résistance's stated goal, what it's trying to do for Paris Nouveau.

Next, decide on la Résistance's **weakness**. This is the one thing that most plagues the Resistance, the thing that most often gets in its way.

La Résistance's manifesto and weakness are both setting aspects, which exist during all scenes.

Put 3 fate points in la Résistance's **Cache**.

What does the Cache do?

Players, you'll be able to spend fate points from the Cache, as if they were your own, during prep scenes (*page 106*) and during scenes that take place in la Cave or another Resistance-friendly location.

Finally, give la Résistance two **advances**. You can choose advances from any of its three advancement trees: Intel, Resources, or Support. However, you can only choose an advance if it is at the top of its tree, or if la Résistance has taken another advance that connects to it. Work together to choose these advances, resolving disagreements with table consensus.

The descriptions of la Résistance's advances start on *page 159*.

Manifesto: LIBERATION. EQUALITY. FREEDOM.

Weakness: BRANDED AS TERRORISTS

Starting Advances: Hijacked Shipments, Hearts and Minds

Table Consensus

"Table consensus" is a fancy way of saying "make sure everybody at the table agrees." If everyone at the table agrees that something should happen, you have table consensus and it should just happen. If there are dissenting opinions, talk it out or go to the dice to resolve the issue. Means rolls are a fine way to resolve some issues, including determining who goes first in a conflict.

You may find that you have one or two people at your table who continually dissent, holding up play by breaking table consensus. If this happens, you have a larger issue on your hands; either not everyone is clear on the expectations for the game, or you have disruptive players in your game. Either way, the best way to resolve such a problem is to step away from the game for a bit and have a conversation about it.

II. APPLICABLE LAWS FOR CITOYENS

We are fortunate to be blessed with a hard-working citizenry with a strong moral center. As a result, we have very few laws in place. We believe in limiting government interference and in the instinct of the system to regulate itself.

Le Silence is for your protection. Between the hours of 20h00 and 06h00, we expect Citoyens to be in their domain. During le Silence, Citoyens must ensure they replenish their neural casings. Don't run out of power halfway through your shift.

There is no business to be conducted at night that cannot be conducted in the light of day. Only criminals and vagrants need the dark to hide their activities. Behave with caution and prudence at all times and it is easy to stay on the right side of the law. For a complete list of laws in effect, see appendix A24-N57.

The Spark That Lights a Fire

Le Silence. Amazing how curtailing our freedoms is presented so mildly by our government. Only a police state forbids their citizenry from doing as they please when they please. Their control is slipping, however.

Needless to say, le Silence is the time when we get our best work done. It's simply a matter of routing around surveillance, avoiding the gendarmes, and moving quickly and silently. I should probably thank them, truly. The more despotic they behave, the easier my job is.

The loss of Arielle is breaking my nerve. I saw her as a younger me, told her too much. Not just Resistance secrets, but my secrets. My heartbreak, my fears. That night with the bottle of wine in the Moulin Rouge. Damn Jean le Roux_it's been years since I've drunk such a delicious red. A bourgogne from before the Fall, so rare and precious. It went straight to my head, loosed my tongue. And Arielle was such a good listener. Hard to believe there's guile behind those bright blue eyes, under those flyaway blonde curls.

But she's an infiltrator, a sniper of the first water, and I forgot that. I forgot being the leader means you don't get to set those burdens down. That they're yours forever. You can befriend people, love them, but you can never ever let them in. I was just tired of dragging all this weight myself. We laughed and talked the length of le Silence and as we headed back to la Cave in the gloom of early morn, she wrapped her arm around my waist and laughed this charming little laugh. We were leaning on each other, staggering, making more noise than was good for us.

That's the last time I'll open up. If I have to kill her, it'll be a higher cost than I'll ever want to pay again.

The Spark That Lights a Fire

Build the Government

Like la Résistance, the government has its own playsheet. Players and GM, you'll both have a hand in filling out the government playsheet. Like with the Resistance playsheet, anyone at the table can look at the government playsheet at any time, though the GM will manage it during play.

First, decide on the government's **slogan**. This represents the public face of the government, its stated goal. Some of this may be propaganda, but it has more than a little truth to it. The slogan is always positive in nature; publicly, the government's purpose is to serve the citizenry.

Next, decide on the government's **scandal**. This is the thing that the government would kill to keep secret from les Citoyens. Unfortunately, la Résistance knows what it is. Initially, agents of la Résistance can only invoke or compel this aspect when they're dealing with others who know the truth of it: other members of la Résistance and certain members of the government and the corporations.

The government's slogan and scandal are both setting aspects, which exist during all scenes.

Finally, the government starts with two advances, just like la Résistance. The players choose one, and the GM chooses the other. These work just like the advances that la Résistance can pick, but the government has its own advancement trees: Corporate, Military, and Security.

The government also has a **Bank** of fate points, though it starts off empty.

What does the Bank do?

Throughout play, the Bank will fill for various reasons, such as when the PCs buy equipment on the open market.

At the start of any mission, the GM can withdraw fate points from the Bank and add them to her Budget of fate points for the mission. Also, during debriefs, she can spend fate points from the Bank to advance the government more quickly.

Slogan: UNITY FOR A BETTER TOMORROW

Scandal: THE KLEPTOCRACY IS REAL

Starting Advances: Taxation, Drone Surveillance Network

[Emergency Message Broadcast: burst text from Sidenge
[ID 38137711] to Arielle [NO ID FOUND]]

Arielle it's Sidenge. It's been ten hours now and everyone's
looking for you. Message me when you get this. They're not
playing. If you don't return in the next six hours, there's talk
of reclassing you as an enemy combatant. I know you're tired
of the rules and restrictions, but if you care at all about me
and our friends you need to come on back. We got a good thing
going here and you can't help out your family and the Naturels
if you're shot on sight. Message me NOW.

[Output: Message UNDELIVERABLE]

Decide on Game Length

Decide, as a group, how long you want the campaign to be. This determines how
many critical advances that a side, la Résistance or the government, must have
before they can gain their endgame advance.

Short Game: The government must have one critical advance (Élite Kickbacks,
Increased Volunteerism, or Drone Neural Network). Likewise, la Résistance must
have one critical advance (Dirty Secrets, Means to an End, or The Will of the
People).

Medium Game: A side must have two critical advances.

Long Game: A side must have three critical advances.

Marya, Sidenge:

I'm now classifying this as an A-level risk. It's been 32 hours
with no contact from Arielle. She's now classified as an Enemy
of the State, la traîtresse. I've been as patient and willing to
negotiate as I can. It's time to act, to protect la Résistance.
She's been tracked to a unit in le Bas. As you know, she's a
highly trained sniper and is both a flight risk and likely willing
to kill upon being discovered. I can't lose any more of my good
people. I'm sending Jules with you, in case drastic measures
need to be taken. Gear up_you leave at 05h00.

Report back the moment Arielle is in custody.

Clare

III. PRIVILEGES OF CITIZENSHIP

By joining the ranks of citizenship, you have automatically taken the most important step in improving your surroundings and lifestyle.

With your new augmentation, you have the ability to overlay visual skins, called **veils**, on your environment. These veils significantly improve your overall daily experience in augmented reality (AR). Sights, smells, sounds, and textures can be customized to fit your tastes. While virtual reality (VR) is a heightened and immersive experience, AR can come close with the benefits granted by your neural casing, and you can use it all the time.

A wide range of veils is available for only a small additional fee of 3×55 credits.

Don't forget, it's important to prepare your children for citizenship. While their brains are not yet developed enough for augmentation, they can train with gyro rigs and headgear.

We have recently been informed that some Citoyens are concerned with the minimal physical interaction between themselves and their offspring, due to the potentially addictive nature of VR. Please remember this is only a concern until they reach the age of eleven, which is the youngest approved age for neural augmentation. Once they achieve full citizenship, they will be capable of moving into their own domain, and any future requirements on your resources will be minimal.

Do I really have to comment on this? It's nice that the half-units are groomed for citizenship and then dumped into another cell block. Remember the Naturels? I once met a family free of augments. They laughed and talked to each other, with actual eye contact. They sang songs and told stories. This is what it once was. This is what we will make it again.

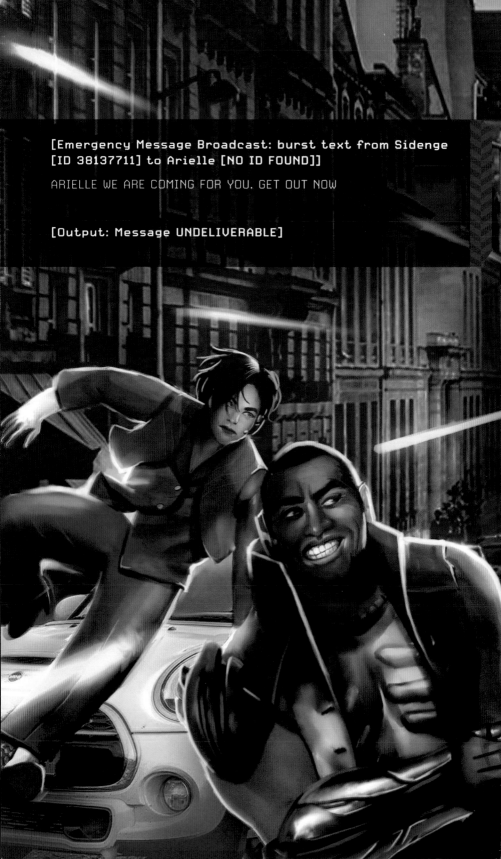

[Emergency Message Broadcast: burst text from Sidenge [ID 38137711] to Arielle [NO ID FOUND]]

ARIELLE WE ARE COMING FOR YOU. GET OUT NOW

[Output: Message UNDELIVERABLE]

The story of Paris Nouveau is complex and shrouded in the fog of history and disinformation. What's true and what's just propaganda? How did the Fall happen, and what *was* the great calamity that forced us all behind the city's walls? What's outside the city? Is it safe? Are there other survivors?

Our answers to these questions, dear reader, are only slightly more accurate than your own.

The following chapter contains snippets—bits of correspondence or communique, an imperfect story for an imperfect world. Piece together what you can from this, and fill in the gaps on your own.

It's your story too, after all.

IV. YOUR ROLE AS A CITIZEN

Your neural casing upgrade is sponsored by **Cryptiq, Inc.**, the leader in manufacturing biological kilojoules (kJs). This sponsorship gives you a 20% discount on your kJ power plugins.

CARE AND MAINTENANCE OF YOUR NEURAL CASING

Immediately after your surgery, you may experience some soreness and swelling. Don't be alarmed. This is normal. Your casing is hard-wired to your brain, replacing a small portion of it.

Be sure to keep your port for power and diagnostics clean and free from obstructions. It is the small hole positioned near the base of your skull, where you insert your kJ power module. Insert the plugin until you hear a faint click. A successfully inserted plugin will emit a soft glow. Blue indicates a full charge. When it starts blinking, it is time to replace it. Because it may be difficult for you to see the indicator showing that your kJ is low, your neural casing will buzz softly when you are low on power. Helpful gendarmes will also tell you when your power is low. Your kJ plugin will last anywhere from a few days to a few months, depending on its latency setting.

WARNING: Do not eject a kJ plugin without immediately replacing it. Otherwise, your augmentation will slowly drain of power, which will disrupt your AR/VR experience.

Thanks to the generosity of Cryptiq, Inc., you can now enjoy enhanced reality, both augmented and virtual. The cost of this upgrade is 68 credits. Citoyens earn 5 credits per hour of labor. After one year of service in good order, this is increased to 7 credits per hour.

I'm curious, does **indentured servitude feel good?** I know, nobody likes that term. But how else would you describe being indebted to a large corporation for an unspecified number of years, with a debt mathematically impossible to pay off? Actually, I take that back.

How does it feel to be **enslaved**?

I powered down my casing years ago. It was brutal; I hallucinated and scratched and bled. But give me a hard truth over a beautiful lie. And what are these corporations but the liars we enable just to make our lives sweeter? You think augmenting your reality changes the fact that our clothes are shabby and our walls are concrete, as the entire city sinks inch by inch, year by year, into the Seine?

It's time to wake up. I know you can do it.

Fortunately, the work you are asked to do is easy to accomplish. It's simply matching a series of patterns, a game. But it is a very important game and your contributions improve our society, powering the machines keeping us all alive and safe.

This is a charming way to refer to les Naturels and Ex-Cits, the people who keep our city running. Naturels are people with no brain augmentation, either because they have insufficient funds or sponsorship, wait too late in life to adopt it, possess moral convictions against it, or have brains that wouldn't survive the surgery.

They're more clear-seeing than our entire citizenry, yet they're treated as untouchables. Ex-Cits are former Citoyens who survived their withdrawals and now live offline—they are criminals and outcasts.

In other words, me and my ilk.

Did you know your tech doesn't age well? That machine you have hooked up to your brain, thinking on your behalf, will die before you do. And then what? Upgrades are difficult and painful, just ask the first-gen casing adopters. If you can find any. Most of them died in the process; the government doesn't really talk much about it. Those who survived simply found their debt to their corporate sponsor tripled.

So you know, we do have access to some wearable tech, when necessary. It's not really a substitute for augmentation as much as a way to hack into the system when necessary. That's how I'm talking to you now. Latency is better, but resolution is crap, so forgive the archaic text chat. Our wearable tech can only be used so many times, though, and it is highly illegal.

A note on your "innocent" pattern-matching: the government deliberately decouples your job from its results. So you never know if your "game" is constructing an apartment, analyzing metadata, executing a criminal, or evicting your neighbors.

If not knowing what you're doing to others bothers you, **read on.**

SURVIVAL DATA

Daily environmental alerts (DEAs) are uploaded to your neural casing to ensure a constant feed regarding the safety of your surroundings.

Electromagnetic radiation levels, biological hazards, tainted food output, fall-out, and extreme weather alerts will automatically blink in your left cornea, as needed. In order to guarantee your safety, never power down your augmentations. If your credit balance is short, the company will loan you the necessary funds to keep your tech operable, at a mere 11% interest rate.*

A polite reminder: we cannot emphasize enough—it is illegal to power down your augmentations. Don't risk being on the wrong side of the law or putting yourself or your family's health at risk by not receiving your DEA.

Fear. It's what keeps them in control and keeps you predictable. The first week my augmentation was powered down, I was terrified, jumping at shadows. They had me so programmed, I was afraid to breathe the air without their little mind box.

...And I lived. Of course there are dangers. But being more aware of your environment, instead of having it overlaid with pretty virtual pictures, makes you **less** likely to get hurt or killed, not more.

It's true, this world isn't as pretty without the gauzy layers of avatars and veils cushioning you. The people smell. The walls are ugly and plain. Life is hard. But sometimes still I'll catch the reflection of the moon in the Seine and remember why living in reality is what I fight for.

11% interest rate is introductory, for the first 30 days. If not repaid in full, the credit interest rate (CIR) increases to 71% and is simply added to the Citoyen's balance owed.

WATER AVAILABILITY INSTRUCTIONS

As you know, water from the Seine is collected and purified at four filtration stations across the city, but water rationing is in effect until further notice. Bathing is to be restricted to a rotating schedule: 1st arrondissement for the first week of the month, 2nd for the second week, et cetera. Each domain is equipped with an automated elimination gutter seat. Urine and waste will be collected weekly; please be sure to keep your gutter free from clogs to prevent overflow.

If you notice the appearance of small, bubbling sores, please report to the nearest medical kiosk; it's possible you were exposed to irradiated water.

ARTIFICIAL PROTEIN EXTRACT

As requested, Vat IV has added an additional flavor to its artificial protein extract (APE). It is now available in unflavored and meat-flavored, to add variety to your diet. Consistency can be improved by adding a few drops of water and mashing your extract so it can be more easily chewed.

Should you wish to enjoy an AR upgrade to improve the taste and texture of your APE, that can be purchased for the low cost of 2×26 credits per meal.

While there are rumors that terraformation has resumed, they are incorrect, as is the suggestion that the countryside, if improved, could sustain farmland. This is simply an unfounded accusation by the criminals terrorizing our city.

Such chilling propaganda. If they'd resume terraformation, it's estimated they could reach citywide food support levels in six months. The earth around Paris Nouveau is still rich; it crumbles dark and lush in your hand. But they lie and say it's irradiated, because they'd rather keep you working eighty hours a week and eating protein, drinking your dribbles of water to survive.

As a side note, your latency in le Bas is so poor that, even with the AR upgrade, it may look like a steak and smell like a steak, but it will taste like APE. Don't think la Societé isn't tricking their brains into tasting steak with their superior latency at l'Apogée. Poor bastards. Wealthy as hell but still pretending life is good.

What is your life worth to you? Your children's lives? Do you want to eke out your existence, or do you want to resist, to make life good again for everyone, not just for the privileged few?

That's what we want. Liberté. Égalité. Fraternité. We will accept nothing less.

ENERGY SOLUTIONS

There are eight hydropower turbines underneath the ruins of four of the historical bridges on the Seine: Pont Alexandre III, Pont des Arts, Pont des Invalides, and Pont Marie. These turbines provide the power for our city, but you can help by powering down your domain to low levels during the day and by using power at non-peak times.

Reports that power is being siphoned off to serve the needs of la Societé in l'Apogée of L'Aerie are simply untrue and scurrilous. Remember, a productive Citizen is one that has no time for illegitimate gossip. All Citizens in our society are valued.

Ha! If I have to explain this one to you, we don't want you.

...But perhaps I should at least tell you the truth about L'Aerie. What you think you know is a lie. What they will tell you later in this module is also a lie.

L'Aerie is Paris Above, though when people speak of L'Aerie they're usually referring to its pinnacle, l'Apogée. The place is constructed in a rough imitation of la Tour Eiffel, that hunk of twisted metal now residing in Paris Below. We Parisians are nothing if not nostalgic. But that's where the similarities end. It's mostly cinder block construction, a warren of low-cost housing. It's rumored that l'Apogée has far more amenities. Hot water, for example.

They still aren't living the high life, but I know for a fact the latency at the tip of L'Aerie (where those in la Societé live) is fifty times better than that at the base. And they keep building higher. If they would simply reroute their resources into terraforming, we could improve life for everyone. But that's not what the Élites want.

Just remember that.

La Cave is Paris Below. It's dark, and even more dirty and dangerous. After the Fall, the catacombs beneath Paris gave way and the city collapsed, folding itself into treacherous origami. Much of it is underwater, but not nearly as much as the government wants you to believe. The catacombs are accessible but hazardous. That's where we live. I won't give you specifics, not till you join us, but I can fill you in on the rough outlines.

We move around primarily at night, in the shadows. The moon becomes your friend in la Cave. You learn to prefer the dark. It's safer. Sometimes when I move around the city at night, poling through the flooded tunnels of la Cave, the moon is my only company. I said that to the group once, and they called me la Lune ever after.

That's my name. But names don't matter much anymore. We aim to change that. You're assigned a serial number on your neural casing, for "ease of information processing" they say, but that number is attached to your metadata flow. That's all you are to them.

DOWNCYCLING

Downcycling is the most practical option for garbage disposal. As you may imagine, a city this size generates a staggering amount of garbage. Until now, it simply would have been buried in the countryside. Now, thanks to our corporate sponsors, we can convert the garbage with peak efficiency to supplement artificial protein extract production.

As always, we are grateful to our sponsors for allowing us to run a cleaner, more efficient city.

D'you hear that? They've got you eating their garbage.

When I was younger, I heard a story once about men who were kept in cages. Everyone wanted the top cage because piss flows downwards. The upper levels send down their trash, and we eat it and ask for more.

SECURITY

We are fortunate to have a strong network of surveillance equipment, linked by le Treillis. When a crime is taking place, an operator in VR directs a drone to resolve the issue. Drones are equipped with the latest in neural paralysis technology. Suspects are then collected and moved to a private location, where their case can be reviewed and punishment meted.

If you are community-minded, we encourage you to consider joining la Gendarmerie, our Citoyen-run constabulary. While you will not receive any credits for your assistance, you can be confident that your contributions assist us in maintaining a peaceful and productive society.

To join, simply complete the form at the end of this orientation, and we will contact you about how you can make a difference in the lives of your fellow Citoyens.

La Gendarmerie is Citoyen-run all right, rife with corruption and prone to excessive force. Most people don't read history anymore—it's forgotten—but it's littered with examples of why it's a bad idea to have a police force of untrained and violent volunteers with free rein.

So why do people join the gendarmes, you might ask. Some of them are bullies, some are criminals, all of them enjoy having authority over others. If the government can get us to police our own, it's less work for them.

Last week, I saw two gendarmes beating a young man to death. His crime? He had illegal hacked technology he's been selling to the Resistance. They dumped his body in the Seine afterwards. I could not save him.

Do you know what their form asks, to determine if you are a good fit for la Gendarmerie? It's only one question: "Do you think extreme measures are sometimes necessary to protect our society?"

V. CITY STRUCTURE

L'Aerie is the only area of the city that is consistently safe. It has been reinforced against the occasional ground-shift as the city continues to sink into itself. Its swooping, narrow-tipped pinnacle is designed to echo the shape of la Tour Eiffel, now unfortunately a crumple of girders in la Cave.

Citoyens can travel up and down L'Aerie via ascenseurs in the structure's central axis. At the tip of L'Aerie is L'Apogée, where our government offices are located, as well as the quarters of la Societé. As you are aware, your domain is located in le Bas; it is essential to remember you are just as important as the members of la Societé, but it is simply not practical to house everyone in l'Apogée.

As far as complaints regarding latency in le Bas, we are working on improving your technology daily.

La Cave is off-limits to all Citoyens. It is a desolate collection of ruins, constantly shifting and sinking. Not only is it dangerous, but it is peopled by the criminals known as Ex-Citizens. If you value your life and property, you will avoid this part of the city.

Should you approach the perimeter of la Cave unknowingly, your neural casing will offer a faint buzz to notify you, and it will increase in intensity the closer you get. We have found that this gentle encouragement reinforces good behavior on the part of our citizenry.

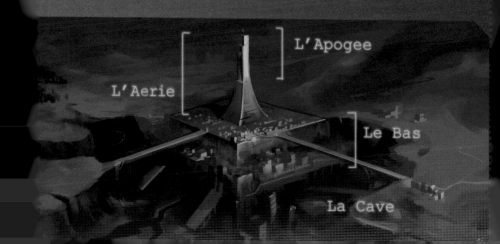

L'Apogee

L'Aerie

Le Bas

La Cave

I suppose I should thank the government. Their little "joy buzzer" keeps out the idle curious. If you truly want to get into la Cave, you have to allow us to hack your neural casing. Even that only works temporarily. If you want to stay, you have to remove your augmentation or else the buzzing will soon drive you mad.

I'm told the warning vibrations get so violent inside la Cave that people have been known to bleed from their nose and ears.

Let us speak of la Cave. Home sweet home. I can't deny some of the government's charges: it's basically a sunken city, a constantly shifting obstacle course of cement and crumpled steel and shattered glass.

But there are still glimpses of the old city, moments when I can recognize the history and grandeur, even sunken beneath the Seine. Yet it is all repurposed now, made into something the Resistance can use.

If you see the red windmill of the Moulin Rouge peeking out from behind that pile of rubble, know that it's now a bar owned by a Resistance sympathizer who calls himself Jean le Roux. He's a giant Moroccan with faded tattoos and a disconcerting habit of inserting wild flowers into the port of his neural casing.

Jean le Roux is essentially a mercenary. He puts up with us and we make sure he's got access to the best alcohol that's still available.

D'accord, this is where I take a chance on you. From here on out, I am risking a lot by telling you all this. But I think you can be trusted. I hope.

If not, we'll just have to kill you. **Kidding. Mostly.**

Our headquarters are located at the Louvre, or what's left of it. As you know, much of the historic building is crumbled and sunken, but the glass pyramid survived. It's now tilted on one side and looks rather drunk, but we gather beneath it because it symbolizes a world that once was. In fact, one of our other missions is to rescue and preserve French culture.

I know globalism is/was a thing, but we are now in danger of being totally consumed by an English-speaking society. The art, the architecture, the very bones of our city are in danger of being lost forever. No one cares about the history anymore. They are concerned with sedating themselves fully against reality. If you should join us, know you'll be doing the occasional rescue mission that involves protecting or retrieving an essential part of French culture. Your children will thank us, if they survive.

Les Naturels are responsible for the salvage operations. They can travel in and out of la Cave effortlessly and they are not tracked by the government, other than by the same surveillance cameras that watch us all. They use makeshift scuba gear and add AR tags to valuables so they can be found on our maps, especially to the pieces too heavy to be moved. Just the other day, they found an armless, headless marble goddess beneath a destroyed charcuterie. This city creates unforgettable contrasts.

When a member of the Resistance needs to meet with a contact or recruit outside headquarters, they often gather at the ruins of the Pont-Neuf. There in the darkness, they can swap information, purchase necessary goods, and pass along messages with relative discretion. We have an elaborate cipher worked out; the underside of the bridge is covered in graffiti, but we are trained to read the messages meant for our eyes only.

"La mort n'est rien, mais vivre dans la défaite et sans gloire c'est mourir quotidiennement." ["Death is nothing, but to live defeated and inglorious is to die daily."] It was Napoléon Bonaparte who said that. No one speaks of Napoléon anymore, but I often think of him. He was maybe an absurd little man at times, but he overcame vast challenges to defeat his enemies and unite France.

The Père-Lachaise cemetery is where we test and train recruits. If you join us, you will experience great struggle there. For one thing, you will be enduring terrible withdrawal pains, while being tested to your physical and mental limits. Some don't survive. But if you do, you will not need their tech again. Or, at least I should say, it's manageable. I liken it to quitting smoking, back when one could still get cigarettes.

I hear smoking used to be considered a French national right. Now? Good luck finding anything green to dry to smoke.

I enjoy sitting in Père-Lachaise, thinking of all the dead who came before us. Their fears and hopes and dreams. Our struggle is just another century in the march of time. Sorry, sometimes I get philosophical in my old age. Another French right.

As for Jardin des Tuileries, those once-famous gardens are now barren, but provide good cover when running to escape the gendarmes or government spies. They are also considered neutral territory, a place to meet those not in the Resistance or even our enemies. It's considered bad form to kill people in the Jardin, even those who probably need killing.

VI. TRAVELING IN PARIS NOUVEAU

For Citoyens, travel within the city is simply a matter of accessing an ascenseur, which is the quickest way up and down L'Aerie. There is, of course, a credit cost which is automatically deducted from your balance with each use. Fortunately, the cost is nominal.

We do not recommend using any non-government-endorsed method of travel, as we cannot guarantee your safety.

There is also a service that runs pataches, small paddleboats that can navigate the waterways and locks of the Seine. Unfortunately, this service consorts with a criminal element, so it is only recommended as a last resort.

There's not much easy portable power remaining: gasoline or electric engines, etc. Planes, buses, and automobiles as they were used before, as individual mobility units, are extremely difficult to find and fix up. Most still-functional vehicles belong to the government or corporations. The pataches are the only way to travel to many areas of la Cave. In certain sections, we have to pole through the darkness, because the rubble level is so high it will crack the paddle mechanism. If that sounds quaint and picturesque, remind yourself that capsizing or falling in the water often means drowning, as it's so dark you cannot tell which way is up.

In the city above, there is a whole system of tunnels, ladders, and chutes to get in and out. It is not always safe and definitely not official, but it's fast and easy and practically the only way to avoid being captured on surveillance footage.

VII. UPDATE ON TERRAFORMATION

While we are cognizant there is disappointment with the deactivation of the terraformation program for reclaiming the outlying areas of Paris Nouveau, it is simply not cost-effective. Investing in this technology with an uncertain result requires far too many resources. It is unclear whether the radioactivity of the soil even allows for successful terraforming.

La Societé has ruled that, in the best interests of our community, we should focus our resources on improving our city within. There is a shortage of quality housing, but there are plans to expand L'Aerie at le Bas that is sure to meet the needs of the people. As well, more money invested in our technology infrastructure leads to improved latency for all.

The old model of city planning and urban development was not working. There have not been shortages since we switched from grown foodstuffs to APE. While we realize it is not an ideal solution, no one has gone hungry since the development of protein extracts. It is important we prioritize what matters to our Citoyens.

First lie: the soil is radioactive. While it's true the initial assault during the Fall involved radioactive weapons, the subsequent years have allowed for any lingering radioactive effects to bleed off.

We have a guy who built a homemade Geiger counter—he's brilliant and builds just about anything we need—and smuggled it outside of the city to test the soil. Nothing. No reading. We thought maybe it was broken or simply didn't work. Until we tested it by the APE vats. The machine pinged like les cloches de Notre-Dame.

I don't know why it reacted to the APE. The cynic in me suggests slow poisoning, but I need to do more digging to see where they are sourcing these proteins. I guess the takeaway is just to not trust everything you're told. But I hope you've at least figured that out by now.

Second lie: the money invested in the infrastructure benefits you. The wealthy up in l'Apogée live like gods, even though nothing is real. Their VR is magnificent. Though none of their existence is grounded in reality, their daily lives have all the edges smoothed off by their superior tech and low latency.

Dear Ephraim,

Thank you for setting up this useful device. I haven't been able to write a proper e-message for a long time. Be sure you wash your shirt before Tanya comes to visit.

Love,

your mother

P.S. What does the gray button do?

Mum,

I'm glad you're enjoying it, but please remember it has a limited number of uses, so it's best if we use it mostly in cases of emergency. In fact, it's illegal, so please don't wear the wrist unit when you go out shopping. The gendarmes look for reasons to beat up nice little old ladies like you, and black market tech is more than enough reason.

Sometimes I feel like things would be easier if we just had neural casings like the Citizens.

The gray button resets the entire unit if you hold it down for ten seconds. Please don't do that. And of course I washed my shirt. I was taught proper.

-Ef

BREAK

Mum,

Okay, okay I get your point. You didn't have to embroider a message on an old potato sack with red yarn to get your message across. Tanya laughed at me when it arrived in my delivery tube and I unfolded it. I think I've found a man who can add charges to your wrist unit_I can trade him some carpentry services for these charges. He wants a new bed frame so you'll be able to use it more. Isn't that exciting?

Btw, mum, you didn't have to spell out Ephraim all the way on your embroidered message. I know you hate 'Ef,' but that's a lot of yarn wasted. But I suppose it did get me to_

You tricked me.

-Ef

BREAK

Dear Ephraim,

Calling it a trick maligns your dear mother. I simply know how to get my boy to accomplish what needs to be done. I've known it your whole life. Besides, you wouldn't want your decrepit old mother to not have a way to communicate with her only son. This life may be hard, but there's no reason to make it harder.

I know you're not a big fan of our current government, but I remember how things were before. We were starving and there's no other way to say it. One time I had to boil some shoe leather to chew on. This was all before APE. It tastes about the same as shoes, to be sure, but it's far more sustaining.

And I'm not afraid of the gendarmes. They see right through me. Once you get to be a lady of a certain age, people in authority don't notice you unless you bump straight into them. Then I usually put on the helpless old lady act and they push me aside and let me go on my way.

When the chance came for the strongest corporations and the government to merge, I thought it'd be a pretty good thing. For one thing, there's regular APE now and the trash gets cleaned up. It gave the government a much-needed infusion of credit. I know you don't remember then, you were too little, but Paris Nouveau used to be far more filthy and dangerous. Those gendarmes have really kept the miscreants off the street. Of course, I didn't get a vote_Naturels have never had the vote_but I thought it'd be a good thing and I was right.

I saw you when I got into my patache headed out of the city. You look thin. Be sure to eat more APE.

Love,

your mother

Mum,

It pains me to say it, but you're wrong about the gendarmes. They are very, VERY dangerous. You're going to have to take my word on that. I saw three of them beat a stray dog to death, just because it was begging for some food. They are vicious and encouraged to be so. Stay away from them wherever you can.

I know you're very pro-government and I wish I could agree with you, but I've been talking to some people that I think can make a change for us. It's not fair Naturels are treated so shabby, just because we're not Citizens. I'm willing to stand up for what's right.

-Ef

BREAK

Dear Ephraim,

I don't want you joining that Resistance. They're liars and troublemakers. Groups like that always seem more appealing because they paint a shiny picture of what life could be like, if you only help them overthrow the current order. I know you don't like the way they treat Naturels, but son, you need to work in the system not outside it. Plus, it's extremely dangerous. I want you outliving your old mother. Promise me you

BREAK

Before I was able to sign my last message, I noticed there was a pair of gendarmes following me from my APE pickup. I think I've outmaneuvered them, but

[Unit deactivated.]

AR and VR: A Crash Course

Clare,

We're getting more and more Naturels in la Résistance lately, and most of them don't seem to understand how AR and VR work for the citizenry. Wearable tech isn't quite the same thing, you know? Given that this information could literally be the difference between life and death when you're working in the city, I figured I'd put together this brief primer for any new recruits who are a little fuzzy on the details. Citoyens won't need this information, of course.

Augmented Reality

Augmented reality, or AR, is an overlay on the real world, similar to what you might experience with AR glasses or goggles. What you're used to is a little box in the corner of your vision that feeds you information as you need it, but doesn't obscure your ability to see the world. For Citoyens, though, even those on the lower rungs of society, AR is a more complete transformation of the world.

You'll notice, as you walk around Paris Nouveau on assignment, that the buildings are pretty boring, furnishings quite utilitarian, and much of what you encounter is obviously old, recycled, or of middling quality. You'll probably be confused by the fact that there are no signs pointing you where to go, telling you what building is what, advising you of hazardous conditions. That's because, for Citoyens, all of that's contained within AR.

When we come of age, every Citoyen is fitted with a neural casing. It's a series of implants in our brain and nervous system that allows us to experience AR using all five senses, at all times. For us, the signs, buildings, and furnishings look more appealing, food tastes better, clothes look and feel nicer.

That's the theory, anyway. In practice, it's an imperfect lie. Our AR experiences are fed to our casings through a cloud interface, and the hub for that interface is in l'Apogée. The closer you are to the hub, the better your connection to the cloud interface is, the lower your latency and the higher your resolution. For the rich folks at the top, this is great; their already very fine possessions look and feel even nicer, and the illusion is very convincing. Or so I'm told, at least.

For the bulk of the citizenry, down in Paris Nouveau proper, it's easier to see through the illusion. The greater latency means the overlay doesn't stick to objects all that well, and even tastes or sounds can get out of sync with our experience. Even the sensory experiences we do get have lower resolution—apples down on the ground just don't taste as real as they do up top. Sometimes AR cuts out altogether, and let me tell you, *that* can be disorienting.

Much of this AR doesn't work with wearable tech like you're used to. We'll rig some goggles to give you mission-relevant data while you're out in the city, but you won't get the full experience. It's just not something we can simulate without a casing, and we're not equipped to install them here; we just remove the parts that allow the government to track and control us.

Virtual Reality

It's pretty unlikely you've experienced anything like VR before. Where AR is an overlay on the real world, VR replaces it entirely. You climb into a rig and it feeds sensory data to you, tracks your movement, and allows you to move about in a virtual world, even while you're stationary in the real world.

VR isn't used nearly as often as AR is, even by the citizenry at the top. In early life, before you get a casing, you spend a lot of time in VR, learning the ropes of society, getting indoctrinated, and so forth. After that, it becomes something of a novelty. Some people perform their jobs in VR, but that's rare. Most Citoyens use it strictly for recreation, though there are parts of the Infosphere that allow full VR. The most famous (infamous?) of these is Tír na nÓg, a hackerspace you can only access through VR.

We have a few VR rigs here in la Cave. You might get to use one of them, if the mission demands it.

The Fall

Is this thing on? I swear, the new wave of recorders makes me feel stupider and stupider. If my voice sounds shaky as I'm speaking this, it's because I'm afraid. This is saved in an encrypted file in my personal data bank, but I'm not so naïve as to think this would keep them from finding it.

My mandate was simple: review the historical archives about the Fall, and file them in an organized manner. I'm an archivist, so this is barely busywork. I mean, we all know what caused the Fall, right? Paris Nouveau banded together against the threat of the outside world. Nuclear proliferation meant we needed to shut our borders. There were so many nuclear weapons. I mean, between the radioactive environment and the roving bandits, we had to protect ourselves from the outside. We weren't the only ones. Everyone shut their doors, battened down their hatches, and prayed for tomorrow. We know for certain two major warheads were launched, but it's inconclusive how dangerous the detonated weapons were or what the net result on the planet was.

Then the dominoes started to fall. Once trade between cities stopped, so did the exchange of information. And that's where the official records become jumbled and insufficient. I'm theorizing that the communications systems were either mostly damaged or seized by the governments in charge.

Around the turn of the century, climate change seemed to be a big issue. I found a lot of studies, but also a lot of arguments from the non-scientific community about whether it was dangerous. Also, there was a time when large parts of North America were not underwater.

Of course, here, we had the end of the world. The Fall for us wasn't just bombardment from the outside world; it was also implosion from within. The city flooded constantly, and records show there was a concerted effort to build floodwalls and reinforce key bridges and parts of the city. It wasn't enough. I doubt there's anyone still alive now from that day, the day the city fell through. The catacombs underneath Old Paris, weakened from the constant erosion and battered by the powerful rising waters, finally collapsed. This is known. There aren't many firsthand accounts of that day, probably because so many were killed, but it's confirmed that historic Paris as it was once known_well, it no longer existed. It was underwater. I would have liked to have seen la Tour Eiffel go. It must have been a spectacular sight.

So many monuments that survived world wars, shattered and forever lost. The windmill of the Moulin Rouge is mostly intact, though it fell through to la Cave. L'Arc de Triomphe, Champs-Elysées, these are just words now. They don't exist as real things anymore.

Anyway, as to what I discovered_I'm gobsmacked. I knew the xenophobia was bad, but had no idea how it fed the steamroller that crushed parts of the world. It is my suspicion that the adverse effects of the Fall are seriously exaggerated by our government, for their own purposes.

Let me repeat that, as I can hardly believe I'm writing it: the adverse effects of the Fall are not as bad as our government tells us. But I work for the government! I'm confident they have no idea I know we've been lied to this whole time. By them.

Let me explain. I found some early studies, post-Fall, testing the levels of fallout on the outskirts of the city. The terraformation was within our lifetimes, probably twenty to thirty years away. Most of the technologies were in place before the Fall, but now many of them have been forgotten. These studies have been suppressed and instead I was redirected to a series of increasingly dire government announcements about the risk of the outside world to public safety. The roads out of the city were blockaded and we retreated behind our walls of rubble. All of our existing news services were replaced by government information systems. Le Silence was tested and then enforced_no one was to go out after dark.

It's that simple and yet complex. They don't want us to terraform, to return to growing our own food. But why? I've wondered for a long time what the tasks of les Citoyens really accomplish. It sounds so conspiracy-theorist, but once they made it difficult for us to discover what it is we're doing…well, we could be ensuring our survival by restoring the land around Paris Nouveau, instead of wasting hours tapping away at these screens because of compounding corporate debt.

But I know there were other reasons. I mean, there are bandits on the outside. Fallout. Hungry animals. Radioactive rain. It's dangerous_or at least that's what we've been told.

Wait, was that a noise?

I'm jumping at shadows now. How stupid_I'm safe in my own unit. Perhaps I should send a quick copy to Luce, just in case. I think he's smart enough to keep this under a lid. He owes me one.

The World Beyond the Walls

This memo was found in the government archives. It has been removed from the current data stream on le Treillis, though there is no explanation as to why.

Each of these cities is ruled independently, though the level of violence it takes to maintain a subdued populace varies wildly, based on the level of militarization and organization of each city.

Our files are, unsurprisingly, highly incomplete. No radio signals or other transmissions can be detected, so a great deal of this document is guesswork and pieced together by word-of-mouth.

Neese

No doubt all the dead French who came before us would be incensed at the now-phonetic spelling of Nice. Blame the modern world. People like simple things that are easy to remember. Neese is a success story for France, though the bar is undoubtedly low. They did not outlaw terraforming and so the ground around the city is allegedly fertile. Also, because they are right on the water, they have been able to farm the ocean for the fish that survived, though the level of radioactivity makes them still mostly unsafe. We have incomplete information because people that we send to Neese generally don't return. It's unclear whether they're killed or simply choose to stay and so abandon their post. They have built a very tall wall around the city and keep mostly to themselves. They don't send out patrols or skirmish with the soldiers we send. We recommend Neese be prioritized as a high threat. The best way to raise support for a military action against them is to stir envy and resentment in the populace. We can also blame the occasional bandit raid on them. Once public opinion is set against them, it's likely we can muster up a significant military operation to overcome them and absorb their resources.

York and the Boroughs

We have established contact with the former state of New York. It seems to have survived the Fall partly intact. Our ambassador has not visited because the tube is still considered unsafe. The last ambassador we sent actually got stuck for about 37 hours. We're not sure whether it was the lack of oxygen or the extreme temperatures in the tube that got him, but the next one has refused to make the attempt. The Office of the Exchange offered to send a volunteer, maybe an ailing Naturel whose family would be compensated in case of tube failure.

Per reports, there is widespread hunger and more than a little anarchy, due to the lack of basic necessities. Part of the city was leveled, but it seems the boroughs are mostly intact. They are each held by a so-called governor, though this seems to simply be the term for the strongman (or woman) in charge of the area.

Upfrancisco

Upfrancisco, formerly known as San Francisco, actually seems to be thriving in its own way. They have successfully maintained desalinization plants, drawing water from the ocean and purifying it to survive. This might explain why some of the other surviving cities after the Fall are those beside bodies of water. The people of the city have rebuilt the damaged areas into a sort of pyramid, with a stalk-like structure blooming up from the top, where their government and wealthy are housed, a little like l'Apogée for us. Some other details of note include that they have successfully sent one of their Citoyens here via the tube, which is why we have a little more information than before about them. Unfortunately, we have yet to be able to send someone back.

Nu Berlin

The people remaining among the ashes seem to be too disfigured to recognize as still human. Or perhaps that's simply stories told by frightened travelers, those who dare to edge beyond our borders.

Prague

Destroyed.

London

No contact, presumed destroyed.

St. Petersburg

Nuclear winter.

Tokyo

Underwater.

Cairo-321

Cairo is still known as a commerce hub, but who knows what they trade anymore? There is a flourishing market, just below their government's notice. They did successfully terraform, though only to a limited extent, so some foodstuffs are available though the prices are far beyond the reach of average Citoyens. It's said the Élite get their occasional luxury through Cairo.

Versailles

These people are doing quite well. Surprisingly so, in fact. A thriving economy, technology on par with our own and, in some cases, more advanced. They still speak French and have maintained the original spelling of the city's name. Recommend against any of our people making contact of any kind. Further recommend using papers to make it clear that Versailles is an irradiated wasteland full of bandits and murderers.

CITOYENS, THIS IS YOUR DAILY REMINDER OF THE MOST IMPORTANT LAWS OF PARIS NOUVEAU

These laws are in place for your safety and the productivity of our society.

- ⊘ It is important that you devote the majority of your day to your civic duties required of you by your sponsoring corporation. Any regular deviation from this schedule will initially prompt a warning, then a fine. Finally, more extreme measures may need to be taken in cases of unyielding noncompliance.

- ⊘ Though it may be tempting to communicate with Naturels, it's important to remember your station. Only the bare minimum of interaction is allowed. Naturels have their place and it is not with Citoyens. Fraternizing with Naturels is strictly prohibited and we needn't remind you that becoming emotionally or romantically involved with a Naturel makes you subject to loss of citizenship and deactivation of your neural implant.

- ⊘ Do not enter Paris Below. It's not only physically dangerous, but also populated by a criminal element. Remember that your neural implant will buzz if you get too close, so better to give it a wide berth.

- ⊘ Do not leave the city without the proper permits, protective radioactive gear, and appropriate security, to avoid unpleasant experiences.

- ⊘ Orders from the lowliest gendarme are law in this city. Do not test the gendarmes, do not joke with them, and do not waste their time. If they are forced to detain you, be sure to cooperate completely. **DO NOT RUN.**

4 Strange Bedfellows
The Nine Playsheets

The playsheets in this chapter allow you to make characters quickly and easily.

That said, you might want to just grab a character and go! To that end, each playsheet includes a premade character with a name, five aspects, a means spread, and three stunts. Feel free to use these characters for inspiration, modify them, or use them whole cloth. Many of these premade characters refer to one another with their aspects. If one of your aspects refers to someone who isn't in the game, simply change it to someone who is.

La Société

We are fortunate, as a city, to benefit from the strong leadership and guidance provided by la Société. Their hard work contributed to the rebuilding of our city after the Fall, and to the invention of neural casings. They have worked ceaselessly to develop our virtual opportunities, which improve everyone's quality of life.

Click here to donate ten credits to a happier, more just society. By improving our virtual economy, the benefits trickle down to everyone.

I am going to be sick. They already have you in hock for hundreds of thousands of credits and now want you to contribute to keep the Élites in power? The last time this happened, Paris created Madame Guillotine. It's time for a change.

People are half-living their lives, locked to their domains and their veils, their virtuality more real than their reality. And that's how the government wants us.

No.

La Société in Play

Members of la Société are the upper crust of Paris Nouveau. You have wealth, privilege, and power.

Members of la Société…

- …have authority over those of lower social standing.
- …have the trust (mostly) of the government and corporations.
- …have numerous powerful allies to call upon.

However…

- …they are often targets of la Résistance, and are viewed with suspicion when they join la Résistance.
- …they are often disliked by les Citoyens.
- …they often have powerful enemies.

Class Stunt

Because I have **great wealth**, equipment that I buy costs 1 point less, to a minimum of 1.

Conditions

- » ANGRY
- » WOUNDED
- » COMPROMISED
- » DEPLETED
- » MARKED FOR DEATH

THE CLEANER

Amongst those who would thumb their noses at the ones in charge of Paris Nouveau, rumors of the Cleaners are told in hushed, fearful whispers. The Cleaners are the most dangerous agents of the secret police: part intelligence operative, part investigator, part assassin. When somebody becomes a problem for the government, or for a powerful corporation, you descend upon that person and ensure that they're never heard from again.

Think: Victor Nettoyeur from *La Femme Nikita*

ASPECTS

Answer these five questions using single words or short phrases. These are your aspects.

- » *What makes you the best Cleaner in Paris Nouveau?*
- » *Why do you kill so often?*
- » *Who is the one person you trust?*
- » *Who do you wish you could remove from play, but can't?*
- » *Why did you join la Résistance?*

MEANS

Pick one means spread from the following.

- » *Fight +3, Manipulate +2, Maneuver +1, Observe +2*
- » *Fight +3, Manipulate +1, Maneuver +2, Observe +2*
- » *Fight +2, Manipulate +2, Maneuver +1, Observe +3*

ADVANCEMENT

ADVANCEMENT TRACK ⬡⬡⬡⬡⬡

During a mission, *if my advancement track becomes full, I can immediately clear it to gain 5 fate points.*

At the end of a mission, *I earn one advancement point per true statement:*

- » *I killed someone without being detected.*
- » *I disposed of evidence of wrongdoing.*
- » *I struck from a position of advantage or hiding.*

During a debrief, *if my advancement track is full, I can clear it to advance.*

STUNTS

You start **with great wealth**. Pick two more. Reduce your refresh by one to pick one more.

- Because I have **stealth augmentations**, I can spend a fate point to disappear from a scene. I can show up during a later exchange in a different zone.

- Because I have an **information network**, when I create a prep advantage with Manipulate, I tie another boost to it as long as I can access my network of spies.

- Because I **serve my masters**, I can call upon my corporate sponsor to get me out of trouble, once per mission. Their help, however, is never free.

- Because I **kill without hesitation**, when I successfully cause physical harm, I can give the GM 1 blowback to force my opponent to mark an extra condition, provided my intent is to kill.

- Because I'm **slippery**, I get +2 to avoid detection with Maneuver.

RENO

ASPECTS
THE ANONYMOUS KILLER; EXPEDIENCY BEFORE MORALITY; SEVEN KEEPS MY SECRETS; UNFRIENDLY COMPETITION; MAKING A BETTER WORLD

MEANS
Fight: Good (+3)
Manipulate: Fair (+2)
Maneuver: Average (+1)
Observe: Fair (+2)

STUNTS
Stealth augmentations, slippery, great wealth

THE BLUEBLOOD

You're a member of the ruling class. Wealthy, powerful, influential, and well-known, you get your way with massive amounts of money. Most nobles are content to live out their lives in luxury, but a rare few can't blind themselves to the suffering of those who don't have access to the same resources. Some of them become philanthropists, doing some small amount of good in the short term; some, like you, join the Resistance, either as active agents or secret benefactors.

Think: Marquise de Merteuil from *Les Liaisons Dangereuses*

ASPECTS

Answer these five questions using single words or short phrases. These are your aspects.

> » *Where does your wealth and privilege come from?*
> » *What do you want, but can't buy?*
> » *Who do you rely upon to get you the things you want?*
> » *Who's looking to usurp your rightful place?*
> » *Why did you join la Résistance?*

MEANS

Pick one means spread from the following.

> » *Fight +1, Manipulate +3, Maneuver +2, Observe +2*
> » *Fight +2, Manipulate +3, Maneuver +2, Observe +1*
> » *Fight +1, Manipulate +2, Maneuver +2, Observe +3*

ADVANCEMENT

ADVANCEMENT TRACK ⬡⬡⬡⬡⬡

During a mission, *if my advancement track becomes full, I can immediately clear it to gain 5 fate points.*

At the end of a mission, *I earn one advancement point per true statement:*

> » *I convinced someone to agree with my way of doing things.*
> » *I used money or influence to solve a problem.*
> » *I used other people to do my dirty work.*

During a debrief, *if my advancement track is full, I can clear it to advance.*

STUNTS

You start **with great wealth**. Pick two more. Reduce your refresh by one to pick one more.

Because **money talks**, whenever I buy equipment, I can reduce the cost by 1, to a minimum of 1. If I do, the GM gets 2 blowback.

Because I **deal in favors**, when I gain the advantage in a social situation, I gain another boost.

Because **the camera loves me**, I can make a Manipulate or Maneuver prep advantage without spending a prep action, but only if I tell the press something juicy, giving 5 blowback to the GM.

Because I have **bodyguards**, I can bring them into any conflict, once per mission. If I do, they're an aspect with a tied boost. I'll work with the GM to make sure their inclusion makes sense in   the scene.

Because **words cut**, when I successfully cause harm in a social situation, I can give the GM 1 blowback to force my opponent to mark an extra condition.

CHLOE

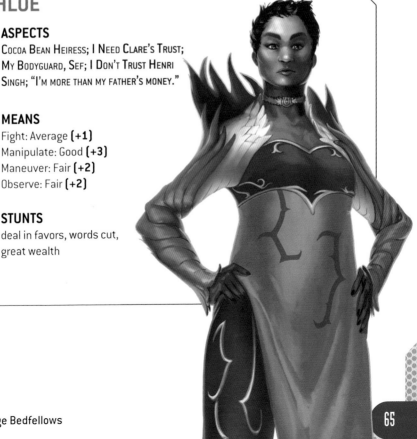

ASPECTS
Cocoa Bean Heiress; I Need Clare's Trust; My Bodyguard, Sef; I Don't Trust Henri Singh; "I'm more than my father's money."

MEANS
Fight: Average (+1)
Manipulate: Good (+3)
Maneuver: Fair (+2)
Observe: Fair (+2)

STUNTS
deal in favors, words cut, great wealth

THE OFFICER

You are at the top of a law enforcement, security, or military organization. Neither a rank-and-file cop nor a mid-tier superior, you command a large number of personnel, all of whom have extensive combat training. Officers are often targets of the Resistance, though assassination is not usually the goal. The Resistance loves to get Officers alone to try to turn them into allies, whether through coercion, bribery, or appeals to morality. There are Officers who bend to these tactics; there are also Officers who play along to infiltrate the Resistance.

Think: M. de Tréville from *Les Trois Mousquetaires*

ASPECTS

Answer these five questions using single words or short phrases. These are your aspects.

» *What militant organization are you in charge of?*
» *Why do you deserve your position?*
» *What do you hide from your subordinates?*
» *Who is your greatest enemy?*
» *Why did you join la Résistance?*

MEANS

Pick one means spread from the following.

» *Fight +3, Manipulate +2, Maneuver +2, Observe +1*
» *Fight +2, Manipulate +3, Maneuver +1, Observe +2*
» *Fight +1, Manipulate +2, Maneuver +2, Observe +3*

ADVANCEMENT

ADVANCEMENT TRACK ⬡⬡⬡⬡⬡

During a mission, *if my advancement track becomes full, I can immediately clear it to gain 5 fate points.*

At the end of a mission, *I earn one advancement point per true statement:*

» *I issued an order, and it was obeyed without question.*
» *I helped create a plan that our group executed.*
» *I used violence to solve a problem.*

During a debrief, *if my advancement track is full, I can clear it to advance.*

STUNTS

*You start **with great wealth**. Pick two more. Reduce your refresh by one to pick one more.*

○ Because I have **authority**, I can have my men accomplish one action for me, without rolling, once per mission. The GM will tell me what consequences I face as a result.

○ Because I have **clearance**, I can enter a secure area openly, with little trouble. The GM will tell me what consequences I face as a result.

○ Because I'm a **warrior**, I get +2 to cause harm with Fight in close-quarters combat.

○ Because I have a **war chest**, I can become <aspect>Depleted</aspect> in order to get equipment with a total cost of 4, without spending fate points. I can do this during a prep scene or even during a mission, provided it makes sense to do so.

○ Because I **command**, I get +2 to gain the advantage with Fight when I'm engaged in combat with allies or subordinates present.

ALISTAIR BARON

ASPECTS
Captain of the Baron's Men;
Living on Borrowed Time;
Robert, My Son; A Chance at
Redemption; "I built this company
from the ground up."

MEANS
Fight: Fair (+2)
Manipulate: Good (+3)
Maneuver: Average (+1)
Observe: Fair (+2)

STUNTS
Authority, command,
great wealth

Les Citoyens

Embedded in your neural casing is a small chip engraved with your serial number. This chip records all your genetic, biometric, and neurological information so that if any health system is noted as out of sync, then medical assistance can be summoned.

You no longer have to worry about reaching medical assistance in time. They will find you. In addition, if you are hungry, your neural casing can suggest nearby sources of APE or the quickest route back to your domain.

Your privacy is important to us, and that's why we have systems in place to protect your valuable information from hackers and dangerous people.

No, no, no, no. Everything you do or say, everywhere you go, the people you meet. Your biostats, including the beat of your heart and the autonomic responses of your body, that information is owned by the corporation that owns the tech in your head. Your information is not only used ruthlessly by corporations and unscrupulous individuals, but they know where you are. At. Every. Moment.

People are in great denial about this simple fact, pointing to how easy and effortless their lives are with this technology. It's true, but the cost is high. If you join the Resistance, the first thing we will do is cut that thing out of your skull. If it's embedded too deeply to remove safely, we can try to hack it and create a false data trail to protect you.

And remember: if we can hack it, they can hack it too.

Les Citoyens in Play

Les Citoyens—the Citizenry—make up most of the population of Paris Nouveau. You have some rights, but not as many as those in la Societé.

Members of les Citoyens...

- ...can go most places without having to take special precautions or explain themselves.
- ...are mostly anonymous.
- ...have corporate sponsors who will sometimes help them, for a cost.

However...

- ...they are expected to obey figures of authority.
- ...they are under constant surveillance through their AR rigs.
- ...they are expected to work every day for their corporate sponsors, and will be missed if they don't.

Class Stunt

Because I'm **just another Citizen**, I can ignore the effects of either COMPROMISED or BLACKLISTED until the end of the scene, once per mission. If I do so, the next time I attempt to clear the condition I ignored, my opposition increases by 2.

Conditions

- » ANGRY
- » WOUNDED
- » COMPROMISED
- » BLACKLISTED
- » MARKED FOR DEATH

THE HACKER

Your neural casing grants you AR, the ability to pretend that life isn't as ugly as it is. But it also means that you're being watched constantly, your actions monitored and logged, assessed for dangerous behavior. You know these things, and know how to subvert your neural casing to make it do what you want it to do. Further, you know how to project into *other* people's neural casings, making them see what you want them to see.

Think: Any member of Urban eXperiment (UX), a French hacker-artist group

ASPECTS

Answer these five questions using single words or short phrases. These are your aspects.

  » *What's your reputation in the Infosphere?*
  » *What hack do you really wish you hadn't pulled?*
  » *Who do you often rely upon for meatspace help?*
  » *Who do you want to take down a peg or two?*
  » *Why did you join la Résistance?*

MEANS

Pick one means spread from the following.

  » *Fight +1, Manipulate +3, Maneuver +2, Observe +2*
  » *Fight +2, Manipulate +1, Maneuver +2, Observe +3*
  » *Fight +1, Manipulate +2, Maneuver +2, Observe +3*

ADVANCEMENT

ADVANCEMENT TRACK ⬡⬡⬡⬡⬡

During a mission, *if my advancement track becomes full, I can immediately clear it to gain 5 fate points.*

At the end of a mission, *I earn one advancement point per true statement:*

  » *I obtained valuable or illicit information.*
  » *I caused havoc within a computerized system.*
  » *I solved a problem by clever application of my hacking skills.*

During a debrief, *if my advancement track is full, I can clear it to advance.*

STUNTS

You start **just another Citizen**. Pick two more. Reduce your refresh by one to pick one more.

Because I can **spoof my markers**, once per mission I can immediately clear my COMPROMISED condition by giving the GM 2 blowback.

Because I have **eyes everywhere**, I get +2 to gain the advantage with Observe, provided I can access security cameras & the like.

Because I can **spike the A/R**, I can spend a fate point to take out all blanks and agents in one zone without rolling, provided they have active neural casings. The GM gets blowback for each one I take out, though.

Because I can **spoof the A/R**, I can enter any scene disguised as someone else. My disguise is an aspect with a tied boost.

Because I post **screeds on the boards**, whenever I gain the advantage in a way related to mobilizing the hacker underground of Paris Nouveau, I gain another boost. After I roll, I can gain more boosts by giving the GM 2 blowback per extra boost.

SEVEN

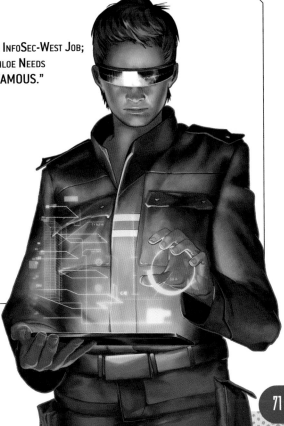

ASPECTS

GHOST IN THE MACHINE; THE INFOSEC-WEST JOB; SOHO, MY BIG BROTHER; CHLOE NEEDS HUMBLING; "I'M GONNA BE **FAMOUS.**"

MEANS

Fight: Average (+1)
Manipulate: Fair (+2)
Maneuver: Fair (+2)
Observe: Good (+3)

STUNTS

Eyes everywhere,
spoof the AR,
just another Citizen

THE SOLDIER

Not all Citizens get the abstraction of pattern-recognition games painted over the reality of their work. Some of them have to get their hands dirty. La Gendarmerie, the Parisian military, and the various corporate paramilitary outfits all require rank-and-file troops, people trained to fight, detain, and kill undesirables, rabble-rousers, foreign threats, and their fellow Citizens when called upon to do so. You are such a person: rigorously trained and conditioned to be loyal and efficient. But not all Soldiers *remain* loyal.

Think: Jeanne d'Arc

ASPECTS

Answer these five questions using single words or short phrases. These are your aspects.

> » *What form of violence or bullying are you an expert at?*
> » *Whose position do you covet?*
> » *Why don't you respect your superiors?*
> » *What causes you to employ violence the most often?*
> » *Why did you join la Résistance?*

MEANS

Pick one means spread from the following.

> » *Fight +3, Manipulate +1, Maneuver +2, Observe +2*
> » *Fight +3, Manipulate +2, Maneuver +2, Observe +1*
> » *Fight +2, Manipulate +1, Maneuver +2, Observe +3*

ADVANCEMENT   ADVANCEMENT TRACK ⬡⬡⬡⬡⬡

During a mission, *if my advancement track becomes full, I can immediately clear it to gain 5 fate points.*

At the end of a mission, *I earn one advancement point per true statement:*

> » *I obeyed an order without question.*
> » *I used intimidation or force to solve a problem.*
> » *I maintained my composure during a chaotic or stressful situation.*

During a debrief, *if my advancement track is full, I can clear it to advance.*

STUNTS

*You start **just another Citizen**. Pick two more. Reduce your refresh by one to pick one more.*

⬡ *Because I have **combat training**, I get +2 to cause harm with Fight if I intend to kill my target.*

⬡ *Because I have been subjected to **behavioral conditioning**, I get +2 to avoid attempts to gain social or psychological advantages against me.*

⬡ *Because I have **friends on the force**, I can call upon them to gain access to a restricted location without too much trouble. The GM will tell me what it costs me.*

⬡ *Because I have **implanted meta-data readers**, I get +2 to gain the advantage with Observe, provided I'm using the metadata of a person I can see.*

⬡ *Because I have **tactical training**, when I cause harm with Fight and spend boosts, I get +3 instead of +2 for each boost spent.*

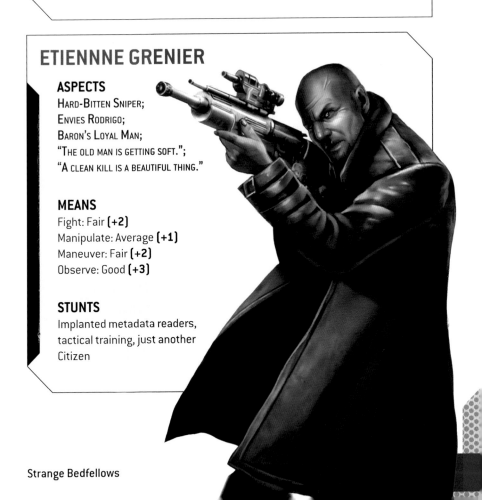

ETIENNNE GRENIER

ASPECTS
HARD-BITTEN SNIPER;
ENVIES RODRIGO;
BARON'S LOYAL MAN;
"THE OLD MAN IS GETTING SOFT.";
"A CLEAN KILL IS A BEAUTIFUL THING."

MEANS
Fight: Fair **(+2)**
Manipulate: Average **(+1)**
Maneuver: Fair **(+2)**
Observe: Good **(+3)**

STUNTS
Implanted metadata readers,
tactical training, just another
Citizen

THE MALCONTENT

Most Citizens are placid, docile. Perfectly happy to live their lives of mind-numbing consumerism and semi-convenience. You are not. You're the classic rabble-rouser: a Citizen who's fed up with the establishment and who is actively working against it. You don't have any skills that are particularly valuable to the Resistance, but you do have passion. Passion that they don't mind using as a weapon.

Think: Ravachol, a.k.a. François Claudius Koënigstein, famous French anarchist

ASPECTS

Answer these five questions using single words or short phrases. These are your aspects.

>> What made you believe that anarchy is the only solution?
>> What corporation or organization do you want to tear down more than any other?
>> What's the worst thing you've ever done in service of your cause?
>> Who is your most reliable ally?
>> Why did you join la Résistance?

MEANS

Pick one means spread from the following.

>> Fight +3, Manipulate +2, Maneuver +1, Observe +2
>> Fight +2, Manipulate +3, Maneuver +1, Observe +2
>> Fight +1, Manipulate +3, Maneuver +2, Observe +2

ADVANCEMENT

ADVANCEMENT TRACK ⬡◇◇◇◇

During a mission, *if my advancement track becomes full, I can immediately clear it to gain 5 fate points.*

At the end of a mission, *I earn one advancement point per true statement:*

>> I killed an agent of the government.
>> I convinced others to rise up and break their shackles.
>> I gave an impassioned speech about overthrowing our corporate overlords.

During a debrief, *if my advancement track is full, I can clear it to advance.*

STUNTS

You start **just another Citizen**. Pick two more. Reduce your refresh by one to pick one more.

- Because **fortune favors the bold**, I gain a boost whenever I succeed at a reckless or impulsive action.

- Because **I'm a charismatic leader**, I gain another boost whenever I gain the advantage with Manipulate, but I must give the boost to someone else.

- Because **violence can be used for good**, I get +2 to cause harm with Fight when I firmly believe I'm doing the right thing.

- Because I have a **reputation**, when I meet an NPC, I can declare that the NPC has heard of me and respects me, once per mission. This respect is an aspect with three tied boosts.

- Because I'm **fighting for a better world**, I can spend a fate point to cause Citizens and Exiles around me to rise up and fight, once per scene. This gives me +2 to cause harm with Manipulate until the end of the scene, but the GM gets 5 blowback.

ILLYANA

ASPECTS

ALL GOVERNMENTS ARE THE SAME;
CORVID ECONOMICS TOOK MY EYES;
MY BROTHER'S BLOOD ON MY HANDS;
RODRIGO UNDERSTANDS ME;
FREEDOM THROUGH INSURRECTION

MEANS

Fight: Average (+1)
Manipulate: Good (+3)
Maneuver: Fair (+2)
Observe: Fair (+2)

STUNTS

Violence can be used for **good**, reputation, just another Citizen

Les Exilés

LES NATURELS

We must empathize with our friends les Naturels, even if we understand they are not our equals. They are, after all, Néo-Parisiens too. Generally, those in this group wished for brain augmentation, but by mischance or simple bad luck were not able to partake of this excellent technology. Some of them suffer from ill health and the operation would kill them, some did not find sufficient corporate sponsorship, some waited too long.

There is a small subset of les Naturels who claim such upgrades are immoral and dangerous. To those so deluded, we can only offer pity that they cannot enjoy the pleasures of neural casing technology.

EX-CITIZENS

These souls are lost to us. At one time they were useful, productive members of society. Now they have joined a criminal element, deactivated their neural casings, and removed themselves from le Treillis.

These people are evangelical and dangerous. If you are contacted by one, it's important to recognize that the loss of their neural casing has clearly unhinged them. The government of Paris Nouveau has classified the Resistance as a terrorist group, one willing to sacrifice Citoyens for what they term the "greater good."

Remember, being convicted of a crime leads to deactivation of your neural casing and to exile. Click here to inform the government of interaction with a suspected Resistance member.

Go ahead. Click. I'll wait.

No? You mean it's possible the government isn't telling you the whole truth? It's good to know I've at least convinced you of their relentless propagandizing.

I envy les Naturels. They will never know the deep horror of waking in sweat and reaching to plug in your neural casing, only to realize it's been cut out of you. They never have the withdrawals. They have learned to adapt to their situation, to live in the real world without the cost of knowing the fake delights that are in reach.

As far as Ex-Cits and the Resistance, well, the government is right about one thing. We **will** sacrifice ourselves to change the world into what we believe it ought to be. When's the last time you heard such a claim from a senior executive at Cryptiq or Paragon Gyromatics?

We are indeed against the law, because the law is wrong and it's dangerous and we won't stand by and watch our city burn the minds of its people into ash.

Perhaps you think that's Resistance hyperbole? Let me ask you: when's the last time you saw an elderly Citoyen? Not a Naturel or Ex-Cit, but a "useful, productive member of our society"? Can't think of one, can you? That's because the neural casing is such a taxing addition to the brain that it savages it in twenty to thirty years. When that happens, sometimes the Citoyen dies, but more often they are quietly removed from their domain by the downcycling technicians.

Don't believe me? I know—it's horrible. I've got some Naturels in our group who could tell you of whole wards of these people, missing and unnoticed by the rest of us. Our corporate masters have taught us that family is immaterial, so what does it matter?

Perhaps now you are rethinking that hunk of microchip in your skull. Good. Keep thinking about it. We want you to join us. This city needs people like you, people willing to ask questions, willing to unplug from le Treillis because their lives are worth more than fifty years of pattern-matching.

So here are our goals, simply:

To wake the people. They are asleep, going through the motions, with no awareness of the corruption they are enabling.

To disrupt la Societé, ultimately dissolving it, and to create a new system of government that allows the voice of the people to be heard.

To force those in power to renew focus on terraforming. Until we improve this world, people will always want to escape it into their virtual lives. Our goal is to restore the farmland around Paris Nouveau so we can begin feeding the populace real food again, instead of the artificial protein extract.

Your choice is clear. **Either feed the Beast or kill it.**

Les Exilés in Play

Les Exilés are the outcasts, the untouchables, those who have no rights and are not considered part of Paris Nouveau society.

Members of les Exilés…

> …are part of a tight-knit community that looks after its own.
>
> …are mostly trusted by la Résistance.
>
> …can avoid most surveillance, because they have no AR rigs and no Shade.

However…

> …they are discriminated against and are automatically suspected of wrongdoing by authority figures.
>
> …they have few resources at their disposal.
>
> …they have trouble functioning in Paris Nouveau proper, because they lack AR implants and citizenship.

Class Stunt

Because I'm a **friend of la Résistance**, when I requisition equipment from la Résistance, I pay 1 point less, to a minimum of 1. I can also requisition equipment with a cost 1 higher than normal.

Conditions

- » Angry
- » Wounded
- » Person of Interest
- » Blacklisted
- » Marked for Death

THE EX-CIT

You were once a Citizen, but you're not one any longer. Some people choose this path, opting to power down their augmentations and have their neural casings removed, so they can live life in the real world. Often Citizens do this in order to join the Resistance, as a show of commitment and solidarity.

Others have this status forced upon them, as punishment for a crime. When the government deems it appropriate, a Citizen can be stripped of Citizen status, have their neural casing forcibly deactivated, and be turned out of their home. With no property, no access to AR or VR, and limited rights, these Ex-Cits, too, often turn to the Resistance out of desperation or desire for revenge. It is possible, however, for these "resident exiles" to earn Citizen status back.

Think: Captain Alfred Dreyfus, French Jewish artillery officer convicted of treason

ASPECTS

Answer these five questions using single words or short phrases. These are your aspects.

- » *Why were you stripped of your citizenship?*
- » *Who were you in your old life?*
- » *What do you do, now that you live in exile?*
- » *Who helped you find shelter after you were exiled?*
- » *Why did you join la Résistance?*

MEANS

Pick one means spread from the following.

- » *Fight +3, Manipulate +1, Maneuver +2, Observe +2*
- » *Fight +2, Manipulate +1, Maneuver +3, Observe +2*
- » *Fight +1, Manipulate +3, Maneuver +2, Observe +2*

ADVANCEMENT   ADVANCEMENT TRACK ⬡⬡⬡⬡⬡

During a mission, *if my advancement track becomes full, I can immediately clear it to gain 5 fate points.*

At the end of a mission, *I earn one advancement point per true statement:*

- » *I faced down adversity on my own.*
- » *I won when the odds were against me.*
- » *I paid kindness back in kind.*

During a debrief, *if my advancement track is full, I can clear it to advance.*

STUNTS

*You start **friend of la Résistance**. Pick two more. Reduce your refresh by one to pick one more.*

- Because I have **nothing left to lose**, I can mark Angry or Wounded to get +2 or +4 to a roll, respectively.

- Because I'm **self-sufficient**, I get +1 to any rolls I make when I'm handling something alone.

- Because sometimes you have to **live to fight another day**, whenever I concede a conflict, I get another fate point at the end of the scene.

- Because **I always settle my debts**, whenever I mark a condition because I took harm, I get +2 to cause harm to whoever caused me harm, until the end of the scene.

- Because I'm **used to adversity**, I get +2 to gain the advantage with Fight when I'm going up against superior enemies.

RODRIGO VALJEAN

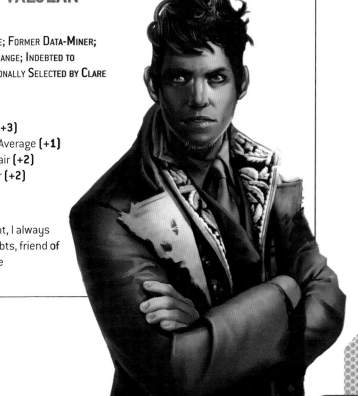

ASPECTS
I Choose Exile; Former Data-Miner; I Fight for Change; Indebted to Illyana; Personally Selected by Clare

MEANS
Fight: Good (+3)
Manipulate: Average (+1)
Maneuver: Fair (+2)
Observe: Fair (+2)

STUNTS
Self-sufficient, I always settle my debts, friend of la Résistance

THE NATUREL

As a Naturel, you've never had a neural casing or any form of augmentation. You live fully in the real world—though that doesn't preclude you from using wearable tech—and you do without many of the conveniences, rights, and restrictions of the citizenry. Naturels are often part of tight-knit communities that grow their own food, look out for each other, teach each other necessary skills, and band together for defense when necessary. Most of this is illegal. As a result, many Naturels are part of the Resistance.

Think: Marie-Angélique Memmie le Blanc, feral child

ASPECTS

Answer these five questions using single words or short phrases. These are your aspects.

> » *Why doesn't your community use implants of any kind?*
> » *How have you learned to be self-sufficient?*
> » *Who taught you the skills you use to survive?*
> » *Who has decided you're a threat?*
> » *Why did you join la Résistance?*

MEANS

Pick one means spread from the following.

> » *Fight +3, Manipulate +1, Maneuver +2, Observe +2*
> » *Fight +2, Manipulate +1, Maneuver +3, Observe +2*
> » *Fight +2, Manipulate +1, Maneuver +2, Observe +3*

ADVANCEMENT

ADVANCEMENT TRACK

During a mission, *if my advancement track becomes full, I can immediately clear it to gain 5 fate points.*

At the end of a mission, *I earn one advancement point per true statement:*

> » *I used the environment to my advantage.*
> » *I supported and cooperated with my allies.*
> » *I made strides to help my community.*

During a debrief, *if my advancement track is full, I can clear it to advance.*

STUNTS

You start *friend of la Résistance*. Pick two more. Reduce your refresh by one to pick one more.

- Because I **move unseen**, I get +2 to avoid detection with Maneuver.

- Because I'm **off the grid**, get +2 to avoid attempts to gain the advantage over me when that advantage would be gained by metadata or biometric scanning.

- Because **I know my environment**, whenever I invoke a situation aspect representing an environmental feature, I get +3 instead of +2.

- Because **blood is thicker than water**, whenever I enter a scene in which I can call upon my community, I can choose to gain an aspect with a tied boost. The aspect must represent something I could gain from my community.

- Because **people underestimate me**, I get +2 to cause harm with Fight against an opponent who believes himself to be my superior.

JOSEPHINE OF THE WOODS

ASPECTS

WE STAND ON OUR OWN, TOGETHER;
THE WILDS ARE MY HOME; MY FATHER,
PIERRE; KELSEA DOESN'T TRUST ME;
THE WALL MUST FALL

MEANS

Fight: Fair (+2)
Manipulate: Average (+1)
Maneuver: Fair (+2)
Observe: Good (+3)

STUNTS

I move unseen, know
my environment,
friend of la Résistance

THE ARMIGER

Armigers are rare, misunderstood, and feared. They often start off as Ex-Cits or Naturels, and seek to take control of their world by making themselves more physically powerful and formidable. You've replaced your limbs with cybernetic prostheses, grafted armor plates to your skin, attached blades and hooks to your body.

Your augmentations all have two things in common. First, they're entirely self-contained. They're usually driven by machinery rather than electronics and advanced software, and they're never connected to the system of AR and VR that powers Paris Nouveau. Second, they're illegal. Armigers are often attacked on sight by gendarmes, but only when the gendarmes have far superior numbers; a single Armiger is an engine of destruction.

Most Armigers are part of the Resistance, and almost all of those live most of their lives in la Cave; it's the only place you find any kind of safety or acceptance.

Think: Sasha Bordeaux, DC Comics

ASPECTS

Answer these five questions using single words or short phrases. These are your aspects.

> » *Why do you rely so heavily upon augmentations?*
> » *What is your most disturbing physical feature?*
> » *Which augmentation is your favorite?*
> » *Who accepts you despite your intimidating presence?*
> » *Why did you join la Résistance?*

MEANS

Pick one means spread from the following.

> » *Fight +3, Manipulate +1, Maneuver +2, Observe +2*
> » *Fight +2, Manipulate +1, Maneuver +3, Observe +2*
> » *Fight +2, Manipulate +2, Maneuver +1, Observe +3*

ADVANCEMENT

ADVANCEMENT TRACK ⬡⬡⬡⬡⬡

During a mission, *if my advancement track becomes full, I can immediately clear it to gain 5 fate points.*

At the end of a mission, *I earn one advancement point per true statement:*

> » *I made someone uncomfortable or afraid.*
> » *I caused significant property damage.*
> » *I solved a problem by using my implants.*

During a debrief, *if my advancement track is full, I can clear it to advance.*

STUNTS

*You start **friend of la Résistance**. Pick two more. Reduce your refresh by one to pick one more.*

Because I'm covered in **armor plating**, I can spend a fate point to avoid marking a condition caused by physical harm.

Because I'm an **engine of destruction**, I can give the GM 1 blowback to get +2 to a Fight roll. I can do this up to three times on a given roll.

Because I'm **enormous**, I get +2 to cause harm with Fight when my size is a factor.

Because I'm **scary**, I get +2 to gain the advantage with Fight when I'm intimidating someone.

Because I'm a **pariah**, I can spend a fate point to draw the attention of any NPCs in my zone. When I do this, each of my allies gains a boost.

KELSEA

ASPECTS
FLESH IS FRAILTY; PROTRUDING BLADES;
MY EYES SEE EVERYTHING; I WON'T LEAVE
JOSEPHINE; MY FATHER IS WRONG ABOUT ME

MEANS
Fight: Fair **(+2)**
Manipulate: Fair **(+2)**
Maneuver: Average **(+1)**
Observe: Good **(+3)**

STUNTS
Armor plating, pariah,
friend of la Résistance

Come out of the bathroom, Sidenge

Got a nervous stomach, leave me alone

We were supposed to leave five minutes ago

She's my friend - I didn't sign up for this Marya

Jules is going to bust down the door if you don't come out soon.
I'm her friend too, but we're out of time.

Not going

Let me put it this way. Do *you* want to be the one to find
Arielle...or Jules?

...

Sidenge?

...be right there

5 Who You Are
Aspects and Secrets

Two fundamental parts of your character are worth more explanation: their aspects and their secrets. In this chapter, we'll go into the details of both, explaining what they are, how they can change, and how they drive play.

Aspects

An aspect is a short phrase, or even a single word, that says something true about your character. It describes her in some way. It could be a physical feature, like exceptional strength; it could be a quirk of personality, like a proclivity for risk-taking. It could also describe a relationship, an issue your character struggles with, or any other thing that's both true about your character and dramatically relevant to the game.

An aspect can be a **noun**: a person, place, or thing. Maybe you have your MOTHER'S LOCKET, or maybe you're a GRIZZLED EX-SOLDIER.

An aspect can be an **adjective or description**: Elayna is TALENTED BEYOND HER YEARS. Henri is CRUEL BUT FAIR.

An aspect could also be a **quote or catchphrase**. You might write one like "RISE UP AND RESIST!" or "THE ONLY GOOD GENDARME IS A DEAD ONE."

How Do I Write Aspects?

When making your character's aspects, write brief, punchy sentences that immediately convey who your character is and what she's like. Though exceptions exist, brevity is your friend; keeping your aspects under five words is a useful guideline.

Choose aspects you think would be interesting or exciting to play in the world of Paris Nouveau. Who are you? Why do you fight for la Résistance? How did you learn the skills you have? What is your relationship with people in the different classes? The questions on your playsheet are there to help you, but feel free to interpret them broadly or answer them obliquely or in unexpected ways.

Think also about how your aspects drive play. Do your aspects ensure that you pretty much get along with everyone? That might seem like a good idea, but in practice it'll minimize conflict. Conflict is where a lot of the interesting stuff happens, so creating aspects that generate tension between characters can lead to fun situations. Make sure, though, that you're not generating tension between *players*. Everyone's at the table to have fun, after all.

A good aspect is also double-edged. It's tempting to make aspects that are purely beneficial, but one chief way you get fate points is by accepting compels or even compelling yourself (**page 92**). So if your aspects complicate your life, you get rewarded for it with a resource that can be hard to come by in **Uprising**.

What Do Aspects Do?

Aspects allow you to influence your story, to change its direction, to make it go your way. You can use aspects by spending **fate points**. Though you start with only a few fate points, you earn more during play when you allow aspects to be used against you in creating trouble or obstacles for your character.

Invoking Aspects

You can **invoke** an aspect to help you accomplish something or establish something as true. Invoking an aspect costs you one fate point or one boost tied to that aspect, and you must be able to explain how the aspect has bearing on the current situation and how it helps you, subject to table consensus. When you invoke an aspect, you gain one of the following benefits:

» Add +2 to your effort.

» Reroll your dice and use the new result.

» Declare a story detail.

» Provide opposition to someone else's roll.

> ### What are boosts?
> Boosts are small, temporary advantages that you gain during play. When you get one, you can spend it before it goes away, pass it on to someone else, or tie it to an aspect to make it last longer. For more on boosts, read "Boosts" (**page 141**).

When you invoke to **add +2 to your effort,** you can invoke the aspect **before or after** you've rolled. You can even choose to invoke an aspect after you've learned the outcome of a roll, if you want a better outcome. The same is true of rerolling the dice, though it makes little sense to invoke to reroll before you roll the dice in the first place.

When you invoke an aspect to **declare a story detail,** this doesn't provide any kind of mechanical advantage, but it does declare something as explicitly true within the narrative. This type of invocation is subject to table consensus, and the GM can veto particularly ridiculous declarations outright.

You invoke your DAUGHTER OF THE COMMANDER aspect to declare that the military official you have to get past is your father, who's likely to be sympathetic to you. The table agrees, so the declaration becomes true.

BREAK

You invoke your DAUGHTER OF THE COMMANDER aspect to declare that your father bursts into the interrogation room you're being held in, summarily executes the guards and interrogator, and secrets you out of the facility. This strains credibility for the others at the table, though, and they don't agree that this happens. You can either withdraw your declaration and keep your fate point, or work with the table to come up with a declaration that **does** make sense.

BREAK

You invoke your ALWAYS WATCHFUL aspect to declare that you spot a meteor streaking out of the sky, which impacts the facility you want to destroy, leveling it utterly. The GM tells you this is a rather silly declaration, and vetoes it. You keep your fate point.

When you invoke to **provide opposition,** you're doing it to block someone else's action. This comes in two flavors: forcing a roll, or making an action harder. You can invoke to provide Fair (+2) opposition or to add +2 to preexisting opposition. In either case, the opposition lasts for only one roll. The fate point you spend to invoke goes to the person you're opposing. As usual, if you spend a boost, they get nothing.

Rodrigo is trying to get behind some cover. The GM wants to make it difficult on them, so she invokes a HAIL OF BULLETS to force Rodrigo to resolve an uncertain outcome with Maneuver first. Now, Rodrigo has to roll against Fair (+2) opposition to get behind cover.

BREAK

Kelsea is trying to break down a door. The GM decides to invoke the HASTILY CONSTRUCTED BARRICADE to make it harder, increasing the opposition she's rolling against by two steps.

Who You Are

You may invoke as many aspects as you like on a given roll, provided you can spend a fate point or boost on each invocation, and provided you can justify each one. However, you can only spend one fate point per aspect on a given roll. You may spend as many boosts to invoke an aspect as you like, though.

> Kelsea is trying to disable some gendarmes quickly, causing harm with Fight. She spends a fate point to invoke her PROTRUDING BLADES to add a +2 bonus to her effort. She can't spend another fate point on PROTRUDING BLADES for the same roll, but she **can** spend a fate point on a different aspect, FLESH IS FRAILTY, or spend any number of boosts tied to PROTRUDING BLADES, to add more +2 bonuses.

Compelling Aspects

Fate points are a finite resource, and you'll want to earn more of them during play by accepting **compels**.

When anyone, GM or player, decides that one of your aspects could complicate the situation, they can offer you a fate point to compel you. When a player compels you, he offers you one of his own fate points. When the GM compels you, though, she offers you a fate point from the general supply.

If you accept the fate point, then your aspect complicates the situation as they've said. You can, however, choose to reject the compel by refusing the offered fate point **and** spending one of your own. They keep their offered fate point, and your spent fate point goes to the general supply. If you reject a compel, the event might still come to pass, but you manage to avoid any complications associated with it.

But here's the thing: you're the person at the table most likely to remember your own aspects. If you want fate points, you can compel *yourself*. When you do this, you make trouble for yourself and point out to the GM how your aspect factored into that trouble. The GM will happily slide you a fate point for doing that.

For example, if you have the aspect **IN LOVE WITH PIERRE**, you could choose to make a complicating decision, such as abandoning your post, to go have a rendezvous with your paramour. Point this out to the GM. You'll likely get a fate point, and it'll cause all kinds of fun trouble later on.

Players, you can even compel an NPC's aspect by offering a fate point to the GM. However, if the GM resists your compel, the fate point she pays will go into the general supply, not to you.

There are two sorts of compels: events and decisions.

When someone initiates an **event compel** something happens that's not wholly within your character's control, but affects you because of an aspect. For example, if you have the aspect CAPTAIN RODERICK IS MY HATED RIVAL, an event compel might involve Roderick showing up at an inconvenient time to get in your way. If you accept such a compel, he shows up and complicates your life as suggested. If you refuse it, perhaps you avoid him, or perhaps he shows up but you have a plan to deal with him already in place.

A **decision compel**, on the other hand, presents you with a complicated choice. If you are a FAMILY MAN, for example, you might get a call from your daughter just before a mission. She needs medicine for your son, and she needs it soon. Now you have a choice: continue on the mission, or go get medicine for your son. If you accept such a compel, you make the choice and your decision leads to complicated things, such as your son getting ill or the mission being compromised. If you refuse such a compel, you might still make the choice but your decision doesn't complicate things in the same way, or you might find a way to solve both problems at once.

Are There Other Kinds of Aspects?

There are three broad categories of aspects in this game: character aspects, setting aspects, and situation aspects.

Character aspects are all of the aspects on the PCs' playsheets.

Setting aspects are la Résistance's manifesto and weakness, and the government's slogan and scandal.

Situation aspects represent the current situation (naturally), whether that means the situation as a whole or a specific someone or something. For example, a gendarme might put you OFF-BALANCE, or the tunnel that you're in might become FLOODED. The GM can introduce situation aspects as she likes, while players can introduce situation aspects by gaining the advantage (*page 132*).

Situation aspects behave the way character aspects do: they're true for as long as they're relevant, and they can be invoked or compelled by anyone who can justify it—and pay for it. If the GM decides that a situation aspect no longer makes any sense, she can remove it from the scene. If you're OFF-BALANCE, for example, the GM might rule that you're only OFF-BALANCE until you get a chance to act, at which point you regain your footing and the aspect goes away.

All Aspects Are the Same

Whether you're talking about your character aspects or someone else's, situation aspects, or the aspects on la Résistance or the government, all aspects work the same, and you can interact with them in the same ways regardless of who or what they're attached to. That means you can invoke someone else's aspect to help yourself, and someone else could compel you with any aspect that makes narrative sense.

The Truth and Lies of Aspects

Regardless of whether your aspects get invoked or compelled, they're always true. Just because you're not getting a mechanical advantage from the fact that you're an **Armor-Plated Living Tank** doesn't make that statement any less true. Keep it in mind, and play your character as if it's true. If you use an aspect to complicate your life, ask the GM if it's worth a fate point. It probably is. So, aspects are true...

...except when they're not. See, agents of la Résistance sometimes lie about who they are and what they think. Aspects are, more accurately, what everybody else *believes* is true about you. They're public information; they don't necessarily represent the real you. To represent this, once per session, you can spend a fate point to change one of your character aspects, revealing that it wasn't true all along, and that something else is true instead. Tie two boosts to that aspect for your trouble.

> A couple sessions in, Lucy decides that one of Luce's aspects, Ex-
> Hunter, Ex-Spy is actually a lie; the truth is that she's an assassin
> sent to kill someone in la Résistance! She pays a fate point, erases
> Ex-Hunter, Ex-Spy, and writes down Contract Killer in its place. Emily
> hands Lucy two boosts to tie to Contract Killer.

Destroying Aspects

Sometimes you'll want to destroy an aspect in play, like if the enemy is **Behind Cover**, for example, or if you have **Romantic Ties** you want to break off.

To try to destroy an aspect, roll to resolve an uncertain outcome (**page 132**) against the mission opposition (**page 124**), adding +1 to the opposition per boost tied to the aspect. Instead of passive opposition, someone else can roll active opposition to try to prevent you from destroying the aspect, as long as they're in a position to do so.

Only situation aspects can be destroyed, not character aspects. If you destroy a situation aspect, you also destroy all boosts tied to it. However, you can't destroy boosts that aren't tied to aspects.

Secrets: That Which Motivates

During character creation, each character gets a secret. Secrets give players another way to advance their characters, but secrets often bring PCs into conflict and breed suspicion. This is good; suspicion is part of *Uprising*.

There are eight types of secrets:

» Blackmail

» Mole Hunter

» Hostage

» Secret Attraction

» Troublemaker

» Rival

» Killer

» Spy

The secret deck has 5 versions of the Spy, and 1 of each other secret. Each secret has three parts:

» The **prompt** provides context for the secret and asks questions. When the players read this text, ask them to think about the answers to the questions and answer them to themselves. These answers can inform how they play their characters.

» The **advancement triggers** tell the player other ways that they can earn advancement points. When a player earns advancement points from fulfilling the advancement trigger, they simply mark the points. They don't have to announce that they're earning points.

» The **reveal clause** tells players what big, dramatic thing they can do to reveal the secret. When a player triggers their reveal clause, they earn an immediate advance and may get other benefits.

Immediate Advances and Table Consensus

At some point, you'll earn an immediate advance from a secret, but an advance simply might not make any sense within the moment. It doesn't make sense for you to declare your love so hard for someone that you suddenly sprout forearm blades, for example.

If you want to take your earned advance immediately, but table consensus is that it doesn't make sense in the moment, feel free to hold your advance until it *does* make sense. Otherwise, you could choose a different advance that makes more sense in the moment.

Characters created at the start of the game get secrets as described starting on **page 22**.

If a new player enters the game, they draw two secrets from the secret deck and choose one to keep, placing the remaining secret back in the deck.

If an existing player has to make a new character, shuffle the old character's secret into the deck, then that player draws two secrets and chooses one, placing the other secret back in the deck.

Blackmail

You were a Citizen in good standing until la Résistance blackmailed you into helping them. What do they have on you? What would happen to you if it got out? How far are you willing to go to keep it covered up?

Earn 1 advancement point whenever the PCs complete a Resistance goal. Keeping them happy is how you keep your skeletons in the closet.

Earn an immediate advance when you reveal the nature of your blackmail to the group, the general public, or both, thus robbing the secret of its power. The focus of your blackmail becomes an aspect with 5 tied boosts. You cannot spend these boosts, but others can use them against you. When these boosts are gone, the aspect disappears.

If you survive to the next debrief, the GM selects and gives you two new secrets. Choose one new secret to keep, then shuffle the other secret and your old secret back into the deck.

Mole Hunter

La Résistance has tasked you with rooting out traitors. How do you feel about that? Why did they choose you?

Earn 1 advancement point whenever you pass la Résistance secret information about your teammates (by passing a note to the GM).

Earn an immediate advance when you correctly accuse someone of being a Spy during a debrief. Being correct means that the accused either turns double or sacrifices themself. When you get back to the table, reveal your secret and earn your advance. Then, the GM selects and gives you two new secrets. Choose one new secret to keep, then shuffle the other secret and your old secret back into the deck.

Hostage

Your loyalty to la Résistance is constantly tested by the fact that it puts some-one close to you—someone who's still a loyal Citizen—in danger. Who is it? Do they know that the government is watching them? What will happen to them if you step out of line? Has the government made threats to that effect?

Earn 1 advancement point when you take out someone in a way that *doesn't* give blowback to the GM.

Earn an immediate advance when you either convince the hostage you're protecting to defect to la Résistance, or the hostage turns against you or dies. Reveal this secret. If the hostage defected, la Résistance earns an advance. If the hostage turned against you or dies, the government earns an advance.

If you survive to the next debrief, the GM selects and gives you two new secrets. Choose one new secret to keep, then shuffle the other secret and your old secret back into the deck.

Secret Attraction

You're drawn to someone else on the team. Who is it? Why can't you let them know? What would you do for them?

Earn 1 advancement point whenever you help the object of your attraction by giving them a boost, defending them, attacking someone they're fighting, or backing them up on a decision they make.

Earn an immediate advance when you declare your attraction to them, conse-quences be damned. Reveal this secret. The aspect **ROMANTIC TIES** enters play with three tied boosts, and it starts each mission with three tied boosts, re-gardless of how many it ended the previous mission with. If the object of your attraction declares that the attraction is mutual, then they, you, and the GM can use the aspect. If they declare that the attraction *isn't* mutual, you can't use the aspect—only they and the GM can use the aspect *against* you.

If you survive to the next debrief, the GM selects and gives you two new secrets. Choose one new secret to keep, then shuffle the other secret and your old secret back into the deck.

Troublemaker

You just want to tear things down and mess things up. Why? Are you following an ideology, or do you just like chaos? What's the worst thing you've ever done? What thing do you most want to do?

Earn 1 advancement point whenever you take an action that gives blowback to the GM.

Earn an immediate advance when you do something incredibly stupid and destructive, regardless of the consequences. Reveal this secret. The GM gains 10 blowback.

If you survive to the next debrief, the GM selects and gives you two new secrets. Choose one new secret to keep, then shuffle the other secret and your old secret back into the deck.

Rival

You have an intense rivalry with someone else on the team. Why do you have it in for them? What real or imagined slight are you avenging? What would you do to them, given the chance?

Earn 1 advancement point whenever you hinder the object of your rivalry, or when you call them out publicly.

Earn an immediate advance when you declare your rivalry publicly. Reveal this secret. The aspect RIVALRY enters play with three tied boosts, and it starts each mission with three tied boosts, regardless of how many tied boosts it had at the end of the last mission. Only the GM can spend these boosts, and she can use them to compel you or your rival **without** giving out a fate point.

If you survive to the next debrief, the GM selects and gives you two new secrets. Choose one new secret to keep, then shuffle the other secret and your old secret back into the deck.

Killer

You have a taste for killing, though it troubles you deeply. What made you this way? How many people have you killed? How many of them didn't deserve it? How does killing make you feel?

Earn 1 advancement point whenever you kill a named NPC.

Earn an immediate advance when you confess your sins to someone, telling them of all the terrible things you've done, and ask them to help you stop. Reveal this secret. An aspect enters play representing your confession and plea for help. It starts each mission with two tied boosts, and only the person you confessed to can use it.

If you survive to the next debrief, the GM selects and gives you two new secrets. Choose one new secret to keep, then shuffle the other secret and your old secret back into the deck.

Spy: Agitator

Your job is to sow chaos within la Résistance. Why are you loyal to the government? What have they promised you? What would you do to pursue their goals?

Earn 3 advancement points whenever you falsely accuse someone else of being a Spy.

Earn 1 advancement point whenever the government earns any number of advancement points at once.

Earn an immediate advance when you reveal yourself to be a traitor. Reveal this secret. The GM gains 5 blowback, and you gain 3 fate points.

If you survive to the next debrief, choose whether your character becomes an NPC or has a change of heart and joins la Résistance.

> » **If your character becomes an NPC,** trigger the betrayal milestone (*page 147*).

> » **If your character stays with la Résistance,** assuming they allow it, then at the next debrief the GM selects and gives you two new secrets. Choose one new secret to keep, then shuffle the other secret and your old secret back into the deck.

Spy: Sleeper

Your job is to lie low, make la Résistance trust you, and strike at an opportune moment. Why are you loyal to the government? What have they promised you? What would you do to pursue their goals?

Earn 1 advancement point whenever a member of la Résistance asks for your help or gives you information in confidence.

Earn 1 advancement point whenever the government earns any number of advancement points at once.

Earn an immediate advance when you reveal yourself to be a traitor. Reveal this secret. The GM gains 5 blowback, and you gain 3 fate points.

If you survive to the next debrief, choose whether your character becomes an NPC or has a change of heart and joins la Résistance.

> » **If your character becomes an NPC,** trigger the betrayal milestone (*page 147*).

> » **If your character stays with la Résistance,** assuming they allow it, then at the next debrief the GM selects and gives you two new secrets. Choose one new secret to keep, then shuffle the other secret and your old secret back into the deck.

Spy: Informant

You've been tasked with feeding information back to the government. Why are you loyal to the government? What have they promised you? What would you do to pursue their goals?

Earn 1 advancement point whenever you pass a piece of sensitive information to the government (by passing a note to the GM).

Earn 1 advancement point whenever the government earns any number of advancement points at once.

Earn an immediate advance when you reveal yourself to be a traitor. Reveal this secret. The GM gains 5 blowback, and you gain 3 fate points.

If you survive to the next debrief, choose whether your character becomes an NPC or has a change of heart and joins la Résistance.

> » **If your character becomes an NPC,** trigger the betrayal milestone (*page 147*).

> » **If your character stays with la Résistance,** assuming they allow it, then at the next debrief the GM selects and gives you two new secrets. Choose one new secret to keep, then shuffle the other secret and your old secret back into the deck.

Spy: Saboteur

You've been told to undermine la Résistance's efforts whenever possible. Why are you loyal to the government? What have they promised you? What would you do to pursue their goals?

Earn 1 advancement point whenever you take an action that gives the GM blowback, or when you convince someone else to do so.

Earn 1 advancement point whenever the government earns any number of advancement points at once.

Earn an immediate advance when you reveal yourself to be a traitor. Reveal this secret. The GM gains 5 blowback, and you gain 3 fate points.

If you survive to the next debrief, choose whether your character becomes an NPC or has a change of heart and joins la Résistance.

> » **If your character becomes an NPC,** trigger the betrayal milestone (*page 147*).

> » **If your character stays with la Résistance,** assuming they allow it, then at the next debrief the GM selects and gives you two new secrets. Choose one new secret to keep, then shuffle the other secret and your old secret back into the deck.

Spy: Embezzler

The government would like you to waste la Résistance's resources and funnel money to the corporations. Why are you loyal to the government? What have they promised you? What would you do to pursue their goals?

Earn 1 advancement point whenever you spend a fate point from the Cache, and whenever a fate point goes into the Bank.

Earn 1 advancement point whenever the government earns any number of advancement points at once.

Earn an immediate advance when you reveal yourself to be a traitor. Reveal this secret. The GM gains 5 blowback, and you gain 3 fate points.

If you survive to the next debrief, choose whether your character becomes an NPC or has a change of heart and joins la Résistance.

> » **If your character becomes an NPC,** trigger the betrayal milestone (*page 147*).

> » **If your character stays with la Résistance,** assuming they allow it, then at the next debrief the GM selects and gives you two new secrets. Choose one new secret to keep, then shuffle the other secret and your old secret back into the deck.

[Electronically filed report from Jules d'Orsay, Level D Cleaner for la Résistance, to Clare]

General,

I accompanied Marya [ID 29145529] and Sidenge [ID 38137711] to the mission location at le Bas, Unit 2241-B. I brought light to medium weaponry, as requested: a shotgun, a pistol, and a modified blackjack, as well as body armor for my torso. Team members were tense and uncommunicative; this is in line with former interactions with me. I don't say this as seeking reprimand for them - we were, after all, hunting their friend.

We didn't encounter any gendarmes on the way, thanks to my prior arrangements with Roger D. W., one of their lieutenants. The cost to la Résistance was 3,250 credits - I will file the reimbursement report in the morning. On a side note, we may want to consider a more permanent arrangement with Roger. His loyalty is clearly for sale and he's not as much of a brute dullard as the rest. Not necessarily to join la Résistance, for I don't think he'd risk his skin, even for money. That said, he would likely help us infiltrate further and he has connections to the Captain. Espinosa is a dangerous ally, but I think he could be swayed.

We approached the unit at 05h25. There was a small delay with the team, but nothing we were unable to handle. As you know, there is not much early morning light that touches le Bas, so it was not difficult to stick to the shadows. Sidenge wanted to knock on the door of the unit; I persuaded him otherwise, by having him stand guard at the end of the hall. I set a small charge on the door, blasted through the hinges. Marya and I proceeded to enter the unit. Through the subsequent smoke, I saw a dark-haired woman fumbling at her bedside table. I shot her through the shoulder - at least, I thought I did. I'm rarely asked not to shoot to kill anymore. She died instantly.

As for Arielle, she started screaming uncontrollably. They were both in sleeping clothes. Blood was everywhere. I had to grapple Arielle to subdue her, as her first instinct was to lunge for her weapon. Her hysterics continued unabated for another five minutes, until I sedated her. I searched the apartment, but was unable to locate any evidence of treason or double-play. Marya and Sidenge led Arielle away, bound. Because the adjoining units summoned the gendarmes, I did not get to sweep the site to my satisfaction and had to leave the body of the dead woman behind.

Upon further reflection, it now seems obvious Arielle had a relationship with this woman, and her unwillingness to communicate may have been a social matter, rather than a political one. I did find the woman's identity clip - Emilie Wu, a sorting specialist for Sun Systems Biotech. It seems she has minor corporate connections, but clearly just a cog rather than an integral piece in the tech-corp governance monopoly. I recommend reconditioning for Arielle. She's obviously very capable, but it seems likely the outcome of this mission could inspire disloyal feelings.

This statement is a clear and accurate reconstitution of the facts as I experienced them.

[Signed Jules d'Orsay]

11 Mai

18h45

6 Before the Storm
Prep Scenes, Equipment, and Favors

Before every mission, the PCs have a **prep scene**. During a prep scene, each PC takes one **prep action** from this list:

» Clear one condition (except for **Marked for Death**, which to clear you must obtain a favor from the Contessa). Roll against Fair (+2) opposition to determine whether you pay a cost to clear it.

» Requisition equipment (**page 108**).

» Request a favor from one of the Élites (**page 109**).

» Create a prep advantage (see below).

After resolving the prep actions, clear the **Angry** condition from all PCs. If la Résistance has taken the Medical Equipment advance, also clear the **Wounded** condition from all PCs.

Players, as you choose your prep actions, roleplay it out. Say what your characters do to gain the benefits they gain, and interact with the NPCs the GM portrays. GM, speak for the NPCs the PCs are interacting with, and ask the players what they say and do. Don't call for a roll unless prompted by a prep action, but feel free to give the players difficult decisions. Prep scenes can be a lot of fun!

If there are fewer than 3 fate points in la Résistance's Cache, increase the Cache to 3 fate points. Players, you can spend fate points from the Cache during the prep scene and during scenes in the mission that take place in la Cave or another Resistance-friendly location.

Prep Advantages

A **prep advantage** is something you prepare or bring into a mission to tip the scales in your favor. It takes the form of an aspect with some number of tied boosts, but the aspect disappears when its boosts are spent. As normal, you can spend fate points to invoke a prep advantage while it still has boosts.

To create a prep advantage, choose which means you're using to get the prep advantage and describe what you're doing to get it. The prep advantage gets boosts tied to it equal in number to the rating of your chosen means. Each prep advantage comes with strings attached, consequences you'll have to deal with later. During the mission, the GM can compel your prep advantage to cause big trouble for you. If the GM compels your prep advantage, you get a fate point; it doesn't tie a boost to the advantage.

A prep advantage created with Fight is acquired through violence or brute force. The GM can compel your prep advantage to make you deal with the consequences of your violence. Perhaps gendarmes have questions about that snitch you roughed up, or maybe a gang member's friends are looking for retribution. The consequences are usually violent in nature.

A prep advantage created with Manipulate is some sort of quid pro quo. At some point during the mission, your bill will come due. Maybe you have to grant a favor in return that puts your team in a bad situation, or maybe the person you got the advantage from betrays you or asks you for something dear.

A prep advantage created with Maneuver is, in some way, volatile. If you have a cloaking device, the GM might compel your prep advantage to say that it shorts out everything electrical in the area, or sets off security systems you're near. If your advantage is information, maybe that information is unreliable or likely to make people mad at you.

A prep advantage created with Observe requires focus and concentration. The GM might compel your advantage to say that the subroutine you're using to hack through the building's security requires a fair bit of user input on your part, making you vulnerable and unaware of your surroundings. Or maybe the information you have requires some interpretation and analysis.

Secret Information

GM, if you want to pass a player a note containing secret information, do so! Secret-keeping is part of *Uprising*. You can even compel someone using a note; all the player has to do is nod or shake their head, and then take or pay a fate point as usual.

Players, likewise, if you want to pass a note to the GM or to another player, do it! Why should the GM have all the fun?

Everyone, if you want to discuss something secretly with another person at the table, just call for a sidebar with them. As long as the fiction supports the secrecy, go ahead and leave the group for a few minutes and discuss things clandestinely. Don't take too long, though! If you do, the other people at the table are within their rights to call you back to the table.

GM, here's a dirty trick: pass a note to a player that says, "Study this note as if it contained interesting information, then nod and pass it back. Take a fate point afterward."

Equipment

Your character has the equipment she needs to use her abilities. If you want to pull out a gun and shoot someone, you don't have to worry about whether you have a gun in most cases; you just cause harm with Fight and leave it at that.

However, sometimes you want equipment that gives you an edge, represented by the following **benefits**:

» Grants +2 on a specific combination of means and end, such as causing harm with Fight or resolving an uncertain outcome with Maneuver.

» Grants the ability to affect everyone in a zone with a specific combination of means and end.

» Allows you to create an aspect with a tied boost, or ties a boost to an aspect already created by the equipment. This must be attached to an effect already on the equipment; for example, a device could grant +2 to cause harm with Fight, and if you succeed on this action, the target gets **Stunned**.

Each benefit on a piece of equipment increases its **cost** by 1. Equipment starts with a cost of 0, so a piece of equipment with three benefits has a cost of 3. You can add any combination of benefits, and you can even add the same benefit more than once.

You can also, if you wish, give a piece of equipment one **drawback**:

» The equipment can be used only once before breaking.

» The equipment costs a fate point each time you use it.

» The equipment has a flaw, represented by an aspect like **Unreliable** or **Indiscriminate**.

Adding a drawback decreases its cost by 1, to a minimum of 1. You can only add one drawback to a piece of equipment.

Here are a few examples of equipment:

» **Machine Pistol (cost 1):** +2 to cause harm with Fight, and you can cause harm to everyone in a zone. However, it's **Indiscriminate**.

» **Cloaking Field (cost 2):** Spend a fate point to gain the advantage with Maneuver, rolling with a +2 bonus. If you succeed, you make yourself **Cloaked**, which gets another tied boost.

» **AR Scanner (cost 2):** You can gain the advantage with Observe over a specific person in a crowd. If you succeed, you make them **Tagged**, which gets another tied boost.

Getting Equipment

There are two primary ways to get the equipment you need: you can **buy** it or you can **requisition** it from la Résistance. You might also find caches of equipment in the field, or get equipment in exchange for a favor from someone powerful.

When you buy equipment, you must do so during a mission, by visiting someone who can sell you the equipment you want. Pay fate points equal to the cost of all the equipment you want to buy. When you buy equipment, the fate points you spend go into the Bank.

When you requisition equipment from la Résistance, you must do so during a prep scene, and you must have access to Resistance Headquarters in la Cave. Pay fate points equal to the cost of all the equipment you want to requisition. When you requisition equipment, the fate points you spend go into the general supply, *not* the Bank. However, there's a catch—how much equipment you can requisition with a single prep action is limited by la Résistance's advances. Unless you've purchased at least the Hijacked Shipments advance, or you are an Exile, you can't requisition equipment at all.

Favors: The New Currency

In a city where money is effectively an imaginary concept created to keep la Société on top and everyone else subservient, **favors** are the only currency that really matters. Sure, money can buy weapons, gadgets, and other toys, but favors make Paris Nouveau *run*.

There are five individuals in Paris Nouveau collectively known as **the Élites**. While politicians and CEOs pretend at making the important decisions, the Élites are the ones behind everything truly important, and everyone in la Résistance knows this.

During a prep scene, a player can use a prep action to ask for a single favor from one of the Élites. This prep action represents making arrangements, using dead drops, and establishing secure channels by which to communicate, all of which allows you to define the details of the favor **at any time during the following mission**.

If you do not use the favor during the current mission, you do not have to pay its cost…but the Élite in question won't be happy that you wasted their time, which the GM will take into account when it comes to future dealings with that Élite. Also, if you ask an Élite for a favor, and the Élite refuses you, you don't use up your prep action.

Portraying the Élites

GM, the Élites are not favor factories, and if your players start to treat them as such, you're perfectly free to teach them the error of their ways. Each of the Élites has his or her own agenda, goals, likes, and dislikes. Each has his or her own enemies and allies, and each sits at the center of his or her own complicated web of social currency.

An Élite will help a PC because of two truths: he or she can use the PC to advance some personal goal, and he or she does not consider the PC a threat. If *either* of these reasons changes, players should expect favors to dry up from that particular Élite, or at the very least they'll become prohibitively expensive. If both reasons change, a PC might find himself on an Élite's hit list.

The Cost

These favors are incredibly powerful, but they are not without cost. Once you've received the benefit of an Élite's favor, their only demand is that you repay them in kind. You immediately gain the aspect **A Debt Owed to...**, specifying the Élite in question. While you have this aspect, you cannot request a favor from another Élite—or the same Élite, for that matter; they all know each other well and scheme against each other, and none of them will grant a favor to someone whose loyalty might be in question.

Also, the GM can compel this aspect to inform you of actions you can take to pay your favor back. This may come in the form of multiple small actions, or a single dramatic act; either way, these compels *do* provide you with fate points when you accept them. You may refuse these compels as normal; however, be aware that none of the Élites likes being kept waiting or being treated as unimportant. If you put an Élite's cost off for too long, the GM can treat the situation as if you'd reneged on the debt (see next page). The magnitude of the debt is commensurate with the favor you request from the Élite in question.

GM, don't let the player off easy here, but also be reasonable. The Élites have better things to do than to keep the PCs dancing like puppets on strings for weeks at a time. When coming up with costs for favors, think of it from the Élite's perspective: what would they want, and what does this cost gain them. There are examples of favors and costs in each Élite's description, starting on **page 112**.

Players, once the GM informs you that you've paid off your debt, you can erase the aspect, and you're free to seek favors from the Élites again. Also, if you're paying for a favor yourself, feel free to keep it as secret from the other players as you like.

Spending Résistance Advances on Favors

Some of la Résistance's advances grant free favors from the Élites. A player can use this to pay the cost of a favor, but this has a catch: the deal for the favor cannot be made in secret. Because the advance is owed to la Résistance itself, not the player, the deal for the favor must be made with la Résistance leadership's full knowledge and acquiescence. This typically means that everyone at the table knows the details of the favor.

Reneging on a Debt

If you put an Élite's debt off for too long, that Élite is likely to get impatient with you and consider you to have reneged. If you renege on a debt, immediately mark your **MARKED FOR DEATH** condition; the Élite has put a contract out on your life.

In addition, change your debt aspect to **ENEMY OF [ÉLITE'S NAME]**. Even if you manage to avoid the Élite's hired killers long enough to clear **MARKED FOR DEATH**, that relationship is irrevocably ruined, so you can no longer seek favors from the Élite you ignored. You may seek favors from other Élites, but they may be leery of someone whose word means so little.

Using Cards from *Coup*

GM, if you have a copy of **Coup**, grab a copy of each character card from that game. During each prep scene, lay the cards out on the table, to act as a visual reminder that the PCs can go to the Élites for aid.

When someone claims a favor from an Élite, you might pass the appropriate card to that player as a reminder. **Coup** contains multiple copies of each Élite's card, so you shouldn't run out.

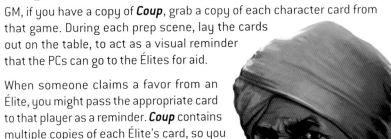

The Ambassador

Ainsi va le monde. Ce n'est pas ma faute.
So goes the world. It's not my fault.

—Vicomte de Valmont, **Les Liasons Dangereuses**, Pierre-Ambroise Choderlos de Laclos

Name: Georges de la Tour
Height: 1m85
Hair: Black, with streaks of gray
Eyes: Dark brown
Build: Broad, with a faint thickness around the middle

The Ambassador simply enjoys watching things unravel. There is little in Paris Nouveau, high or low, that he does not know. His eyes and ears extend from the depths of la Cave to the tip of l'Apogée. The title is one he's assumed—there are no official ambassadors in Paris Nouveau. What cities are there left to negotiate with? Yet the title fits, here. Even those who dislike him have to grudgingly admit his influence.

He's quite the striking figure, tall and broad, with burnished bronze skin and a perfectly trimmed moustache. There are laugh lines around his eyes, but also deep furrows around his nose. The fanciful might actually call it a cruel mouth. His teeth are shockingly white. He speaks well, with crisp intonation.

Just like the Contessa, he appreciates physical finery. That way, even if someone does not have the correct tech installed, his appearance is impressive. The fabrics he wears are always luxurious, fabrics not seen in Paris since the Fall: damask, silk, and wool soft enough to rub against your cheek.

For those who know a bit of history, the Ambassador's name seems rather familiar. It's one he's assumed, to give himself an air of quality. No one knows his real name, and it seems he'd like to keep it that way.

The Ambassador's Favor

The Ambassador knows nearly everyone worth knowing in Paris Nouveau, and he can get you the access you need. When you claim your favor from the Ambassador, name a person or a location; the Ambassador will arrange for a meeting with that person or access to that location. The GM will tell you how long it takes for the Ambassador to make these arrangements, but the Ambassador does work quickly. The Ambassador may place restrictions on your behavior, such as not making a scene or ensuring a person's safety during a meeting; these come in the form of situation aspects.

Cost: The Ambassador typically asks for access in return. He may ask you to provide access to a location or person, either for himself or for an individual he specifies. The more difficult your favor was to arrange, the more inconvenient it will be to provide this access.

The Assassin

Peut être que j'avais besoin de lui pour me montrer que même les anges n'échappent pas à la guillotine.

Maybe I needed him to show me that even the angels do not escape the guillotine.

—Malak El Halabi

Name: 'Nette Lécuyer
Height: 1m63
Hair: Light golden blond, pulled smooth into a tall tail on top of her head, with thick-cut bangs
Eyes: Incandescent blue
Build: Athletic, with taut calves and a surprisingly potent punch

People underestimate 'Nette the first time they meet her. Some don't get a second chance to be wrong. With her mile-high boot heels, high-collared jumpsuit, and golden hair, she could be mistaken for a cheerleader before the Fall. And yet…

Many believe she has the most power in all of la Société. Death walks with her, and those smart enough move aside.

She has distinctive facial tattoos, pale blue splotches spread across her cheekbones like wiped-away tears. Or war paint. As a private joke, she's had an antique piece of ivory carved into a skull; she wears it as a cameo. She also wears wine-red lip stain, which has led to some uncharitably accusing her of drinking the blood of her victims.

That is, of course, nonsense. She has a job to do and she does it very well. The Assassin rarely has to kill someone herself anymore; rather, she has a little red book of names, people who owe her the darkest of favors.

The Assassin's Favor

The Assassin's favor is simple—name a person. By the end of the current mission, that person will die. Typically it will happen sooner rather than later.

Cost: The Assassin's cost is equally simple—at some point in the future, she will name a person. You have until the end of the current mission to ensure that person's death.

The Captain

El castigo más justo es aquel que uno mismo se impone.

The most just punishment is one that is self-imposed.

—Simon Bolivar

Name: Alejandro Espinosa, Captain of la Gendarmerie
Height: 1m83
Hair: Black, combed back into a small, tight ponytail, shaved high up on the sides with thin sideburns
Eyes: Pale, watery blue
Build: Broad and muscular, coiled perfection

There are a lot of snipes passed around about members of la Société. Not so about the Captain—his presence gives anyone pause.

He doesn't talk much, but he listens. He hears everything you say, and there are those who'd swear he can fix you with that gaze and know what you're thinking too. To be in the sight of that cold, dead eye…many have faltered.

What happened to his eye? No one knows. A vicious, old scar runs from the bottom of his cheekbone through the eye socket and deep into his scalp. He didn't lose the eye, but it's a dead eye nonetheless. Some claim he's augmented it with tech. That could be rampant speculation, though it does have an icy gleam.

The Captain is always seen in his cobalt blue gendarme uniform, even in social settings. At most, he might wax his moustache and goatee for a formal event. The uncharitable might whisper it's because he's never off duty, but they wouldn't dare whisper that within his hearing.

Under his command, the gendarmes have transformed from a loose rabble of Citizen thugs into a constabulary to be feared. People who disappear into their care never come back the same.

The Captain's Favor

The Captain can get you muscle when you need it. Pick a time and place—here and now is an acceptable answer—and you'll have the assistance of a large contingent of armed men and women when you get there. This gives you **BACKUP** with five tied boosts. You can spend these boosts as normal, but you can also spend them to cause harm to someone without using an action. When you do so, don't roll; instead, treat your effort as Mediocre (+0), adding +2 for each boost you spend. The GM may even rule that the Captain's muscle allows you to bypass a conflict entirely.

Cost: As commander of the gendarmes and the secret police, the Captain must make arrests and interrogate dissidents on a regular basis. As such, his cost usually involves names: the names of people involved in illegal or subversive activities. He may ask you to deliver a specific person or people, or a specific number of people.

The Contessa

J'ai retrouvé la parole et l'art de m'en servir, et le vocabulaire qui sied.

I have found my voice again and the art of using it…

—Colette, *The Vagabond*

Name: Karina, Comtesse de la Rouge
Height: 1m68
Hair: Pale auburn
Eyes: Hazel
Build: Thin, almost fragile

The Contessa refers to herself in the third person as La Divine. She's definitely a woman who knows her worth, which is significant in both wealth and power. In a city where everyone and everything seems dirty, she's found a way to make the sheen of sweat transform into a glow. Her personal grooming is impeccable, and her closet…it's whispered she has a whole cadre of Citizens living near her in l'Apogée, repurposed to sew her physical fashion, not just virtual, tailoring it to perfection. Where does she get the fabric? Nothing in this city is fair or sensible.

Titles mean nothing when you have no land, but she's referred to as *la Comtesse de la Rouge* (the Countess of the Red) by those native to Paris Nouveau. It's impossible to know her original nationality, same as so many in this city. Some say her pale skin and red hair make it likely she's Western European. Others say she's more Mediterranean up close, with olive tones and dark roots to that hair. Either way, little is known of her antecedents. She likes it that way. Where did her wealth come from? If she clawed her way up, little of it shows now. Her voice is measured and mellifluous, but her slightest utterance carries the weight of a command.

Though sympathetic to la Résistance, she refuses to join it officially. She says it would be political suicide, but it's equally likely that she has no interest in leaving the carefully cultivated veils of her personal compartment to go running, dirty and fearful for her life, to la Cave. She is an Élite through and through.

Should you request the Contessa's help, it's best to bring her a gift. Any small luxury will do, though an impressive present may improve your result. She doesn't want money; she has more than you could amass. Something curious and whimsical is a bonus. Really, she wants homage, an acknowledgment of her superiority.

She is one of the few who can block the actions of all of her fellow Élites, including the work of the Assassin. Her work is delicate, which makes it instantly identifiable. But even when it's known she must have been behind some machinations, the trail dissipates like dust.

The Contessa's Favor

Though she cultivates an air of passivity, the Contessa is quite possibly the most powerful of the Élites. Her favor is simple but potent: she can protect you from anyone, once. Think of the Contessa as a "get out of jail free" card. If you suffer incarceration, retribution, or scrutiny of any kind, the Contessa can make it go away with no consequence.

This doesn't mean you'll never be subject to a similar circumstance in the future; the Contessa protects you from a particular person or organization in a specific circumstance, not indefinitely. For example, if you're being chased by Corvid SecSpec for burning down their warehouse, the Contessa can make them give up the chase. If you burn down another warehouse, though, you may be on your own.

You can even use the Contessa's favor to clear the **Marked for Death** condition; in fact, it is the only way to clear that condition.

Cost: The Contessa does what she does because she knows as much as she can about everyone. Information is her stock and trade, and she uses it to exert leverage. As such, her cost comes in the form of secrets, typically secrets that force you to violate someone's trust. Her cost may be one big secret or several small ones; it depends on the magnitude of the favor she did for you.

The Duke

Was ich besitze, seh ich wie im Weiten, Und was verschwand, wird mir zu Wirklichkeiten.

What I possess seems far away from me,
And what is gone becomes reality.

—Dedication, *Faust*, Johann Wolfgang von Goethe

Name: Tsiu (pronounced "Tsoo")
Height: 1m68
Hair: Black, shaved high up onto the crown of his head
Eyes: Brown, with flecks of green
Build: Slender, with a concave chest

The Duke is l'acquéreur, he who acquires things. He is a collector, and has access to tremendous gear, technology, and equipment. There is no duchy in Paris Nouveau, but he is called Duke nonetheless. You can ask him why, but he's likely to just purse his mouth in a smirk.

Because he is small-framed, his garb pads out his shoulders and his neck, making him feel physically more impressive than he is. It's said Henry the VIII used the same technique. Unlike Henry, the Duke has no interest in collecting wives. Rare and precious things bring out his inner magpie.

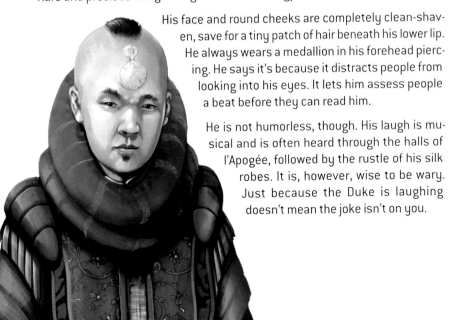

His face and round cheeks are completely clean-shaven, save for a tiny patch of hair beneath his lower lip. He always wears a medallion in his forehead piercing. He says it's because it distracts people from looking into his eyes. It lets him assess people a beat before they can read him.

He is not humorless, though. His laugh is musical and is often heard through the halls of l'Apogée, followed by the rustle of his silk robes. It is, however, wise to be wary. Just because the Duke is laughing doesn't mean the joke isn't on you.

The Duke's Favor

The Duke's favor is all about toys. He can get you any piece of equipment you need, gratis. Well, almost gratis. You can name any pieces of equipment with a total cost of 8 or less and get them without paying anything at all, other than the Duke's own cost. He can even get you specific items you might need, such as the key to a specific door or incriminating photo evidence on a particular politician.

Cost: The Duke is a collector. He'll name something he wants. It's your job to get it for him. You have until the end of the mission. Typically, the Duke will ask for one hard-to-get thing. Often it's something you're uniquely suited to get because of your position and access.

I just snapped my stylus in two, digging it so hard into my tablet. How could things have gone so wrong? Arielle was in love, she'd run away to be with her girlfriend. Marya told me I was wrong, was too blinded by fear and paranoia to hear her. I've failed her, failed the people who trusted me to lead them in the right direction.

No one told me it'd be like this, that leading a revolution would be unending loss, losing everyone who ever meant something to you, to follow a gold and shimmering light on the far horizon. And even if you reach that light, it's cold and it hurts your eyes. When the curtain falls on the dauntless rebels, it never shows the crushing aftermath, as despair sets in. You're always doomed to disappoint someone, and when you mess up, people die.

This is true of every military leader in history, but I never wanted to be a Nero, squealing a violin as the world burns around me. I did this because I had to, because it was the right thing to do, because not doing it and instead looking the other way meant the obliteration of all my country once was. I look around and I see the blank stares, the dull faces of les Citoyens, and I know I have to keep going until they wake up, see what their complacency costs them.

When I read Jules' report, I tore through my office, kicking furniture and breaking my last teacup against the wall. I know what has to be done. I just don't want to do it. Don't make me do it.

7 In the Thick of It
Running Missions and Taking Action

After finishing the prep scene, the mission begins.

GM, at the start of the mission, fill your **Budget** (*page 178*) so it has fate points equal to the number of PCs participating in the mission plus one. You can withdraw fate points from your Bank to add to your Budget.

During a mission, the PCs work toward **Resistance goals** given to them by la Résistance. Completing Resistance goals gives advancement points to la Résistance, and advancing la Résistance gets you closer to glorious revolution! As the PCs work through the mission, they will attempt to accomplish the Resistance goals while also trying to earn advancement points for themselves by completing goals listed on their playsheets and secret cards.

In addition, each mission has **government goals**, which if completed give advancement points to the government. As the government advances, it grows more powerful. And if it grows too powerful, it will find la Résistance and crush them once and for all.

All the while, the GM will be accumulating **blowback** (*page 180*). Each mission has its own list of **transgressions**: things that the PCs can do or allow to happen that give the GM blowback. Players, at any time during a mission, you can give 3 blowback to the GM in exchange for a fate point from the general supply. She can spend blowback to make the PCs' lives harder by triggering the mission's **complications and discoveries** and perhaps even by killing PCs.

Run the mission as a collection of connected **scenes**. A scene is just a series of events and actions that take place in the same general location or time frame; it can be as long or as short as you need it to be. There's no magic number of scenes that a mission should consist of; if you can run a mission in one scene, great! If it takes you twenty scenes, great! It all depends on the story's needs.

Once the mission ends, everyone does a debrief scene, described in *At Mission's End* (*page 149*).

How Many Missions?

You might ask yourself: "How many missions should I run in a session?" Our answer is "As many as you want!" Typically, a single session is enough time to allow you to get through one mission in its entirety, including the prep scene and the debrief. Sometimes your PCs will get through a mission quickly, though. Sometimes they won't. It's perfectly okay to end a session on a cliffhanger and pick back up in the middle of a mission. Likewise, if you get done early, it's fine to run another mission, or even part of one. There are plenty of missions starting on *page 200*, so it's easy to just grab one and go!

Conflicts

When two or more people have opposing goals, this can prompt a type of scene called a **conflict**. Naturally, this means that many scenes in missions are conflicts.

GM, you don't have to start a conflict every time people disagree; you can resolve many disagreements in the game with a single roll, by making two players roll against each other, or by making a player roll against an NPC. When you want to drill down on the action more, such as during a dramatic fight scene or a tense negotiation, use the conflict rules here.

In order to run a conflict, follow these steps in order:

- » 1. Determine Sides
- » 2. Frame the Conflict
- » 3. Run the Conflict

Step 1: Determine Sides

Figure out who's working together and who's opposing who. Most often there will be two sides: members of la Résistance, played by the players, and the gendarmes, agents, and other members of society who oppose them, played by the GM. Things can get a little muddy when you introduce double agents and other forms of betrayal, but it's fine if people switch sides during a conflict. In fact, that's part of the fun of *Uprising*!

Step 2: Frame the Conflict

Once you've figured out what sides you're dealing with, work together to decide the boundaries of the conflict. Typically this means figuring out what ends the conflict in success for the players, and what ends it in failure. For example, if the PCs are raiding a warehouse to steal medical supplies for la Résistance, and it erupts into a firefight, you might collectively decide that the conflict ends when the PCs escape with the medical supplies, are defeated by the guards, or run away. You might decide that a conflict leads to another conflict, such as escaping leading to a chase scene, and that's fine. It can be a lot of fun to have cascading conflicts!

Step 3: Run the Conflict

In this step, everyone in the conflict takes **turns** working toward their side's goals. GM, you'll determine who takes the first turn in the conflict. Generally speaking, the person who acts first should be the person who is being most proactive, and whose actions are most likely to dramatically change the situation. Try to make this one of the PCs, but it's okay if it's an NPC. Resolve any disputes with table consensus.

When the first character finishes their turn, their player—or the GM, if it's an NPC—chooses who will take their turn next from the characters who have not yet acted. Characters continue taking turns until everyone has taken one, which signals the end of the **exchange** and begins a new one. To begin it, the character who took a turn last in the previous exchange chooses who takes their turn first in the next exchange, and can pick themselves if they want to.

When one side accomplishes its goals in the conflict, it **wins the conflict**. The conflict immediately ends, and the winning side gets to narrate how the conflict comes to a close. Players, if your side wins, you each get to contribute details to the narration. As always, use table consensus to determine what is and isn't possible.

If a conflict isn't going your way, though, you can choose to **offer a concession** on your turn, forfeiting it. If the table thinks your concession is reasonable, you concede: you exit the scene, and you get to narrate how you do so. At the end of the scene, you gain one fate point for each of your marked conditions, if any.

If the GM decides to concede, she adds one fate point to her Bank for every named antagonistic NPC in the scene who hasn't been taken out yet. GM, only count named NPCs who were actively opposing the PCs in the conflict; you don't get fate points for bystanders or allies.

If an entire side concedes, the other side wins the conflict.

Concessions and Table Consensus

All concessions, including GM concessions, are subject to table consensus. If someone offers a concession and it doesn't pass table consensus, they'll have to revise the concession so it does.

This does *not* mean that someone can prevent your concession outright via table consensus. If you choose to concede, you concede; table consensus only has authority over the fictional form that the concession takes.

Taking Your Turn

Players, during your turn in an exchange, you can take one **action**, and you can move to a new **zone** if doing so makes sense. However, moving into or out of some zones might spend your action as well. GM, your NPCs take turns in the same way.

While you can only take one action per turn, you might make rolls to avoid things on other turns during the exchange, as prompted by the GM.

Often, taking an action will prompt a roll, though sometimes it won't. You may also do things that don't take an action at all, like opening a door or shouting instructions to an ally. Follow these guidelines if you're in doubt:

» If what you're doing **takes little time or effort or is trivial**, it does not require a roll and does not use an action. Good examples are talking to an ally during a firefight, drawing a weapon, or opening a window.

» If what you're doing **requires time or effort, but won't put you in danger**, it requires an action but not a roll; it just succeeds. For example, searching for data on an unlocked terminal takes time but does not carry risk on its own.

» If what you're doing **might put you in danger**, it requires an action and a roll. Lying to someone, hacking a locked terminal, or opening a window while under fire are all good examples.

Rolling for Action

When you take an action that prompts a roll, you first select a means and an end:

» Your **means** is how you accomplish what you want: Fight, Manipulate, Maneuver, or Observe.

» Your **end** is what you want: causing harm, gaining the advantage, avoiding something, or resolving an uncertain outcome.

When you announce your means and end, the GM may judge that your means is suited or risky, described more on **page 125**.

After you are satisfied with your means and end, roll four dice and read them as follows:

» Every ➕ adds 1 to your result.

» Every ➖ subtracts 1 from your result.

» Every ⬛ adds nothing to your result.

Add together your roll and the rating of your chosen means to get your **effort**. At this point, the GM compares your effort to the **opposition** and tells you the result of your action:

» If your effort is **three or more higher** than the opposition, you **succeed with style**. Describe what you're doing as being that much cooler. You get exactly what you want, and you get a bonus. If you're causing harm, you force your opponent to mark an extra condition (*page 142*). Otherwise, you gain another boost (*page 141*).

» If your effort is **higher** than the opposition, you **succeed**. You get exactly what you want—no more, no less.

» If your effort is **equal** to the opposition, you **tie**. Nobody gets what they want, and the situation changes—people will have to reevaluate and come at things from a different angle. The GM might offer you success at a minor cost.

» If your effort is **lower** than the opposition, you **fail**. You don't get what you want, and things get more complicated for you. The GM might offer you success at a major cost.

Where does opposition come from?

Opposition is either **passive**, meaning a number set by the GM, or **active**, which is the effort of someone else's roll. An NPC or another PC might provide active opposition. If you're rolling against active opposition, the GM will narrate the opposing character's actions.

Often, the passive opposition is the **mission opposition**. If you're playing a premade mission (*page 200*), it's listed near the top of the mission's description. Otherwise, it's set by the GM. Fair (+2) is a reasonable mission opposition.

If you're not satisfied with the result of your action, you can invoke aspects to add +2 to your effort or to reroll your dice, and friendly characters can **help** you, forgoing their next action to add +2 to your effort. However, hostile characters can **hinder** you and can invoke aspects against you, forgoing their next action to add +2 to your opposition.

After everyone is finished with invoking aspects and with helping and hindering, the GM announces the final result of the action.

You'll find more details on invoking aspects in *"Invoking Aspects"* (*page 89*) and more details on helping and hindering in *"Helping and Hindering"* (*page 126*).

The PCs are trying to convince a gendarme to let them into a restricted area, and it's not going well. Berne decides to take a different tack.

"I'd like to offer him some money, and I want to heavily insinuate that not taking it would be very bad for his career."

Emily nods. "That sounds like you're causing harm with Manipulate. Sound right to you?"

"Sure." John rolls for Berne, getting ⊞⊞⊟⊟ for a roll of Mediocre (+0). His Manipulate is rated Good (+3), though, so his effort is Good (+3).

"Well, that beats the gendarme's opposition, which is Fair, +2. You cause harm, and he seems pretty shaken by your words. He marks off his STAGGERED condition. Who's next?"

Suited and Risky Means

Sometimes a particular means is **suited** to the situation, such as using Manipulate to bribe a gendarme who's known to be greedy and corrupt. When you succeed with a suited means, you'll gain a greater benefit, as follows:

» **If you succeed with style,** you gain the normal benefits *plus* another boost.

» **If you succeed,** you succeed with style instead.

Sometimes, though, you'll use a means that is **risky**, such as using Fight to beat and bully information out of a government contact. It might work, but it carries more danger. When you tie or fail with a risky means, you'll suffer a greater penalty, as follows:

» **If you tie,** the situation changes as normal, and you also pay a minor cost.

» **If you fail,** you suffer the normal penalties, and you must mark a condition or be taken out.

When you announce which means you're using, the GM can announce that it is risky or suited. A given means can be **both** suited and risky at the same time. Resolve any disagreements with table consensus. Players, you have the right to change your approach to a situation (and your means and end) up until you roll the dice. Once the dice are cast, your choice is made. That said, don't bog the game down by second-guessing every roll. A revolution allows little time for navel-gazing.

Risky and Suited Means for NPCs

If an NPC brings active opposition to a roll—that is, if the GM is rolling for them, too—the GM uses their action and combination of means and end to inform whether your means is risky or suited. However, **an NPC's means is never risky or suited; it's always a straight roll.**

GM, this rule is in place to keep things quick and simple during conflicts; if you and your players want to give NPCs risky and suited means, doing so won't break the game. But it *will* make conflicts more complicated and potentially slower. If you decide to do this, simply assess whether the NPC's means is risky or suited as you would a player's.

Helping and Hindering

Sometimes you might want to ensure someone's success. . . or their failure. That is, you can **help** or **hinder** them.

After someone in your zone rolls for an action, you can choose to help or hinder them. You can choose to do so during the same time when aspects can be invoked to modify the roll or add to its opposition.

When you help someone, you add +2 to their effort. When you hinder someone, you add +2 to their opposition. When you help or hinder someone, you forgo your next action, though you can still move on your turn as long as it doesn't cost an action to do so.

If you wish to help or hinder someone without their knowledge, pass a note to the GM indicating that you're doing so. Then feel free to lie about what you did.

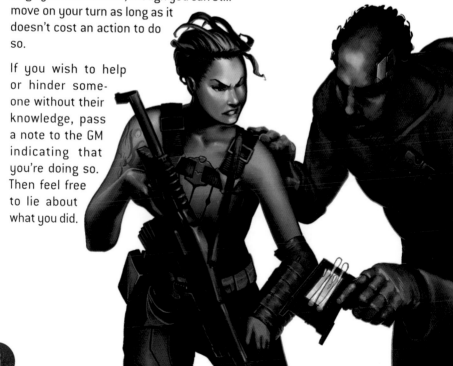

Major and Minor Costs

Players, when you fail or tie on a roll, the GM can offer you success anyway, but it always comes with strings.

When you tie, the GM can offer you success at a **minor cost**. A minor cost, like a simple tie, changes the situation in some way, but it's usually not something that is immediately terrible. Rather, a minor cost is a preview of the terrible thing that's going to happen or arrive soon. Minor costs don't usually have mechanical impact, but they do have an impact on the story and the situation. Some example minor costs are:

» The alarm sounds, and you can hear gendarmes mobilizing around the property.

» The commander barks an order into his radio, along with his exact coordinates.

» An oil lamp falls over onto the floor, setting it on fire. The fire's not bad now, but it will spread.

» The facility goes on lockdown, steel shutters covering the windows and doors.

» The capsule in your hands falls to the ground and skitters across the floor, likely jostling the sensitive biological sample inside.

When you fail, though, the GM can offer you success at a **major cost**, which is the immediate badness. Major costs don't always have a mechanical effect, but they can. Introducing new enemies, creating new aspects with free invokes for the GM, and even causing harm are all perfectly allowable major costs. Here are some examples:

» A second squad of gendarmes arrives on the scene, ready for a fight.

» The sniper on the roof (the one you didn't see) fires a shot that catches you in the shoulder, dealing harm.

» The small blaze becomes a conflagration, engulfing most of the house and becoming a participant in the conflict.

» Your group is now surrounded by SecSpec, guns aimed your way.

» The indicator on the capsule flashes, alerting you that the biological sample is no longer viable.

GM, you can spend 2 blowback to upgrade an established minor cost to a major cost. However, you can only upgrade a minor cost that was introduced in an earlier exchange during the scene, not the current exchange.

The Four Means

When you take an action that requires a roll, you'll use one of the four **means**: Fight, Manipulate, Maneuver, or Observe.

Fight

Fight embodies direct confrontation, whether it's physical, psychological, or social. Whether you're fighting a person, a wall, an onrushing motorcycle, or an organization, you're rolling Fight.

You can use cause harm with Fight by using physical violence, or with direct social pressure, like intimidation or torture. You can gain the advantage with Fight by using tactical acumen or surprising someone with blunt words. You can avoid with Fight by physically blocking or enduring. You can resolve uncertain outcomes with Fight when doing so requires physical force or direct tactics.

Fight can be used to...

> . . . shoot an enemy in the back.
> . . . bully someone into backing down.
> . . . intimidate someone into giving you valuable information.
> . . . bypass a firewall with a brute-force approach.
> . . . kick down a locked door.
> . . . take a punch and look back at the interrogator with a smile.

Fight is the means you use when you want to take **direct action** or accomplish something with **pure force**.

Manipulate

Manipulate is subtle, indirect, and often underhanded. You can use it to lie, disguise yourself, charm someone, or distract.

You can cause harm with Manipulate by sullying people's reputations or with subtle coercion or psychological warfare. You can gain the advantage with Manipulate by putting others in disadvantageous situations before they realize it. You can avoid with Manipulate by misdirecting or deceiving. You can resolve uncertain outcomes with Manipulate when doing so requires deceit, disguise, or other forms of trickery.

Manipulate can be used to...

> ...trick someone into giving up a secret.
> ...play one enemy against another.
> ...feint left, then stab your enemy when he goes the wrong way.
> ...force someone to take a disadvantageous position.
> ...publicly embarrass someone.
> ...cause a security system to work for you instead of the enemy.

Manipulate is the means you use when you want to **put someone else at the disadvantage** or **use cunning and misdirection** to get your way.

Maneuver

When you Maneuver, you're changing your position, whether physical or social. You can use it for stealth, athletic ability, and so forth, but you can also use it to alter your social positioning.

You can cause harm with Maneuver by using the environment against someone or using your enemies against each other. You can gain the advantage with Maneuver by using physical or social positioning. You can avoid with Maneuver by dodging out of the way, or by hiding and sneaking. You can resolve uncertain outcomes with Maneuver when doing so requires quick footwork, athleticism, or clever wordplay.

Maneuver can be used to...

> ...take the high ground.
> ...escape a gendarme patrol.
> ...sneak through a secure facility.
> ...convince someone that you're exactly what they need.
> ...mask yourself from watchdog programs in cyberspace.
> ...block an incoming punch.

Maneuver is the means you use when you want to **put yourself in an advantageous position** or **use stealth, mobility, and quick thinking** to accomplish your goals.

Observe

Observe is about physical awareness, but also about social awareness, deduction, and the ability to put all the pieces together.

You can cause harm with Observe by attacking with precision and targeting weak spots. You can gain the advantage with Observe by noticing things that others don't. You can avoid with Observe when you spot dangers or call out hazards before stumbling into them. You can resolve uncertain outcomes with Observe when doing so requires noticing things or making deductions and leaps of logic.

Observe can be used to...

> ...line your shot up just right.
> ...spot a weakness in an enemy's fighting style.
> ...read a person in a social situation.
> ...say just the right thing in just the right way.
> ...notice a back way in.
> ...find all kinds of juicy data on a secure system.

Observe is the means you use when you want to **notice advantageous information, and act on it** or **achieve your goals with perception and analytical thinking**.

The Four Ends

Whenever you use one of your means to do something, you're trying to achieve one of the four **ends**.

Cause Harm

Say who you're attacking and roll the dice. If you succeed, they must mark a condition (*page 142*) or get taken out (*page 146*). If you succeed with style, they must mark an extra condition or get taken out.

When you cause harm, you...

> ...shoot someone.
> ...break someone's arm.
> ...intimidate someone into getting out of your way.
> ...cause enormous damage to someone's reputation.
> ...get someone in trouble with the law.
> ...bring a system to a crashing halt.

Conditions represent injuries to one's body, social status, legal status, and finances. Taking someone or something out means removing the character or obstacle from the scene.

Avoid

Say what you're trying to avoid and roll the dice. If you succeed, you avoid it, no problem. If you succeed with style, you also gain a boost.

Often, you won't choose to avoid during your turn. Instead, when someone else tries to do something to you that you don't like, you'll roll to avoid unless there's a good reason you wouldn't be able to. That said, there *are* situations, such as sneaking past a guard, where you actively choose to avoid something.

When you avoid, you...

> ...dodge a gunshot.
> ...catch a pipe swung at your head.
> ...assure the gendarmes that the arrest warrant is simply a mistake.
> ...coax a political enemy into halting her attack.
> ...stay out of sight of the watch patrols.
> ...stay under the computer's security radar.

Sometimes you avoid negative situations altogether, while sometimes you suffer a partial effect. You also use avoid to keep from being detected, whether by guards, security systems, or automated turrets mounted around a building.

Gain the Advantage

Say what you're doing and how it'll help you in the future, then roll the dice. If you succeed, you gain a boost. You can keep this boost for yourself, hand it to another character, or tie it to an aspect. You can even create a new aspect to tie it to. If you succeed with style, you gain another boost.

If you're trying to gain the advantage over someone else, they roll active opposition against you. Otherwise, you'll roll against the mission opposition (**page 124**).

When you gain the advantage, you...

> ...spend some time lining up your shot before you pull the trigger.
> ...get to high ground so you can stay above the gendarmes' line of sight.
> ...put your enemy off balance so you can follow up with a killing blow.
> ...bribe an official so you can sneak past a security checkpoint later.
> ...fluster your political opponent to make him easier to discredit.
> ...install a backdoor into a system so you can exploit it later.

Gaining the advantage is what you choose when you want to set up a big success later. "Later" here can mean in a few hours or on your next turn. These advantages don't last past the end of the mission, but stacking things in your favor can be crucial to taking down seemingly unbeatable opposition.

Resolve an Uncertain Outcome

The GM will tell you what you're trying to resolve, and what might happen if you fail. Roll the dice. If you succeed, the situation resolves in your favor. If you succeed with style, you also gain a boost.

When you resolve an uncertain outcome, you...

> ...hack the keypad so you can open the door.
> ...jump from rooftop to rooftop, across the alley, without falling.
> ...disarm the bomb that's about to explode.
> ...find the incriminating evidence in the politician's room before she gets back.
> ...scale the outer wall of the building so you can enter through the window.
> ...find the data you're looking for in the secure system.

You resolve an uncertain outcome when you try to accomplish something that can be resolved with a single roll and that doesn't fall under any of the other three ends. If you're doing something that requires multiple rolls to represent, it falls under one of the other ends. Typically, the GM will ask you to resolve an uncertain outcome when one of the other ends doesn't cover your action.

Narrating Actions

You can narrate and describe an action in a number of ways, and your description can change which means and end you use, and whether that combination is suited, risky, or neither. This section has many examples of different ways to narrate your actions.

> Elayne wants to get past a guard, but she doesn't want to make a scene. She scans the guard's metadata, examines his accounts, and comes up with a plan. She walks up to the guard and whispers harshly, "I know you've been stealing from your employers. Move aside and nobody has to know." The GM decides Elayne is resolving an uncertain outcome with Observe. If she succeeds, the guard simply lets her past, though he remains in the scene and may come back later.
>
> *BREAK*

Luce wants to get past a guard, but she doesn't want to make a scene. She walks up to the guard, stares him dead in the eye, and says, "Move. Now." Luce's hand is resting on her pistol. The GM decides Luce is causing harm with Fight, and that using this means is risky. If she succeeds, she might take the guard out, causing him to panic and run off. If she fails or ties, though, the consequences could be quite bad.

BREAK

Berne wants to get past the guard, but he knows he can't do it alone. He walks up to the guard and says, "You seem to be all alone here, and I've got friends on the way. You should probably just step aside." The GM decides Berne is gaining the advantage with Manipulate, and that the action is suited. Success here doesn't mean he gets past the guard; instead, he's setting his friends up to finish the job. He'll get an extra boost or two out of the action, and he can pass them to Luce, who's waiting on a nearby hill with a silenced sniper rifle.

BREAK

Rodrigo wants to get past a guard, and they don't want to make a scene. They decide to sneak around the guard, bypassing him altogether. The GM decides Rodrigo is avoiding the guard with Maneuver, and that the action is both risky and suited. The guard isn't very attentive, so if Rodrigo manages to sneak past him, they'll also gain a boost or two for their trouble. However, if they get caught, things could get very bad indeed.

There are two basic ways you can decide on your means and end: leading with description and leading with your means and end.

If you lead with description, you simply say what you want to do without thinking about which means and end you're using. Then, you and the GM work together to find the means and end that make sense, unless you have a good idea already.

Luce is trying to bypass an electronic lock that's hard-wired into the security system. She says, "I pull a little flash drive out of my pocket and plug it into the secure port on the side of the lock. That port is meant for an electronic key, but my little flash drive has some great malware I cooked up that'll help me get past it."

"Okay," says the GM. "What are you rolling, and to do what?"

"I'd like to handle this with one roll rather than a back-and-forth exchange, so I'm resolving an uncertain outcome. This is malware I wrote so, because I'm relying on knowledge and information, I'll roll Observe."

"That sounds good," says the GM. "You've had time to prepare your malware, but their firewall is pretty strong. This is neither risky nor suited."

If you lead with your means and end, come up with a description that makes narrative sense and justifies that combo. The GM will work with you to make sure your description makes the game better for everyone.

Luce is trying to bypass an electronic lock that's hard-wired into the security system. She says, "I want to try to bring the whole security system down, so I think I'm causing harm to the system here. I'd like to cause harm to it with Manipulate."

"Okay," says the GM. "What does that look like?"

"I use the wireless transponder in my neural casing to interface directly with the security system, then I exploit critical vulnerabilities to get it to tear itself apart."

"That's super cool, but interfacing directly is going to be risky."

Narrating Means and Ends in Different Situations

Regardless of whether you're shooting a rifle, sweet-talking your way past corporate security, sneaking around an old warehouse, or hacking a secure system for vital intel, you can use any of the means and ends at your disposal. Here are some examples of how.

Physical Situations

You use Fight to **overcome people and obstacles with direct force**. You might cause harm by shooting someone, gain the advantage by knocking the wind out of them, avoid something by simply gritting your teeth and enduring it, or resolve an uncertain outcome by pushing it out of the way or knocking it down.

You use Manipulate to **create disadvantageous situations for others**. You might cause harm by striking from behind, gain the advantage by throwing sand in someone's eyes, avoid something by faking left and going right, or resolve an uncertain outcome by finding a critical weakness in an obstacle.

You use Maneuver to **put yourself in a better position**. You might cause harm by engaging in hit-and-run tactics, gain the advantage by seizing high ground, avoid something by ducking behind cover, or resolve an uncertain outcome by going over something instead of through.

You use Observe to **capitalize on your knowledge of the environment and your tools**. You might cause harm by taking careful aim with your rifle, gain the advantage by fighting on ice you know is thin, avoid something by predicting it, or resolve an uncertain outcome by reasoning your way through it.

Social Situations

You use Fight to **strong-arm people into doing what you want**. You might cause harm by threatening violence, gain the advantage with a hard stare, avoid something by refusing to engage with it, or resolve an uncertain outcome by bullying your way through.

You use Manipulate to **exploit the weaknesses of others**. You might cause harm by planting a vicious rumor, gain the advantage by mentioning a scandal at the right time, avoid something by guiding the conversation in another direction, or resolve an uncertain outcome with lies or fast-talk.

You use Maneuver to **make yourself look good**. You might cause harm by using your reputation against someone else, gain the advantage by mentioning a favor you've done someone, avoid something by extricating yourself from the conversation, or resolve an uncertain outcome by trading on your status.

You use Observe to **pay attention to social cues and capitalize on them**. You might cause harm by deducing that someone is having an affair, gain the advantage by noticing someone's tell, avoid something by knowing what someone's going to say before they say it, or resolve an uncertain outcome by pointing out a clever observation.

Stealth Situations

You use Fight to **leverage your physicality**. You might cause harm by choking someone out, gain the advantage by staying in a difficult position for a long time, avoid something by holding something heavy in front of you, or resolve an uncertain outcome by enduring it.

You use Manipulate to **employ misdirection**. You might cause harm by setting a trap, gain the advantage by creating a distraction, avoid something by not being where you're expected to be, or resolve an uncertain outcome by deceiving someone into going the wrong way.

You use Maneuver to **move with grace and agility**. You might cause harm by stabbing someone from the shadows, gain the advantage by moving quickly and quietly, avoid something by hiding in an alcove, or resolve an uncertain outcome by escaping quickly.

You use Observe to **take advantage of your surroundings and tools**. You might cause harm by tossing a knock-out grenade to just the right spot, gain the advantage by memorizing guard patrol routines, avoid someone by hiding somewhere you know they won't look, or resolve an uncertain outcome by knowing the layout of the facility.

Chase Situations

You use Fight to **go through things and endure**. You might cause harm by tackling someone, gain the advantage by refusing to slow down, avoid something by crashing right through it, or resolve an uncertain outcome by never stopping.

You use Manipulate to **make the chase harder for others**. You might cause harm by throwing obstacles in the way, gain the advantage by forcing your pursuers onto a bad patch of road, avoid something by tricking someone, or resolve an uncertain outcome by sabotaging the path behind you.

You use Maneuver to **move faster and with more agility**. You might cause harm with a quick sideswipe or jump kick, gain the advantage by pulling ahead, avoid something by dodging around it, or resolve an uncertain outcome by weaving through obstacles.

You use Observe to **use your environment to your advantage**. You might cause harm by leaping over a hidden trap you know about, gain the advantage by taking the more dangerous but shorter road, avoid something by expecting it, or resolve an uncertain outcome by knowing exactly where you're going.

Hacking Situations

You use Fight to **brute-force your way through a system**. You might cause harm by employing a DDOS attack, gain the advantage by flooding the system with junk data, avoid something by blocking it with a firewall, or resolve an uncertain outcome by persisting.

You use Manipulate to **use the system against itself**. You might cause harm by exploiting a critical weakness, gain the advantage by creating a critical weakness, avoid something by exploiting a flaw in the programming, or resolve an uncertain outcome by leveraging the system's weaknesses.

You use Maneuver to **move quickly through a system**. You might cause harm by attacking the system too fast for others to respond, gain the advantage by using multitasking subroutines, avoid something by getting out before security finds you, or resolve an uncertain outcome by being adaptive.

You use Observe to **exploit your knowledge of the system**. You might cause harm by using an attack app designed specifically for this system, gain the advantage by knowing how the system fights intruders, avoid something by using a backdoor, or resolve an uncertain outcome by predicting exactly what the system will do.

Transcript of Arielle's confession

Recorded by Jules d'Orsay, 12.5 0800

JD: Please state your name and ID number for the record.

A: My name is Arielle Bonaventure and I don't have an ID number. I'm a Naturel.

JD: Okay, can you confirm you have been offered both food and drink, which you have declined?

AB: I can confirm I'm not eating anything this organization gives me. The piss bucket was a nice touch, but I'd rather go without.

JD: Arielle, I can understand you're angry, but we need to follow protocol.

AB: I answered your question. (mumbling) Can you take off these restraints?

JD: This interview is being recorded, as I said earlier. Please speak loudly and clearly.

AB: How's this? (yelling) Why am I being interrogated by my girlfriend's killer?

JD: As senior cleaner, this task falls to me.

AB: I want to talk to Clare. I want some answers.

JD: I'll see what I can do. First, I need you to answer a few questions. When did you first start meeting with Emilie Wu?

AB: Last Janvier. I saw her at a rally.

JD: A political rally?

AB: No! This was one of those bogus community spirit rallies Sun Systems hosts four times a quarter. Employee attendance is mandatory. Clare had me stake it out, because she was watching the top brass, but my scope kept tracking to this girl. I watched her for a long time. She wasn't into it.

JD: You think she may have been a Resistance sympathizer.

AB: I wouldn't go that far. Emilie was pretty apolitical. She just... was elsewhere, her sign drooped down, read something idiotic like SUN SYSTEMS, IMPROVING YOUR DAILY ROUTINE. God, their marketing people aren't worth_

JD: Anyway, you were the one who initiated contact.

AB: Yeah, I followed her home. She was freaked at first, preferred to meet people virtually, but she gave me instructions on how we could hang out in VR. I've never liked portable tech, but I scrounged around and called in favors, so I could see her there. We met that way for six months. Then she agreed to start meeting in person and_god, she was so pretty and funny and ridiculous. She had a pet turtle she called Snopes, I smuggled in black-market noodles, and it was just_real, you know?

Zones

In many conflicts, space is divided into zones. On your turn, you can move to a new zone if doing so makes sense. The GM might rule that getting to certain zones requires extra effort because they're far away or because getting to them is difficult. In this case, you have to spend your action to move to the new zone, and you might have to roll against the mission opposition (*page 124*).

Zones are aspects, and they show who's where, who can act against who, who can see each other, who can talk to each other, and so forth. They're fictional constraints on what's happening. If one person is on **THE ROOF** and the other is in **THE STREETS**, they can't punch each other, but they *can* shoot each other. They can talk to each other, but not quietly. And so on. While a situation aspect is broadly true, a zone is only true for those in the zone.

There are two kinds of zones: physical zones and abstract zones.

A **physical zone** represents a physical space, but it doesn't have to be any particular size. Rather, zones are used to break conflicts down into easy-to-understand areas.

> A firefight has broken out in the streets! The GM decides that the zones are THE STREET, THE ALLEYS, THE BALCONIES ABOVE, BEHIND THE BARRICADE, and BEHIND COVER.

Likewise, an **abstract zone** represents an abstract concept, like BLENDING IN or HUNTED. They're particularly useful in social situations and stealth missions.

> The players are infiltrating a masquerade ball so they can meet their contact and get the information they need. The GM decides that the zones are THE DANCE FLOOR, BLENDING IN, STANDING OUT, GAUCHE, NOTICED BY THE CONTACT, OUT OF THE WAY, and NOTICED BY THE GUARDS. All of these, except for THE DANCE FLOOR, are abstract zones.

A character can occupy multiple zones at once, if it makes sense in the story. You might be in THE HALLWAY and also TRAPPED, for example.

Just as with other aspects, you can invoke zones when doing so makes narrative sense. For example, if you're perched on THE ROOFTOPS with a sniper rifle, it makes perfect sense that you can invoke THE ROOFTOPS when you take a shot at someone below. It does not make sense to invoke the same zone when you're running as fast as you can away from the gendarmes on street level, though.

GM, it'll be easier on everyone if you write your zones down on index cards or scraps of paper. Place zones near each other if characters in those zones can move between them or affect characters in nearby zones; place isolated zones far away from the rest. You can even decide to create and destroy zones during the conflict.

Players, you may find it useful to represent your characters with small tokens, like glass beads or extra dice. When you're in a zone, put a token on that zone. When you leave it, move it.

In the Thick of It

Boosts

From time to time, performing actions will give you **boosts**. You can spend a boost to get +2 to an action **before** you roll the dice. You can spend as many boosts as you want on a given action.

When you gain a boost, you can do one of three things with it:

» **Keep it.** You can only spend it on your next turn during a conflict, or on the next roll you make during the same scene.

» **Pass it** to a PC or NPC. That character can spend it, but not tie it to an aspect, but only on their next turn during a conflict, or on the next roll they make during the same scene.

» **Tie it** to any relevant aspect, as explained below.

At the end of your turn, you lose any boosts that you had at the start of your turn.

When you **tie** a boost to an aspect, describe what that means in the story and put the boost token on that aspect, so everyone knows it's there. Doing this changes the boost in a few ways:

» The boost now lasts as long as the aspect does, until the end of the scene, or until someone spends it, whichever comes first.

» The boost can now be spent by *anyone* to invoke that aspect, provided they can justify it in the narrative.

You can spend boosts tied to an aspect to invoke it as if the tied boosts were fate points. So, you can spend the tied boost to get the +2 bonus **before or after** the roll, to reroll your dice, to declare a story detail, or to provide opposition.

However, the boost is *not* a fate point. It's still a boost, so you can still spend as many boosts as you want on a single roll, even if they're all tied to the same aspect.

Aspects, Aspects Everywhere

Tying a boost to an aspect is a good way to make the boost last longer, so you have it when you need it. You can even make up a new aspect to tie it to, provided it makes sense within the story. However, there are a few restrictions on this ability. First, if you gain a boost by succeeding with style on an action, you can't create a new aspect unless you're already creating an aspect with that action. You also can't create more than one aspect per action.

Even when you do get the chance to create a new aspect, it's often simpler and more effective to tie boosts to an existing aspect. If what you really want is to create a **SURPRISED** aspect on your enemy and tie boosts to it, that's fine. You might want to tie those boosts to one of your character aspects, though. Similarly, when you gain boosts, see if you can tie them to any aspects already on the scene before you make up new ones. It can be tempting to make up new aspects every time you get the chance, but that can lead to a situation where there are too many aspects to keep track of in the scene.

Marking Conditions

When someone causes you harm and succeeds, you must mark one of your conditions. If they cause you harm and succeed with style, you must mark two conditions.

If you can't or won't mark the required number of conditions, you get **taken out** (**page 146**). To mark a condition, you must be able to explain how marking that condition helps you remain in the scene. If you cannot explain how any of your unmarked conditions would help you remain in the scene, then you cannot mark any of them, so you must get taken out.

Marking a condition does three things:

» A marked condition becomes a character aspect. The GM can invoke it and compel it like any other aspect, and so can you.

» A marked condition prompts a specific effect, which may be immediate or may last until the condition is cleared.

» A marked condition cannot be marked again until you clear it.

Each condition also specifies a way that you can **clear** it. Satisfy a condition's requirements to clear it, and you can erase the mark, ending all of the above three effects: it ceases to be an aspect, its lasting effect (if any) ends, and it can be marked again.

There are six conditions in the game, but you'll only have to worry about five. The social class of your character determines your conditions:

» Members of **la Société** have ANGRY, WOUNDED, COMPROMISED, DEPLETED, and MARKED FOR DEATH.

» Members of **les Citoyens** have ANGRY, WOUNDED, COMPROMISED, BLACKLISTED, and MARKED FOR DEATH.

» Members of **les Exilés** have ANGRY, WOUNDED, PERSON OF INTEREST, BLACKLISTED, and MARKED FOR DEATH.

> Many of these conditions refer to major and minor costs, which are described in more detail on **page 127**.

Angry

You're upset, emotional, and prone to making mistakes. You might be able to use that anger to your advantage, but it's also going to be a liability.

Effect: The person who made you ANGRY gains a boost.

Clear: ANGRY clears at the end of the scene.

Wounded

You've suffered lasting injury, whether emotional, psychological, or physical. It'll make it hard for you to function, but you might be able to use it as fuel for your cause.

Effect: While you're WOUNDED, the GM adds 1 more fate point to her Budget at the start of each mission.

Clear: Spend a prep action seeking treatment, and roll against Fair (+2) opposition. WOUNDED clears regardless of your result. If you tie, you also pay a minor cost; if you fail, you also pay a major cost.

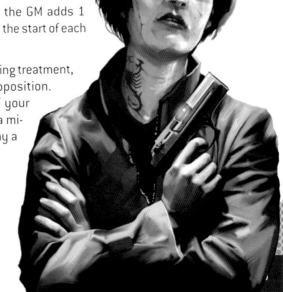

Compromised

The government no longer trusts you. This will make you an ally to some, an enemy to others.

Effect: While you're **Compromised**, whenever you buy equipment, the GM gains blowback equal to the cost of the bought equipment.

Clear: Spend a prep action greasing palms and convincing people you're not a threat, and roll against Fair (+2) opposition. **Compromised** clears regardless of your result. If you tie, you also pay a minor cost; if you fail, you also pay a major cost.

Depleted

Your resources are dangerously low, and you're going to have a hard time bringing them to bear. You might be able to use this to play on sympathies, but that's a dangerous game in Paris Nouveau.

Effect: You lose half of your fate points, rounded up. While you're **Depleted**, your refresh is 0.

Clear: Spend a prep action juggling investments, liquidating funds, and otherwise spending money to make money, and roll against Fair (+2) opposition. **Depleted** clears regardless of your result. If you tie, you also pay a minor cost; if you fail, you also pay a major cost.

Person of Interest

The government has turned its eye toward you. This might get you notoriety or trust in some circles, but it'll definitely make your life harder. They want to talk to you, probably vigorously.

Effect: While you're a **Person of Interest**, the GM gets 1 blowback at the start of every scene, except prep scenes and debrief scenes.

Clear: Spend a prep action trying to cover your tracks and erase your identity, and roll against Fair (+2) opposition. **Person of Interest** clears regardless of your result. If you tie, you also pay a minor cost; if you fail, you also pay a major cost.

Blacklisted

The citizenry no longer wants to help you, and will do so only grudgingly. You might be able to leverage your reputation to make people do what you want, but more often they'll simply refuse to talk to you.

Effect: While you're **Blacklisted**, each piece of equipment you buy or requisition costs another fate point. When you requisition equipment, use the original cost to determine whether la Résistance has access to it.

Clear: Spend a prep action convincing the Citizens that you're not as bad as they think you are, and roll against Fair (+2) opposition. **BLACKLISTED** clears regardless of your result. If you tie, you also pay a minor cost; if you fail, you also pay a major cost.

Marked for Death

People (probably the government) want you dead or otherwise permanently gone. This might earn you allies, but you're going to have to fear for your life.

Effect: If the GM takes you out while you are **MARKED FOR DEATH**, she can spend 5 blowback to remove your character from play permanently. If another player takes you out, they can spend a fate point to do the same.

Clear: Spend a prep action calling in a favor from the Contessa. Only she has the necessary influence to remove the kill order from your profile.

JD: Arielle, when did you start sharing Resistance information with Emilie Wu?

AB: She was just curious, you know? She thought it was cool she had a girlfriend who was a freedom fighter. Not really sure what I'm fighting for now.

JD: Did you tell her Le Chat Noir was our contact point for weapons deals?

AB: I don't know! I mean, maybe, just casually.

JD: Were you aware that location is now compromised, due to government takeover?

AB: I'm sure Emilie had nothing to do with it!

Taking People Out

When you successfully cause harm to someone, they must either mark a condition or get taken out. Players, if you take someone out, you get to say what happens to them, within the limits of the fiction and table consensus. GM, if you take a player out, you can say what happens to them, but you can't remove them from play permanently *unless* they've marked their MARKED FOR DEATH condition *and* you spend 5 blowback. Regardless of how you take them out, they're out of the conflict. They might still be present in the scene, but they can no longer take actions or contribute to accomplishing goals.

> Juliette is facing off against a pair of gendarmes, and she's taken a bit of a beating. All of her conditions are marked, except for MARKED FOR DEATH. One of the gendarmes takes a shot at her and rolls Great (+4). Juliette rolls to defend and only gets a Fair (+2) result, and has no fate points or boosts to spend.
>
> Juliette could mark her MARKED FOR DEATH condition to stay in the fight, but she doesn't like her chances against these two. She chooses instead to be taken out. Because MARKED FOR DEATH is clear, the GM can't kill her character or otherwise remove her from play. She **can**, however, describe the two gendarmes beating her senseless, putting a bag over her head, and hauling her off to a detention facility for questioning... which she does.

GM, describing how a PC gets taken out can be a delicate subject. You do have the right to take them out how you want to, but remember that though you control the government, you're not the players' enemy. Respect their boundaries, and listen when they say "brake." When in doubt, follow these three guidelines:

» **Taking out a PC is dramatic.** It's never a way to simply get a PC off-camera quickly. When you take a PC out, that's a spotlight moment for that player. Let them have it. After all, they just got taken out.

» **Taking out a PC follows the fiction.** Playing an RPG already requires a hefty amount of suspension of disbelief; don't strain that further by taking a PC out in a nonsensical or ludicrous way. Make sure the way you take a PC out stands up to table consensus.

» **Taking out a PC moves the the story forward,** particularly that PC's story. If a PC gets taken out, that's an opportunity to put them in a new, interesting, complicated situation. Even if a PC dies, it's an opportunity to tie up loose narrative threads and shake things up a bit.

Death, Sacrifice, and Betrayal

There are two ways your character can be permanently removed from play: you can be taken out while you have **Marked for Death** marked, or you can opt for the **glorious death**.

If you're killed by being taken out, there's a good chance you'll trigger the sacrifice milestone or betrayal milestone, though you might trigger neither if you don't go out in the way described by either milestone. If you opt for the glorious death, you *will* trigger one of these milestones; a glorious death is one that, by definition, has purpose.

Sacrifice Milestone

Players, when your character dies in service to la Résistance, add your remaining fate points to la Résistance's Cache, and make a new character with the same number of advances as your previous character had.

Betrayal Milestone

Players, when your character dies undermining la Résistance, make a new character with one more advance than your previous character had.

The Glorious Death

Sometimes things are *really* not going your way. When all else fails, or when you want to give your character a spectacular exit, you can choose to give them a **glorious death**.

On your turn, you can declare that you are taking a glorious death. Narrate what you do and how it kills you. You also succeed automatically, without rolling, at one action that would require a roll, though you don't succeed with style.

If you go out in service to la Résistance, each surviving ally gains a fate point *and* a boost, and you trigger the sacrifice milestone.

If you go out betraying la Résistance, the GM gains 10 blowback, and you trigger the betrayal milestone.

JD: When did you start sharing Resistance information with this subject?

AB: Don't call her a subject_you killed her, you [REDACTED].

JD: Arielle, your chair is wired. I'd rather you'd calm down on your own accord.

AB: [crying sounds]

8 At Mission's End
Debriefing and Advancement

After a mission ends, everyone participates in a **debrief scene**. During the debrief, accumulated advancement points may prompt the PCs, la Résistance, or the government to advance. The debrief also gives players a chance to level accusations at each other.

> ### How do immediate advances work?
> Various rules may prompt a player, la Résistance, or the government to earn an **immediate advance** during play. In this case, do **not** clear the associated advancement track.

Fictionally, the debrief represents the PCs returning to la Cave or a Resistance safehouse, talking with their superiors about how the mission played out, and using the information at their disposal to figure out who they can and can't trust. Debriefs can be great opportunities for character drama and development, just like in prep scenes.

To go through the debrief, do the following steps in order:

» 1. Check if PCs advance.

» 2. Check if la Résistance advances.

» 3. Check if the government advances.

» 4. Check if any PC wants to accuse another.

Step 1: PC Advancement
Players, check to see if your character's advancement track is full. If it is, choose one of the following advances and clear your track:

» Increase your refresh by 1 (maximum 5).

» Increase one of your means ratings by one step. You cannot increase a means rating beyond Great (+4). You can have a maximum of one means rated at Great (+4) and two means rated at Good (+3).

» Gain a stunt from your playsheet.

» Gain an augmentation (***page 153***).

» Gain a contact (***page 158***).

Step 2: Resistance Advancement

If la Résistance's advancement track is full, the players choose a new Resistance advance together and clear its track.

The list of la Résistance's advances and their requirements are in *"Resistance Advances"* (**page 159**).

Step 3: Government Advancement

If the government's advancement track is full, the GM chooses a new government advance and clears its track.

If the government's advancement track is not full, the GM may spend fate points from the Bank to earn an equal number of advancement points. If doing this fills the government's advancement track, the GM chooses a new government advance and clears its track.

If the government has already advanced during this debrief, the GM cannot spend fate points to earn advancement points.

The list of the government's advances and their requirements are in *"Government Advances"* (**page 161**).

Step 4: Accusations

GM, ask each player in turn if they'd like to make an accusation. If a particular player seems antsy to make an accusation, let them start; otherwise, just start with the player to your left. If they say "no," move on. If they say "yes," follow the rules below. Multiple players can make an accusation during a debrief.

Players, you can accuse another PC of being a Spy for the government, but only if you spend all of the advancement points on your advancement track (minimum 1). Making an accusation against a fellow Resistance agent is not to be taken lightly.

If you do accuse another PC, you become the **accuser**, they become the **accused**. GM, take the accuser and the accused aside, somewhere the rest of the group can't hear you, to run the interrogation. Accused, bring your secret with you. GM, bring the secret deck with you.

Accused, you must choose one of the three following options.

» You can choose to **clear your name** if you're not actually a Spy. Show the accuser and the GM your secret, proving you're not a Spy. You *may* get a new secret, but you don't have to. If you keep your old secret, it works as normal, but now somebody else knows what it is. Either way, false accusations waste time and allow the government to grow stronger: the government gets an advance.

» You can choose to **turn double** if you are a Spy. Show your secret to the accuser and the GM. You get a new secret. The accuser earns an immediate advance; gaining la Résistance a double agent is well rewarded.

» You can choose to **sacrifice yourself**, whether or not you're a Spy. You tell them nothing, forcing la Résistance to kill you. Your character dies. Trigger the sacrifice milestone (*page 147*). You get a new secret, and then la Résistance gets an advance.

If you need a new secret, the GM selects and gives you two new secrets. You choose one new secret to keep, and then shuffle the other secret and your old secret back into the secret deck.

Talking After the Fact

Both the accused, if still alive, and the accuser are free to talk about the content of the accusation process when they return to the table. Neither, however, is obligated to tell the truth.

Augmentations

Augmentations are roughly as powerful as stunts, and some of them provide benefits similar to playsheet stunts, so they're a good way to gain the abilities of other playsheets—for example, if you're playing a Malcontent and you want to gain elements of the Hacker.

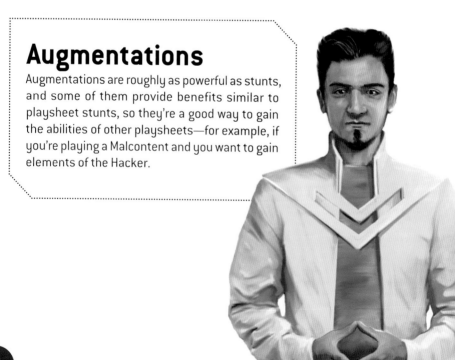

Augmentations use cybertechnology, nanotechnology, or bioengineering to enhance human capabilities. The GM can offer compels to you based on the types of or specific augmentations you have:

» Cybertech augmentations are considered gauche in Paris Nouveau, but they get the job done.

» Nanotech is virtually invisible, but is vulnerable to electromagnetic effects.

» Biotech is impossible to detect, but is experimental and often has side effects.

Some augmentations are also illegal. The GM can compel this, too.

Blood Scrubbers (Biotech)

You are immune to most toxins and diseases, thanks to specialized microorganisms in your blood. Even against particularly virulent maladies, you get a +2 to avoid their effects.

Bone Reinforcement (Cybertech)

Your bones are reinforced with carbon steel. Once per mission, you can avoid taking the **Wounded** condition.

Cyber-Eye (Cybertech)

Your cybernetic eye allows you to see in low-light conditions without too much trouble. You also get +2 to gaining the advantage with Observe by noticing small details or taking careful aim.

EMP Cluster (Illegal Cybertech)

You have a small cluster of batteries at the base of your skull. Once per mission, you can activate your cluster to produce a localized electromagnetic pulse that affects your zone. All security systems are taken out, anyone using AR or VR becomes **Disoriented**, and all electronics (including nanotech and cybertech augmentations) are deactivated. The EMP *does* affect you, too.

Hidden Blades (Illegal Cybertech)

You can unleash blades hidden in your arms, giving you +2 to Fight rolls made to cause harm with lethal intent.

Local Field Receiver (Illegal Nanotech)

You have nano-receivers in your brain that can tap into security feeds and even AR feeds. If you're in a zone with any security systems or characters using AR, you get +1 to gaining the advantage with Observe for each such security system or character.

Local Field Transmitter (Illegal Nanotech)

You have nano-transmitters in your brain that you can use to remotely hack and spoof security and AR feeds. You can gain the advantage with Manipulate by creating visual illusions and anomalies. They're obvious, but distracting. You get a +2 bonus to do this.

Muscle Enhancers (Nanotech)

You have nanites in your muscles and blood that can stimulate adrenaline production and boost muscle efficiency. At any time, you can spend a fate point to activate your muscle enhancers. While they're active, you gain +2 to Fight rolls that rely on strength. Each time your turn begins, you must either deactivate your muscle enhancers or mark one condition to keep them active.

Pheromone Enhancement (Biotech)

You've been given acute control over your biochemistry and can use it to sway people more easily. You gain +2 to gaining the advantage with Manipulate in social situations.

Stealth Field (Illegal Nanotech)

You can alter AR to blend into your surroundings. You gain +2 to Maneuver rolls you make to avoid detection, provided you're hiding from people using AR or from security systems.

Augmented reality is accessible to anyone with a neural casing. It allows you to set overlays (like a skin or filter) on your perception of your environment. Senses can be controlled: sight, smell, taste, touch, and sound.

You can still perceive reality, but it is markedly improved. Experiences may vary, based on the latency of your part of the city. Upgrades to resolution are available, for a small credit cost. Consult the tables in Appendix A33 to calculate your final cost. If you would like to upgrade now, please click here.

As it is likely you've only experienced AR up till now, we are excited to introduce you to a far more powerful tech experience, which is of course virtual reality (VR).

Once you've tried VR, you won't be satisfied with anything less. Your VR reflects your real-life appearance, yet enhances it satisfyingly. In your VR domain, you can interact with other avatars, accomplish your work tasks, and experience high-level entertainment. If you have a business, you can set a veil to mask the current state of your building. This is far cheaper than offering actual improvements and makes your business stand out in a sea of competitors.

In your personal domain, veils can be customized to make your surroundings more palatable, and you can adjust the settings on your avatar. Please remember, your avatar must resemble you within +/-10%, in order to make identification by security forces in VR easier. For example, you can adjust the color of your eyes or hair, but you need to have roughly the same height and facial features. The exception is age. Most people prefer to set their avatar to appear to be in their twenties.

Le Treillis is accessible for a variety of programming. With VR, you can participate in your favorite shows, talk to the characters, and explore their worlds. You can be underwater, on a mountaintop, in any era of history (some restrictions apply).

Why spend any time in this world, when all you desire is within your mind?

Why indeed? This world is smelly and dirty. Your fellow Citoyens forget to bathe and are dressed in ugly, forgettable clothes. The walls of your domain are blank cement. Every place here looks like every other place; it's easy to get lost in Paris Nouveau.

Yet, are we not creatures of this reality? Are we to lose ourselves in a rose-tinted virtual daydream? Can we not achieve more, learn more, improve our world instead of anesthetizing ourselves against it?

On a bleakly humorous note, restricted eras of history include our revolution in 1789 and our resistance against the Nazis during World War II.

Rigs are available for your VR upgrade. These rigs are best for short runs in VR. A company representative is available to meet with you to train you on your rig and show you how to strap yourself in. The gyroscopic model is by far the most popular.

For longer runs in VR, we highly recommend spending the extra credits to lease a tank unit. These are entirely immersive and can actually remove the need for eating, sleeping, or elimination. They trigger what we describe as a "catatonic dream state." Before embarking on a long VR run, it is important to ensure you have sufficient APE to survive your time away.

Our newest and most exciting feature is the upgrade to Shade programming, the latest and most sophisticated in artificial intelligence interactivity. Put simply, your Shade is now your personal AI. It behaves like a person and is voice-activated. Need to research something? Simply ask your Shade. For Citoyens who do not get the opportunity to leave their domain before le Silence, your Shade is ideal company. The more you interact with it, the more it "understands" you and your personality. It can even learn to laugh at your jokes.

Lafleur Digital Media lists the Shade upgrade on their guide to "don't miss" tech.

The Shade, l'Ombre. I had one, back when I had my neural casing. It was less sophisticated then, but I already was uneasy around it, as if it were recording what I did and said. One night I woke up and realized it was watching me while I slept.

After that, the decision to unplug was an easy one. "l'Ombre." It is always with you and is yet another way for Cryptiq and your government to keep tabs on you.

The Shade in Play

Citizens of Paris Nouveau have Shades; however, most members of la Résistance excise them from their brains because the Shades spy for the government. A few manage to hack them, subverting l'Ombre to work for them and not report information back to the government. Some keep their Shade as-is, taking the risk.

If you want to have a Shade, tell your GM. Work with them to describe the Shade by answering these questions:

Who or what does your Shade look like? Is it someone you know? A unique person? Does it even look human?

How does it speak to you? Does it appear to communicate verbally? In pictures? Is it more like telepathy?

How does your Shade assist you in your daily life? What one thing does it frequently help you with?

How does your Shade get in your way in your daily life? What is one way it frequently hinders you?

Then, write a new aspect on your playsheet that represents your Shade.

Contacts

Contacts are NPCs who can help you…for a cost. A contact isn't your servant; they have their own agendas and needs, and they help you because they expect to gain from it and because they expect that their help won't come back to haunt them.

Arielle, Sniper

Sardonic and always smiling, Arielle is one of the best shots around.

During prep scenes, you can create a prep advantage called **ARIELLE** by using Maneuver or Manipulate. There's no downside to this prep advantage, and the GM can't compel it.

During missions, you can spend boosts tied to **ARIELLE** to cause harm to enemies you designate, provided they're in zones that a nearby sniper could hit. Arielle's effort to cause harm starts at Mediocre (+0), adding +2 for each boost you spend. When **ARIELLE** has no tied boosts left, she escapes and the aspect disappears.

Jean le Roux, Bartender and Information Broker

All the illicit information in the city comes through Jean sooner or later.

When you create a prep advantage with Observe, tie 2 more boosts to it.

Henri Singh, Quartermaster

Henri has access to all the best goods; it's useful to know the quartermaster.

During prep scenes, you can requisition equipment without spending your prep action.

Marya, Black Market Dealer

Marya can get you what you need, no questions asked.

During prep scenes, you can requisition equipment with a cost 1 higher.

Once per session, you can buy a piece of equipment retroactively, spending fate points as normal, and have it left for you in a convenient place. Those fate points go to the Bank, though.

Selise, Knife Sisters Lieutenant

The Knife Sisters are one of the most vicious and brutal gangs in Paris Nouveau, and Selise commands many of them.

Once per session, you can spend a fate point to call in the Knife Sisters. When you do, chaos erupts. All nameless NPCs in the scene are brutally killed, granting the GM appropriate blowback. The Knife Sisters then depart.

Sidenge, Problem Solver

Whether you need to get patched up or you need the gendarmes off your tail, Sidenge knows people who can help.

During prep scenes, if you spend your prep action to clear a condition, you can clear an extra condition.

Resistance Advances

When you choose a new advance, it must either be at the top of a tree or be connected to an advance that la Résistance has already.

You'll find these advancement trees on **pages 296–297**.

Intel

Web of Informants: Whenever a player creates a prep advantage with Observe, tie 2 more boosts to it.

Interrogation Techniques: Whenever a player creates a prep advantage with Fight, tie 2 more boosts to it.

Inside Man: At the start of each prep scene, the GM must tell the players one transgression in the coming mission.

Government Contacts: At the start of each prep scene, the GM must tell the players another transgression (2 total) in the coming mission.

Training Archive Access: Once per mission, before a player rolls, the players may collectively decide to discover the passive opposition to the roll or the ratings of the actively opposing NPC's four means.

Favor of the Ambassador: La Résistance can call in one free favor from the Ambassador. You must still request the favor during a prep scene, but this does not cost a prep action, and the favor carries no cost from the Ambassador.

Favor of the Contessa: La Résistance can call in one free favor from the Contessa. You must still request the favor during a prep scene, but this does not cost a prep action, and the favor carries no cost from the Contessa.

Dirty Secrets: You have the proof you need. You can invoke the government's scandal as if it were any other aspect, and invoking it for a bonus adds +3 instead of +2. This is a **critical advance**.

Resources

Hijacked Shipments: Players can requisition equipment with a cost of 1 or less per piece of equipment.

Armory: Players can requisition equipment with a cost of 2 or less per piece of equipment.

Black Market Contacts: Players can requisition equipment with a cost of 3 or less per piece of equipment.

Remote Supply Caches: Players can access the Cache outside of la Cave.

Medical Equipment: At the start of each prep scene, clear the **WOUNDED** condition from all players.

Favor of the Assassin: La Résistance can call in one free favor from the Assassin. You must still request the favor during a prep scene, but this does not cost a prep action, and the favor carries no cost from the Assassin.

Favor of the Duke: La Résistance can call in one free favor from the Duke. You must still request the favor during a prep scene, but this does not cost a prep action, and the favor carries no cost from the Duke.

Means to an End: La Résistance finally has the equipment it needs to make a move. At the start of every prep scene, add 1 fate point to the Cache. Players can requisition equipment with a cost 1 higher. This is a **critical advance**.

Support

Hearts and Minds: Whenever a player creates a prep advantage with Maneuver, tie 2 more boosts to it.

Promises and Bribes: Whenever a player creates a prep advantage with Manipulate, tie 2 more boosts to it.

Gendarme Contacts: The GM must spend 2 more blowback than normal to bring gendarmes into a scene.

Grassroots: The players get +1 to all rolls made to deal with Citoyens without using violence.

Citizen Saboteur: Cross out any one advance that the government has taken. The GM can no longer use its effects, though the advance still counts as a pre-requisite for taking later advances.

Favor of the Contessa: La Résistance can call in one free favor from the Contessa. You must still request the favor during a prep scene, but this does not cost a prep action, and the favor carries no cost from the Contessa.

Favor of the Captain: La Résistance can call in one free favor from the Captain. You must still request the favor during a prep scene, but this does not cost a prep action, and the favor carries no cost from the Captain.

The Will of the People: Les Citoyens support you fully now. The revolution can begin! At the start of any scene in which nonmilitarized Citizens are present, the PCs get the situation aspect CITIZEN SOLDIERS with two tied boosts. This is a **critical advance**.

The Revolution

La Résistance has a special advance, The Revolution. Taking this advance means that the next mission the PCs will undertake is "The Revolution," found under *"Endgame Missions"* (*page 201*). Players, you can take this advance after you've taken a certain number of **critical advances**, depending on your game length:

» **Short Game:** La Résistance must have 1 critical advance.
» **Medium Game:** La Résistance must have 2 critical advances.
» **Long Game:** La Résistance must have 3 critical advances.

Government Advances

When you choose a new advance, it must either be at the top of a tree or be connected to an advance that the government has already.

You'll find these advancement trees on *pages 298–299*.

Corporate

Taxation: At the start of each prep scene, add a fate point to your Bank.

Wage Negotiations: At the start of each prep scene, add another fate point to your Bank (2 total).

Mandatory Charitable Donations: Whenever a PC buys equipment, add 1 fate point to your Bank per piece of equipment bought.

Anti-Piracy Measures: Whenever a PC requisitions equipment, add 1 fate point to your Bank per piece of equipment requisitioned.

Infrastructure Investment: During each debrief, you can put up to 2 leftover fate points back in the Bank.

Shell Companies: During each debrief, you can put up to 4 leftover fate points back in the Bank.

Clever Accounting: During each debrief, put all of your leftover fate points back to the Bank.

Élite Kickbacks: Whenever a player gets a favor from an Élite during a prep scene, add 2 fate points to your Bank. This is a **critical advance**.

Military

Gendarme Recruitment: At any time in a mission, you can spend 5 blowback to bring in gendarmes equal to twice the number of players, as well as a gendarme sergeant.

Gendarme Training: Gendarmes and gendarme sergeants get +1 to all rolls.

Security Allocation: At any time in a mission, you can spend 5 blowback to bring in SecSpec equal to the number of players, as well as a SecSpec commander.

SecSpec Training: SecSpec and SecSpec sergeants get +1 to all rolls.

Mandatory Military Service: At any time in a mission, you can spend 7 blowback to bring in soldiers equal to the number of players, as well as an elite soldier.

Military Training: Soldiers and elite soldiers get +1 to all rolls.

Mercenary Recruitment: When you spend blowback to use Gendarme Recruitment, Security Allocation, or Mandatory Military Service, you can spend fate points in place of blowback, at a rate of 2 blowback per 1 fate point spent.

Mandatory Volunteerism: Whenever you spend blowback to bring NPCs into a scene, it costs 2 less blowback. This is a **critical advance**.

Security

Drone Surveillance Network: You start every mission with +2 blowback.

See Something, Say Something: You start every mission with another +2 blowback (+4 total).

Spy Network: You start every mission with another +2 blowback (+6 total).

Militarized Gendarmerie: The mission opposition of every mission increases by +1.

Constant Vigilance: The mission opposition of every mission increases by another +1 (+2 total).

Drone Security Force: At any time in a mission, you can spend 5 blowback to bring in security systems equal to the number of players.

More Drones, Better Drones: Your security systems get +2 to cause harm.

Drone Neural Network: You can spend boosts created by your security systems in place of blowback. This is a **critical advance**.

The Purge

The government has a special advance, The Purge. Taking this advance means that the next mission the PCs will undertake is "The Purge," found under *"Endgame Missions"* (**page 201**). GM, you can take this advance after you've taken a certain number of critical advances, depending on your game length:

» **Short Game:** The government must have 1 critical advance.

» **Medium Game:** The government must have 2 critical advances.

» **Long Game:** The government must have 3 critical advances.

JD: Were you aware I found encrypted messages on Emilie's hardware, to top Sun Systems officials?

AB: I'm sure they encrypt all their messages - it's only smart.

JD: You're a natural.

AB: Yeah, but not an idiot.

JD: You realize that in order to continue with this organization, you'll have to be reconditioned.

AB: No, I don't want to.

JD: The government will execute you as Resistance, and you're no good to us as you are.

AB: You have shattered my [REDACTED] heart and now you want to wipe my mind. Go ahead, you [REDACTED] horror show. I don't want to remember her anyway. I don't want it to hurt anymore.

JD: It won't hurt at all. I promise. Don't be afraid.

[End transcript]

9 Your Corporate Sponsor: A Citizen's Guide

The Corporations of *Uprising*

REPORT SUSPICIOUS ACTIVITY TO THE GENDARMERIE

You are lucky to be alive right now, after the Fall. This guide offers a listing of the successful corporations located in Paris Nouveau. There are myriad choices here to help you and make your life more appealing, less stressful, and overall smoother.

For your convenience, this catalog has been laid out with your needs in mind. All you need to do is touch your chosen corporation offer to redeem, and instantly your software will be updated and the appropriate benefit unlocked. As your fingerprint is already in the database, for your security, it is impossible for other Citizens to purchase items using your account.

Once you have completed the transaction, the cost in credits will be added to your OCRD (outstanding Citizen rolling debt).

Good news—you have been preapproved for upgrades worth up to 100,000 credits! If you wish to check your eligibility for increasing your debt limit, merely hover your thumb over the Corvid Economics help button and a representative will be with you shortly.

But enough about boring debt and interest rate details! Please read on to see the scintillating array of entertainment options, AR/VR skins, L'Ombre personality settings, and much, much more.

Corporations: Mix and Match

GM, throughout this chapter, you'll see write-ups of some of the more powerful and prominent corporations in Paris Nouveau. If you're stuck for a corporation and you don't want to use one of those provided here, just follow these steps to create your own.

To come up with its concept, ask: What does the corporation do? What do they make? You can pick from this list or make up your own. For particularly big corps, pick two or three things from this list. Don't worry if they don't make sense together; it'll all make sense in time.

» Transportation	» Clothing
» Armaments	» Prefabricated Homes
» Nanotechnology	» Security
» Biotechnology	» Wearable Tech
» Food Production	» AR and VR Equipment
» Health Services	» Educational Products
» Home Goods	» Waste Disposal
» Luxury Goods	» Labor Services

Your corp also needs a name. If you don't have a strong idea for a name, grab one, two, or three things off this list, mash them together, and add "Systems," "Technologies," "Holdings," or "Corporation" at the end, or nothing at all.

» Smith	» Guillard
» Takeda	» Omni
» Branson	» Poullet
» Star	» Omega
» Prime	» Pinnacle
» Research	» Argenot
» Production	» Tower
» Adawele	» Biotics

And you're done! Don't worry about fleshing the corporation out just yet; that'll come with time.

CORVID ECONOMICS

Focus: Banking, OCRD

While banking doesn't exist the same way as it did before the Fall (which some might say is a good thing!), Corvid Economics does provide the grease to keep the wheels of Paris Nouveau running. They also run the central bank and operate as the primary moneylenders of the city.

"The pound of flesh which I demand of him / Is dearly bought. / 'Tis mine, and I will have it." That's a line from *The Merchant of Venice*. Not many readers of Shakespeare left. Who has time for poetry, when you are so busy with your pattern-matching games?

If you can't guess, it's Clare here. I know you must be weary of the snark, so I'll simply say this. The government is run by corporations. This is not a secret. What is an open secret is how it deliberately entraps its citizens in an ocean of debt, so much so that it's easier to swim down than to rescue yourself. They toss around terms like "self-sufficiency" and "fiscal independence for all," but what they really mean is that you'll work for them, for free, forever, to eliminate a debt you can never pay.

Many corporate sponsorships use the same equation credit card companies used before the Fall. The only difference is a small one—they shifted the number from a relatively small one to a sizably larger one. They rely on your ignorance, your inertia, your willingness to sign away your time for access to services that will improve your life. What if we all worked together to make life better for everyone, instead of just the ones willing to take on crippling debt? I know, shocking idea. But that's one of our beliefs. Improving the system that confines our people into a prison of their own making.

I don't mean to say the people at Corvid Economics (or really, any of these corporations) are all evil. That'd be ridiculous. For the most part, they are just your fellow Citizens, doing what they are told for the greater good, a.k.a. the enrichment of a select few.

And evil…what does that word mean? I've seen a great deal of selfishness, greed, and cruelty. But the government is not some faceless Evil Empire. In fact, quite the contrary. The faces of the government are the faces you see every day. But just because the cogs in a machine only do their little part doesn't mean the machine itself isn't destructive.

We're going to break the machine and build a new way, offer the people an alternative to this endless twilight of owing. And we will try to sacrifice as few lives as possible. Will the government make the same promise?

At Corvid Economics, there is a whole host of financial products offering flexibility to help you live your life the way you want to. We know survival in Paris Nouveau takes a lot of energy, so let one of our debt officers find a plan that fits your needs.

CRYPTIQ, INC.

Focus: Energy, manufacture of biological kilojoules (kJs)

Thanks to the repeated investments of Cryptiq, Inc. into our society, we now have a citizenry that is 91% connected to le Treillis. Their mission statement is to reach 100% of our city's citizenry, so no Citizen is left behind without necessary tech upgrades. Fortunately, as our society progresses and former non-tech advocates are phased out, we're certain this goal is completely attainable!

Kilojoules come in a safe, efficient plugin, the affordable and mobile way to power your neural casing. Tired of plugging your head into a power cable? Biological kilojoule plugins are the answer. They are discreet, easily covered by your hair or a hat, non-toxic, and high-performance, lasting up to 48 hours.*

* Personal performance may vary.

Don't be left in the last century! Tap here to receive a 20% discount on your kJ power plugins.

INFOSEC-WEST

Focus: Security for le Treillis, AR and VR

You wouldn't want to lose all the resources for AR and VR that you've purchased with your hard-earned credits! It's important to always have backups of your data, as well as to protect yourself from the many dangerous and unscrupulous hacker groups who are working to break in and steal your data *right now*.

...Okay, I'm sorry. I tried to be quiet and let you read, but **seriously**? People will always be governed by fear. It's one of the strongest emotions. But please tell me you can see how they're manipulating you here. They threaten you with the BIG SCARY HACKERS, but conveniently leave out the fact that's buried in their small print: by authorizing their security systems, you are giving permission for a back door to be placed in your home systems, one that their corporation and (surprise, surprise) the government can access for any little reason.

I'm not saying that there are no hackers out there who would steal your data—that would be disingenuous. And yet, they want you to go further in debt to allow them to spy on you. It's outrageous overreaches like this that keep me up late, working away to dismantle the relentless creep of the government into our lives. Take that as you will, words from someone who's hacked into your system.

InfoSec maintains a tireless team of virtual protectors, ready to shield you from the predators lurking in le Treillis. Think about your favorite veils you've placed in your home area, suddenly stripped away without warning. All the beautiful artwork, fine furnishings, and delicious food stripped away to reveal bare walls, cold floors, and APE. This could be your endless reality, if you don't take care to safeguard your digital purchases. Tap here to experience the peace of mind of a 30-day trial of our security services.

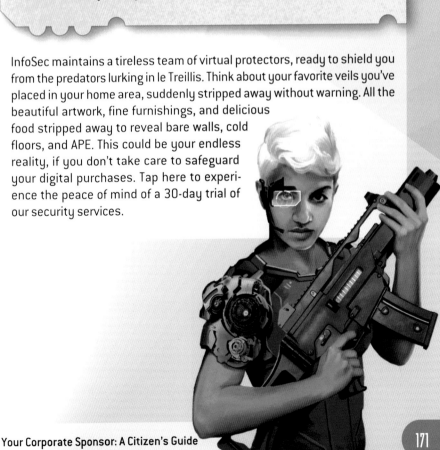

LAFLEUR DIGITAL MEDIA

Focus: Entertainment, news, veils, and l'Ombre programming

Bored? Lafleur Digital Media has the solution for you. Tune in 24 hours a day. There's no need to unplug—simply use our fitted earpiece to stream archival music and news into your consciousness while you sleep. Now you don't even have to be awake to keep up with current events! We are constantly at work designing new and innovative veils for your home or business, upgrades for your avatar, and new functionality for l'Ombre.

Tap here to win a free personality pack for your Ombre. Winners may choose from Romance or Soldier options.

PARAGON GYROMATICS

Focus: Wearable tech, tech implants

From visual key overlays to mecha limbs, Paragon Gyromatics offers the most reliable wearable tech in Paris Nouveau, pairing cutting-edge technology with your life. Want to be stronger? Faster? More focused, more resilient to pain? We have a product for your problem. The human body is a weak bag of flesh, but our upgrades make sure your tech lasts as long as you do. All Paragon Gyromatics products have a Lifetime Service Warranty—that's how strongly we believe in what we make!

Look how easily ideas are twisted. They offer a warranty with the duration of your lifetime because, often, their tech is what leads to your demise. There are no studies on it, due to the stranglehold Paragon Gyromatics keeps on their data, but there are a lot of stories out there of people dying because they wanted a mecha arm or a reinforced chest. The human body instinctively rejects inorganic matter; a splinter is pushed out of the skin. That doesn't keep Paragon from trying, though. They offer a lot of financial incentives to wear their products, often hiring admired members of the community to proudly display their latest implants or wearable tech. This lends it cachet, but doesn't change the dangers, which they downplay.

Don't get me wrong. If you can survive it, the tech can length-en your life, make you capable of impressive feats. We have several Armigers in la Résistance, but they tend to be peak specimens of physical health. Paragon downplays the dan-gers to anyone at risk, for their bottom line.

Tap here to qualify for a free health scan to see if you are eligible for any of our many specialty implants.

QUESADA MÉCHANIQUES ÉLITE

Focus: Miniaturized tech

We've all seen them, those gauche mecha limbs and absurdly outsized chest pieces. In fact, is there anything more *Citoyen* than a bunch of visible mech? For those who don't need to count their credits, Quesada Méchaniques Élite offers a select variety of tiny machines. How about a featherweight lens, fitting over your eye so you can see your preferred veil settings no matter how drear your surroundings? Or perhaps a tiny ear implant which allows you to contact others by pressing your thumb and forefinger together? You know the value of invisible tech. We wouldn't want anyone to think you lived in le Bas.

This is a laugh—we hacked this entry in here. It's actually only included in the Élite guide to the city, which is why the ad copy is extra condescending. See what they think of you? You're only a means to an end, a way to get a limitless, volun-tary labor force. Such disdain for those whose backs they ride.

Tap here for a free credit check to see if you qualify for any elite Quesada product.

RATHBURN CHEMICAL LABORATORIES

Focus: Downcycling, drainage

While it's true Paris Nouveau has lost a lot of the luster of pre-Fall Paris, it's thanks to the hard work of Rathburn Chemical Laboratories that it's relatively free of garbage and waste. Thanks to our government-sponsored Clean Our Rue (Street) program, we've quadrupled the amount of converted waste in Paris Nouveau. Not only are our street processors relatively compact, they also are continually refined in order to improve our already exceptional technology.

Paris always stank of cat piss and old river water, at least after the Fall, but at least it smelled real. Like an actual city. I hear at one time it smelled like baking bread, like flowers and lovers' kisses, but that sounds like fanciful nonsense. Thanks to the disgusting Rathburn Street compactors and their "perfumes," the streets now smell like artificial roses. It smells like death, like rotting flesh, like decay in the sun. Fleurs du Mal, that's the fragrance of our lives.

Tap here to request your own compact waste processor.

SUN SYSTEMS BIOTECH

Focus: Artificial protein extract manufacturing

As long as Sun Systems Biotech is in business, you and your family unit will never starve. Simply order sufficient quantities delivered to your door, load it into your APE gun, and you can serve it on a platter or inject it directly into your mouth, however you prefer. Our menu of flavors and grit saturation is fully customizable.

Now offering lemon-flavored APE! Touch here to have a free sample delivered now.

VERDI TRANSPORTATION

Focus: Public transportation, government vehicle contracts

How lucky you are to be alive right now, when there are so many nonpolluting methods of transportation in Paris Nouveau. If you tire of walking, you can either access l'Ascenseur for a small deduction of credits or rent one of our handy pataches to float down the Seine. As you know, for space and safety reasons, personal vehicles are forbidden without express government authorization. On the positive side, whenever you do see such a vehicle, you can be sure it's your government hard at work!

Ah ha ha! Well, this is a mostly true factoid. The government does own practically all personal vehicles, with the exception of those Élites who have called in a great deal of favors. They want you staying in your homes, like nice quiet little lab rats, punching your touchscreen for your pellets. After all, you might see something they don't want you to see if you leave home. Like your next-door neighbor being beaten by gendarmes. Like them dumping those street-waste processors into the Seine.

We see. We're watching. **Will you watch too?**

IX. Miscellanea and Closing

Though it's likely, as a Citoyen, you will never get the opportunity to visit our sister city, Upfrancisco, it is worth your time if you do get the chance. Sometimes it is helpful to realize we are not alone in this world.

Travel between city-states is not recommended. For the most part, only les Naturels or Ex-Citoyens are equipped to make the trip. We encourage you to stay within the city limits unless absolutely necessary. Even if you survive the extreme weather and biohazards, food is scarce and there are dangers in the form of bandits and wildlife maddened by biological factors.

The other problem is your neural casing, once outside the shielding capabilities of Paris Nouveau, will be subjected to uncontrollable electromagnetic radiation.

Notice to Citoyens: while the quarantine is not currently in effect, it can be resumed by the government with a 24-hour notice. Keep safe and be aware of potential dangers.

If you simply must travel to another city-state, and have the credits to purchase a ticket, there is the space elevator. It is quick but harrowing, and maintenance is always an issue, despite our best efforts to keep the tubes in good repair. As you can imagine, being stuck in a space elevator can traumatize even the most stable of Citoyens.

In closing, thank you for reviewing this document. You can mark your assent to the information herein with your biometric scanner. We would like to offer a heartfelt thanks to Cryptiq, Inc. for compiling this document.

I guess the moment has come, the time to decide. I've told you all you need to know to make the most informed decision. If you wish to join us, you simply need to leave your domain right now and come to Père-Lachaise cemetery. We will meet you there and explain what else you need to know.

The Resistance needs you. Your time is now; it's time to awaken...**if you are ready.**

-Clare

10 Black Bags and Jackboots
Rules and Advice for the GM

GM Fate Points: The Budget and the Bank

GM, you get fate points just like the PCs do. At the start of a mission, you get a pool of fate points called the **Budget** equal to the number of participating PCs plus one. So, if there are three PCs in the scene, you start with a Budget of 4 fate points.

Also, you can withdraw as many fate points from the government's **Bank** as you wish and add them to your Budget for the mission. Your only chance to do this is at the start of the mission—once it begins, you cannot withdraw from your Bank.

Whenever you **invoke** an aspect—whether it's a character aspect or situation aspect—you must spend a fate point from your Budget. If you invoke a PC's aspect against them, give them the fate point you spent. If your Budget is empty, you can't invoke aspects.

Whenever you **compel** an aspect, you offer a fate point from the general supply, not your Budget. This means you can *always* compel the PCs' character aspects. You can also compel NPCs' character aspects, but you don't get a fate point for doing so.

Whenever a player compels an NPC's aspect, though, the offered fate point goes into your Bank, not your Budget. To resist a compel, you must spend a fate point from your Budget, and this fate point goes into the general supply, not to the player who offered the compel.

At the end of a mission, any leftover fate points in your Budget are lost, unless you have taken government advances that allow you to put unspent fate points back in the Bank.

Black Bags and Jackboots

Raoul Allard, Guerrilla

People say Raoul Allard has a hard face, but most people in Paris Nouveau have never even seen its lower half. When he's in Paris Above, he's wearing a tattered black scarf over his mouth and chin.

All that most people remember is salt-and-pepper hair, shorn to just an inch from his scalp. His eyes, deep set, are not friendly. He's strong and free of hesitation in a fight and his voice, when he speaks, is short and sharp like a bark. If he likes you, he may talk a little about his lady friend in the gendarmes, Elisabeth.

He's all business, as Clare's most loyal sergeant in the Resistance. People say he's a dick, but he's a dick who keeps other Resistance members from getting killed. And as he'd probably argue: why are you listening to what people say, anyway?

If you have ***Coup: Rebellion G54*** (G54), you can use the Guerrilla card to represent Raoul Allard.

RAOUL ALLARD

ASPECTS

GRIZZLED VETERAN; COLD, HARD EYES; IN LOVE WITH ELISABETH (pick two)

MEANS

Fight: Fair (+2)

Maneuver: Good (+3)

Manipulate: Mediocre (+0)

Observe: Average (+1)

CONDITIONS

☐ STAGGERED

☐ REELING (optional)

☐ DESPERATE (optional)

Blowback

Blowback is a GM resource that represents la Société's desire to see the PCs brought to justice, and you can spend blowback to tighten the net around the PCs as they try to complete their mission.

At the start of a mission, you have however much blowback you had at the end of the previous mission. Certain government advances can give you more blowback at the start of a mission, too.

During a mission, you get blowback when the PCs cause **transgressions**, conditions listed in the mission. Also, at any time during a mission, a PC can give you 3 blowback in exchange for a fate point from the general supply. Make sure they know this. Feel free to offer fate points to them in exchange for blowback.

You can spend blowback to make the PCs' lives more difficult. Spending blowback goes a little bit beyond a compel in two ways. First, it can affect the entire group, not just one person or a small part of the group. Second, spending blowback always produces a specific mechanical effect.

Here are the things you can spend blowback to do:

» When you take out a PC who is **Marked for Death**, you can spend 5 blowback to kill, imprison, or otherwise permanently remove that PC from play.

» You can spend blowback to trigger a **complication** of the mission.

» You can spend 2 blowback to upgrade a minor cost into a major cost, as long as the minor cost was introduced in an earlier exchange.

» Certain government advances give you other things you can spend blowback on, such as bringing gendarmes into the scene. You can spend blowback to use these advances at any time during any mission.

Loreena Lu, Politician

It's hard for those who want power, when the Élites so clearly have the majority of it on lockdown. But there's still room for Citizens who want to have their fingers in different pies. Loreena Lu is one of those Citizens. She has a reputation for not accepting government cruelty, so the people are quite fond of her. It's likely she would be willing to accept a bribe from the Resistance, should the price be right.

Amongst the grim and gritty of Paris Nouveau, Loreena stands out. Like an Élite, she manages to look very well-groomed, despite a paucity of ways to do so. Her razored bob clings to her cheeks. In fact, she has perfectly groomed eyebrows, something you rarely ever see in this city.

She is, of course, part of the government, and that's something to keep in mind before you lean too heavily on her or her favors. If it suits her and won't burn her reputation, she's just as likely to betray you. After all, it's just business.

If you have G54, you can use the Politician card to represent Loreena Lu.

LOREENA LU

ASPECTS

AMBITIOUS UPSTART POLITICIAN; FLEXIBLE MORALS; IMPECCABLE APPEARANCE (pick two)

MEANS

Fight: Mediocre (+0)

Maneuver: Average (+1)

Manipulate: Good (+3)

Observe: Fair (+2)

CONDITIONS

☐ STAGGERED

☐ REELING (optional)

☐ DESPERATE (optional)

Spending Blowback Effectively

Blowback serves two purposes for you, the GM. First, it gives you a concrete, fair way to do terrible (and interesting) things to the PCs. Because the rate at which you get blowback is (mostly) in the PCs' control, their actions allow you to do these terrible (and interesting) things. To ensure PCs don't feel unduly punished for their actions, make sure they know that their actions will give you blowback. Give them an opportunity to reconsider. Once everyone's comfortable with how blowback works and what kind of actions will give it to you, you'll find yourself having to remind them less and less.

Second, blowback is a way to increase the tension during a mission. When you gain blowback, the PCs know that something bad is coming. Further, they know that something bad is coming because of something they did. Used well, blowback puts ever-escalating pressure on the PCs as they try to accomplish their goals. To amplify this feeling, keep your blowback tokens right out in the open where everyone can see them. Fiddle with them during conflicts.

There are many ways to use blowback effectively. Here are a few:

» **Hoard it for a while.** Let your pile build, and keep (subtly) directing the players' attention to it. Spend it occasionally to bring in reinforcements or cause other complications. When the players are feeling complacent or confident, spend a lot of blowback to catch them off guard.

» **Spend it as soon as you get it.** If the PCs are in a firefight, spending blowback can force them to change tactics when you bring in stronger reinforcements.

» **Save some blowback for taking out PCs permanently.** Look for players who seem to be angling for a glorious (or ignominious) death, and give it to them. Or take out PCs with incarceration rather than death. Then, once the PCs have had a chance to move on from their companion's capture, bring that character back as a named NPC antagonist.

Peter Gladwell, Foreign Consular

The consular from Upfrancisco is fairly striking. You don't see a lot of pale, red-headed, blue-eyed men in Paris Nouveau. Consular Gladwell knows he's distinctive and does not hesitate to use it; when he turns those no-bull blue eyes on Citizens, they are happy to make way. His orange-red haircut is close-cropped and he generally wears his uniform jumpsuit. He seems to always be on duty.

Most famous for the Treaty of the Remainder of Nantes, Consular Gladwell might have some insight to offer about America and the state of the rest of the world. He survived the tube and that's no small feat. Unsurprisingly, though, he doesn't seem to be in a rush to return. He doesn't care a whit about Paris city politics, so if a Resistance member approached him regarding an alliance, he might listen.

If you have G54, you can use the Foreign Consular card to represent Peter Gladwell.

PETER GLADWELL

ASPECTS

CHARMING DIPLOMAT; GOOD-LOOKING, BUT TROUBLE; NO STOMACH FOR POLITICS (pick two)

MEANS

Fight: Mediocre (+0)

Maneuver: Fair (+2)

Manipulate: Average (+1)

Observe: Good (+3)

CONDITIONS

☐ STAGGERED

☐ REELING (optional)

☐ DESPERATE (optional)

Making and Playing NPCs

Non-player characters (NPCs) can be categorized into various types.

Nameless NPCs are the extras of **Uprising**. They exist to populate Paris Nouveau, to provide opposition during conflicts, and little else. They're mechanically simple, and many nameless NPCs don't even need mechanics.

Named NPCs are NPCs who play a more important role in the story. If a character has a name, that character is important in some way. She could be the gendarme commander continually harassing the PCs, or the shop owner who sells the PCs supplies under the table. A nameless NPC can become a named NPC if that NPC suddenly becomes important.

Nameless NPCs

Nameless NPCs, naturally, don't have names. Instead, you refer to them as "gendarme" or "shop owner" or "corporate stooge" or whatever broad archetype fits. Often, you won't need mechanics for a nameless NPC. If the PCs interact with a corporate stooge and never have to roll the dice, then that NPC doesn't need stats or rules yet.

Sometimes nameless NPCs *do* need rules, though. Most frequently, this is because the PCs are engaging in a conflict with them. When this happens, you'll turn each relevant nameless NPC into a **blank** or an **agent**.

When you take out a nameless NPC, you can narrate it in any way, subject to table consensus.

Blanks

Each blank has a **type**, such as GENDARME, MERCENARY, or CORPORATE AGENT. When the blank performs an action that relates to its type—such as a gendarme attacking someone or following a direct order—it rolls with a Fair (+2) rating. The type is also an aspect, so you can invoke it, as normal.

Each blank also has a **flaw**. The gendarmes the PCs are fighting might be FOLLOWERS, or the mercenaries might be UNSUBTLE. If the blank performs an action that could be complicated by its flaw, such as a mercenary trying to sneak up on the PCs, it rolls with a Terrible (-2) rating. The flaw is also an aspect, so you can invoke it, as normal.

If a blank performs an action that relates to **neither** its type nor flaw, or to **both** its type and flaw, it rolls at a Mediocre (+0) rating.

Blanks have no conditions; successfully causing harm to a blank takes out that blank. If you succeed with style, you take out **two** blanks, provided doing so would make sense.

Agents

Agents have a type and flaw, as blanks do, but all of their ratings are shifted up by one step:

» An agent acting within its type rolls at Good (+3).

» An agent acting within its flaw rolls at Poor (-1).

» An agent acting within both or neither rolls at Average (+1).

Agents also have one condition, **STAGGERED**. If you successfully cause harm to an agent, the GM can choose to mark the **STAGGERED** condition. If you succeed with style, you take the agent out. Unlike conditions for PCs, conditions for NPCs do not cause a specific effect when marked, though they still become aspects.

Mobs

GM, sometimes there are quite a few nameless NPCs in a fight, and you don't want to roll actions for each individual NPC. If you wish, you can group nameless NPCs of the same type into a **mob**. When a mob takes a turn, it can take an action against one target or against all enemies in the same zone.

If the whole mob acts against the same target, roll only once but add +1 to the roll for every two nameless NPCs in the mob, to a maximum of +4, for any action other than avoid. Add this to any other bonuses they might get on the roll, such as from their type.

If the mob targets all enemies in the zone, you still only roll once, but you don't grant them the extra bonus, and each enemy in the zone must defend against that roll. There must be at least three nameless NPCs in the mob in order to cause harm to an entire zone.

Players, if you cause harm to a mob of nameless NPCs and succeed with style, you can give the GM 1 blowback in order to take out the entire mob. The GM still gets any blowback they'd get for transgressions triggered by taking those NPCs out.

Named NPCs

When you want to make a particular NPC important to the story, give them a name, high concept, trouble, and means spread.

NPCs That Aren't People

You can represent things like security systems, vault doors, and other such objects that can get in the PCs' way as NPCs. Though they're not people, they can still roll to oppose the PCs and can take actions.

A named NPC has a **high concept**, an aspect that sums up who the NPC is in a few words. If your NPC already has a type, turn it into a high concept by adding detail. For example, a MERCENARY might become a SADISTIC SOLDIER OF FORTUNE. A gendarme might become a HESITANT ROOKIE.

A named NPC also has a **trouble**, an aspect similar to a nameless NPC's flaw. Unlike a flaw, though, the NPC's trouble is specific to that NPC, and it's very personal. What gets that NPC in trouble most frequently? Maybe the SADISTIC SOLDIER OF FORTUNE has PROBLEMS WITH AUTHORITY. Maybe the HESITANT ROOKIE has a FAMILY TO PROTECT.

Unlike nameless NPCs, named NPCs don't automatically roll at a higher rating for acting in accordance with their high concept, nor do they automatically roll at a lower rating when their trouble complicates things. However, their high concept and trouble can be invoked and compelled, as normal.

Also, named NPCs have a full means spread. Use one of the spreads below, or assign the following ratings to the four means: Good (+3), Fair (+2), Average (+1), Mediocre (+0).

- » **Fighter:** Fight +3, Manipulate +0, Maneuver +2, Observe +1
- » **Talker:** Fight +0, Manipulate +3, Maneuver +2, Observe +1
- » **Ghost:** Fight +1, Manipulate +0, Maneuver +3, Observe +2

You can give a named NPC up to 3 stunts, but you don't *need* to give them any. The more stunts you give a named NPC, the more challenging that NPC will be for the PCs to deal with.

The easiest way to give an NPC stunts is to use stunts from the playsheets. However, you can make your own stunts quickly by filling out these templates:

» Because I **[reason]**, I get +2 to **[end or means]** when **[circumstance]**.

» Because I **[reason]**, I can **[dramatic, powerful ability]** once per mission.

All named NPCs have the **Staggered** condition. If you want to make a named NPC tougher, you can give them up to two more conditions: **Reeling**, then **Desperate**. As with nameless NPCs, if you take out a named NPC, your narration is limited only by table consensus.

Renaming NPC Conditions

GM, you should use the default names for NPC conditions unless you have a good reason not to. That said, if you *do* have a good reason to change an NPC's conditions, go ahead and do so. Changing the names of these conditions doesn't change how they function, but it can add some interesting elements to the narrative if an NPC has **Glitching Cyberware** as a condition instead of **Reeling**.

Named NPCs can be assisted by mobs of nameless NPCs. In this case, roll using the named NPC's appropriate means. If you're affecting only one target, the named NPC gets a +1 for every two nameless NPCs assisting her. If you're targeting a zone, the named NPC can do so as long as at least two nameless NPCs are assisting her. The assisting mob still gets an action on its turn. Finally, named NPCs can work together just like PCs can.

Damien the Pious, Priest

Father Damien is known amongst the Resistance as something of a sympathizer. He will not endanger himself or his parish by joining the fight, but occasionally he will arrange for some supplies to "disappear" or will shelter a Resistance fighter on the run for a single evening.

He has an almost gaunt appearance, emphasized by his close-shaved head. His ritualistic forehead tattoos—two white ovals, a small one stacked above another, much larger one—make it hard to focus on the burnished brown of his eyes. He is usually dressed very simply, in the black jacket and tunic of the clergy, with the white stripe down the front. Most of the world's religions don't exist anymore in Paris Nouveau. Since the Fall, there's not much salvation to hope for.

His face is quite well known in Paris Nouveau, for he has a weekly show offered on the Neural Entertainment Network. He alternates between the showmanship of a salesman and the quiet piety of a true believer. Through this program he funnels in a great deal of tithing credits, though no one knows quite where it all goes. He must have some powerful patrons.

If you have G54, you can use the Priest card to represent Damien the Pious.

DAMIEN THE PIOUS

ASPECTS

RESISTANCE-SYMPATHETIC PRIEST; CONSUMMATE SHOWMAN; "I WON'T ENDANGER MY FLOCK." (pick two)

MEANS

Fight: Mediocre (+0)

Maneuver: Average (+1)

Manipulate: Good (+3)

Observe: Fair (+2)

CONDITIONS

☐ STAGGERED

☐ REELING (optional)

☐ DESPERATE (optional)

Acting and Opposing with NPCs

When you act with an NPC, they'll often accomplish their action without you needing to roll, if a PC isn't opposing the NPC. If a PC **is** opposing the NPC—such as if the NPC is shooting at a PC—follow these steps:

» 1. GM chooses the NPC's means and end, and describes their action.

» 2. Player chooses the PC's means and end, and describes their action.

» 3. GM and player roll and compare the NPC's effort to the PC's opposition.

» 4. GM and player choose whether to invoke aspects or not.

» 5. GM announces the final result.

Often, NPCs will provide active opposition against the PCs. When an NPC provides active opposition against a PC, follow these steps:

» 1. Player chooses the PC's means and end, and describes their action.

» 2. GM chooses the NPC's means and end, and describes their action.

» 3. Table consensus decides whether the player's action is risky, suited, or both.

» 4. Player and GM roll and compare the PC's effort to the NPC's opposition.

» 5. Player and GM choose whether to invoke aspects or not.

» 6. GM announces the final result.

Bringing Missions to Life

When you're running a mission, your job as the GM is to provide interesting challenges for the players to deal with. This means providing and controlling opposition for them (each mission will talk about what opposition is available, and how to bring in more), but it also means providing the PCs with interesting, difficult choices to make.

Missions are mostly just collections of aspects, zones, NPCs, and so forth. It's your job to embody the characters in the scene not portrayed by the PCs, to make the scenes feel cohesive, and to tie them together using transition scenes.

A big part of what you're doing in a scene is working with the PCs to get them to describe what they're doing in order to achieve goals. If a player says, "I'm going to take those guys out, and I'm using Fight," then ask, "What does that look like?" Get them into the habit of saying *what their characters are doing* to complete goals rather than saying *what mechanics they're using*.

Berne is in the middle of a tense warehouse shootout, and he needs to get at the medical supplies across the room. There are two guards in the way. John, his player, says, "I want to try to get through them with Fight."

"What does that look like?" asks Emily, the GM.

"Well, I fire off my rifle and take out the two guards, then run over to scoop up the supplies."

Emily thinks for a moment. "Hmm. That sounds more like you're causing harm to those two guards, and you'd have to use something else to get the supplies once they're down. Do you still want to do that?"

"That's two actions, right? No, I want the supplies now. Can I just plow through them to get the supplies?"

"Sure, and that would be Fight alright. It's going to put you in a tight spot afterward. Is that okay?"

"Well, Berne **is** BETTER LUCKY THAN GOOD," John says, grinning.

Emily smiles back, nods, and pushes him a fate point for his self-compel.

The elements of a mission are not straitjackets. If something doesn't fit with the version of the story that your table has come up with, change it. Drop NPCs, add new ones, replace the zones in order to make the scene take place somewhere else. Reskin existing elements where you can in order to ease your cognitive burden, but many of the elements of these missions are simple enough that you can quickly come up with some on your own. If you need to rewrite or restructure a scene, just call for a ten-minute break and do so. Your players will understand, and sometimes everyone needs a quick commercial break to go to the bathroom, refill beverages, and talk about that awesome thing that happened last scene.

Using Clare in Missions

Clare gives the PCs their marching orders at the beginning of each mission, but you can use her beyond that, as a character within the game. She's the leader of la Résistance, so she won't talk to the PCs anytime they like, but she will when important things are afoot. Use her sparingly. She's a no-nonsense woman, and very pragmatic. She sacrifices people when necessary, and will not coddle the PCs. That said, she gives credit where credit is due, and she rewards those who are valuable to la Résistance.

Should you need them, Clare's stats are below. You'll notice she's a bit more powerful than most NPCs; that's intentional.

CLARE, LEADER OF LA RÉSISTANCE

ASPECTS

CHANGE AT ANY COST; TRUST NO ONE

STUNTS

Because I **lead la Résistance**, I start every conflict with **LA RÉSISTANCE SOLDIERS** with one tied boost.

Because I intend to **tear down the establishment**, I get +2 to cause harm with Fight when I'm fighting agents of the government or a corporation.

Because **I believe**, I start each scene with a boost tied to one of my character aspects.

MEANS

Fight: Good (+3)

Maneuver: Great (+4)

Manipulate: Average (+1)

Observe: Fair (+2)

CONDITIONS

☐ STAGGERED

☐ REELING

☐ DESPERATE

Tips and Tricks for Running Missions

For any GM running missions, here are some tips and tricks you can keep in mind to make things easier and more fun at the table.

» Allow the players to be proactive. Typically, missions will involve the PCs going out and trying to accomplish something, with NPCs in the world reacting to what they do. This is good! As much as possible, allow the players to decide how they want to accomplish their goals. If things stray a little (or a lot) from what's provided in the mission, it's okay to make things up to keep the game moving.

» Provide difficult choices whenever you can. Nothing should be simple on a mission, and nothing should ever go entirely according to plan. If the PCs have a great plan, allow them to execute on it, but make sure they run into situations they don't expect and didn't plan for, and that those situations force them to answer questions that aren't necessarily easy to answer.

» Don't go easy on them. You've got blowback; use it. Put the PCs in danger. Make them work for what they get.

» You're not their enemy. Your job isn't to screw the PCs over; it's to complicate their lives in ways that drive fun play for everyone at the table.

» Find ways to keep them involved. If someone at the table has been silent for a while, ask them what they're doing. If they're not sure, give them something to deal with. Make sure everyone's having a good time.

» You can ask the players what happens next. If you're stuck for an idea, poll your players about it. If a new NPC has just walked on the scene, it's fine to point at someone and say, "Who is this guy, and why does he hate you?"

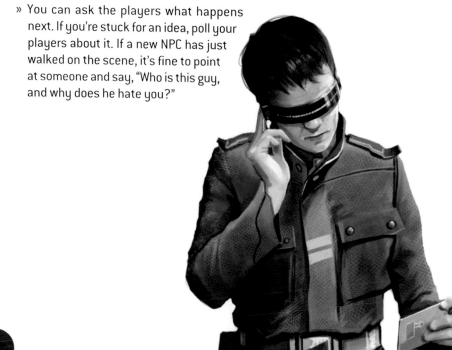

Grégoire Lemarque, APE Dispensary Technician

Grégoire appears all business when encountered at the APE dispensary. His facial recognition visor allows him to scan people in line instantly, bringing up useful data such as Total APE Units consumed to date and Last Dispensary Visit. Unfortunately for Grégoire, he's also got a reputation for being a soft touch. The truly hungry in Paris Nouveau know to go to his line. Even if they're not entitled to another APE portion, he rarely will turn them away.

He's actually being currently blackmailed by the system admin who covers for the shortages in his stores. The Resistance knows of his activities, but for now simply watches him. His charity suits their purposes, but he may become a liability.

If you have G54, you can use the Customs Officer card to represent Grégoire.

GRÉGOIRE

ASPECTS

COMPASSIONATE BUREAUCRAT; BEING BLACKMAILED; PROFILING VISOR (pick two)

MEANS

Fight: Mediocre (+0)

Maneuver: Fair (+2)

Manipulate: Average (+1)

Observe: Good (+3)

CONDITIONS

☐ STAGGERED

☐ REELING (optional)

☐ DESPERATE (optional)

Making Your Own Missions

Making missions in **Uprising** isn't all that hard. If you take the structure provided in the missions in this book, you can easily modify them, reskin them, or make new ones whole cloth. There are, however, a few things to keep in mind as you're doing so.

Resistance goals are clear and attainable. Vagueness, cleverness, and obfuscation are not your friend here; tell the PCs exactly what they're trying to do and exactly how many advancement points it'll get them.

If the PCs do everything right, la Résistance advances. Minor goals that help la Résistance in the short term are worth 1 advancement point. Major goals that contribute directly to la Résistance's long-term success are worth 3. Some goals are worth 5, though these are few and far between. If the PCs do everything right, completing every goal, la Résistance should advance during the debrief, even if it didn't have any advancement points going in.

Government goals directly oppose Resistance goals. Where possible, make government goals and Resistance goals mutually exclusive. Someone should come out on top in each mission.

Government goals are generally worth more than Resistance goals. The same basic guidelines for point values apply, but most government goals are worth 3 advancement points. Because most missions will end in success for the PCs, allowing the government to advance quickly despite not achieving all of its goals keeps the game tense and the opposition threatening.

Mission opposition is typically Fair (+2) or Good (+3). Very rarely it's Average (+1) or Great (+4). A starting character has a means spread of Average (+1) to Good (+3), meaning that, in general, they'll have somewhere in the neighborhood of a 50% chance of success when rolling against mission opposition. In addition, the government has taken advances that increase the mission opposition, to compensate for the fact that PCs can increase their own means with advances.

Around five or six zones is good. Sometimes you want more. Rarely do you want fewer. Too few and everyone's in the same place all the time. Too many and too much time gets wasted on moving around, trying to get near people. If you decide you need more, add them on the fly.

Don't start off with too many NPCs. A good guideline is to start with nameless NPCs equal to two or three times the number of PCs. Nameless NPCs are easy to take out, so large numbers are good. Too large, though, and you risk bogging the conflict down. You can always bring in more with blowback when the PCs start thinning them out.

Use transgressions that are likely to occur. If a transgression is an edge case, it may never get triggered; make sure edge cases are things the PCs are likely to do. A fun trick is to make the most expedient way to handle a situation into a transgression. For example, the PCs tossing a grenade into a room full of NPCs might bypass a conflict altogether, but it'll give you a mess of blowback.

Complications and discoveries make the PCs' lives harder and your job more fun. Always give yourself ways to bring more threats into the scene. Spending blowback is also a great way to model things like lockdowns, alarms, and other changes in security status, or to justify mission targets escaping without making the PCs feel like they've been cheated. In addition, compel-based complications and discoveries are a great way to introduce moral grays and tough decisions into a situation. Sometimes it's fun to make the PCs sweat over their choices a little.

Do your own thing. The previous pieces of advice are just that: advice, not rules. If you've got a better idea, run with it! The government isn't going to knock your door down for not playing by the book (probably).

Advice for GMs

As the GM, your job is to keep players engaged, make sure everyone's having fun, and provide a thrilling, tense experience for the group. Here are some techniques to help you do that.

Respectful Play

Your first, and most important, rule is that the people at your table are more important than the game. **Uprising** is a game about betrayal, intrigue, injustice, violent revolution, interrogation, and other themes that can veer into uncomfortable territory. Have a discussion at the beginning of the first session about this, and let your players tell you if there's anything they don't want to see in the game. Respect their choices. Similarly, you can tell them about things you don't want to see in the game.

That said, sometimes people get carried away unintentionally. If anyone, for any reason, feels uncomfortable because of something happening in the game, that person can say "Brake." When someone says "Brake," it's everyone else's responsibility at the table to skip past the uncomfortable scene and move on to something else. There is no judgment or pressure involved with this; it's everyone's job to respect everyone else's boundaries.

Engaging Taken-Out Players

When a PC gets taken out, it usually means sitting some amount of the game out. Sitting out a scene, or even the rest of the session, isn't a lot of fun, but there are ways you can make it fun.

If the PC is taken out for a short time, like the rest of the current scene, you can keep that player engaged by occasionally asking the player what's happening to her character. Ask leading questions like, "You wake up groggy. What did you lose in the chaos?" or "The gendarme holds a gun to your chin and tells you to talk, a gleam in his eye. What do you say to get rid of him?" If the taken out PC isn't going to face any real consequences for being taken out, keep that in mind.

If the PC has to sit out an entire scene, jump back to that PC periodically throughout the scene. Remember that the PC *is* going to face real consequences before she re-enters play. Talk to the PC about how the interrogation is going, or where she stumbles, bleeding and injured, for help. Each time you jump back to her, amp up the pressure a little bit. At the end of the scene, present that PC with a difficult choice, and ask her to make her choice in secret by writing her decision down and handing it to you.

For example, the secret policeman questioning her might give her the choice of telling him where la Résistance is going to strike next, or being shot behind the woodshed. Either choice is valid. An equally valid choice is for the PC to say, "I feed him false information so he'll let me go," or "I escape my bonds, get the jump on him, beat him senseless, and flee." If the PC says something like this, it's fine to let it happen. But remember: while the answer to the choice must be private, between just you and the PC, the choice itself is public information. All the other PCs know is that she was given the choice to inform or die. When she shows up later, alive and well, they'll wonder why.

If a PC has to sit out an entire session, give her the opportunity to make a new, temporary character for the rest of the session. This isn't the same as permanent removal; this character doesn't take a benefit forward for the previous character's death…yet. Let her play that character for the rest of the session. Then, in between sessions, talk to that player about what happens to her taken out character. Does she want to stick with the new character and let the old character be removed from play? If so, let her have the appropriate benefit for her previous character's exit. Does she want to resume playing her old character? If so, figure out how she comes back and let her start playing again at the beginning of the next session. Hang on to the other character, use it as an allied NPC. You can even let someone else play that character if their regular character gets taken out for a long time.

Elisabeth Bouret, Peacekeeper

Without her gendarme peacekeeper suit on, Elisabeth seems like a conventional, even pretty blond young woman. With it on, she has the capacity to level a city block. She is a gendarme, because her brother was before her, and her father before that. She was the first female peacekeeper and she's quite proud of that. There are now a handful of others, thanks to her. It's dirty, nasty work, but she genuinely believes she's keeping the streets of Paris Nouveau safer.

Though it's unclear how she ignores the obvious brutalities of others in her squad, she doesn't appear needlessly violent herself. In fact, it's rumored she might be sympathetic to Resistance members, or at least look the other way at a critical moment. This is likely because her lover is Raoul Allard, a high-ranking member of the Resistance. It's a real Romeo and Juliet situation. Or is it?

If you have G54, you can use the Peacekeeper card to represent Elisabeth Bouret.

ELISABETH BOURET

ASPECTS

THE ONE GOOD GENDARME; WOMAN IN A BOYS' CLUB; IN LOVE WITH RAOUL (pick two)

MEANS

Fight: Good (+3)

Maneuver: Fair (+2)

Manipulate: Mediocre (+0)

Observe: Average (+1)

CONDITIONS

☐ STAGGERED

☐ REELING (optional)

☐ DESPERATE (optional)

Invokes and Compels

You have a pool of fate points in each scene that you can use to invoke aspects for a benefit. Use these fate points to put pressure on the players and make them work for their goals, but your job is not to win. It's okay if you do, as long as that makes the game fun for everyone, but remember that you can always bring in more opposition later. Let them earn their victory. Make them work for it, but let them earn it.

Compels are another way to put pressure on a player or increase tension. Compelling an aspect against a player is *not* a way to cheat the player out of something or to be a jerk to a player. It's an opportunity for that player to be in the spotlight in a complicated way. A good compel is one that the player will agonize over a little, but will ultimately accept because they want to see what happens.

11 We Shall Die with Our Arms Unbound

Pre-Made Missions

What follows is a long list of missions that you can just grab and run as-is, right out of the book.

You don't *have* to use any of these missions; in fact, there's advice on making your own missions starting on ***page 194***. However, sometimes you just want to grab something exciting for the PCs to do without a lot of prep beforehand. When that's what you want, just turn to one of the missions in this book and run it. There's still plenty of room for improvisation and PC choice in each of them.

Each mission is divided into several parts, as follows.

First is the mission's **briefing**. In this book they're written as if Clare were giving the players their briefing; however, GM, you can feel free to paraphrase, or to use a different character to deliver the briefing. Each briefing explains what goals the PCs must accomplish, why the mission is important to la Résistance, and might outline other things like restrictions, secondary goals, or threats.

Its **set** describes where the mission's primary action takes place. All of the information in the set can be invoked or compelled as if it were a collection of aspects, as can anything implied by the set. That is, if there's a good chance that something is true about the location of the mission, then everyone can treat that thing as if it were an unwritten aspect.

A mission also has a **mission opposition** rating. Whenever a PC attempts an action and you need passive opposition, use the mission opposition. This doesn't necessarily mean that the opposition is always the same; as the GM, you have fate points and aspects you can invoke with them. Just as a PC can invoke aspects to increase the opposition an NPC must roll against, so too can you invoke aspects to increase the mission opposition when a PC takes an action.

Missions also have **Resistance goals**, given to the PCs by la Résistance. Completing Resistance goals gives advancement points to la Résistance, and gets la Résistance closer to advancing.

You'll also find a collection of **zones** in each mission. This will give you an idea of what the mission's location looks like and what's present. This isn't an exhaustive list; if it makes sense to add a zone, do so.

The mission's **cast** is the collection of statted NPCs in the mission—but, again, this isn't an exhaustive list.

The **setup** tells you how many NPCs exist in the mission at the start, and where they are. There might be other, mission-specific rules here too.

The **government goals** give you, the GM, ways to earn advancement points for the government. Many of these goals are mutually exclusive with la Résistance's goals. Keep these goals secret; you can announce that you're gaining advancement points if you want, but you don't have to.

The **transgressions** tell you how you get blowback during the mission.

Finally, the **complications and discoveries** tell you what you can spend your blowback on during the mission, in addition to the things you can always spend blowback on, like killing PCs or using government advances you've taken. There are occasionally also compels listed here; you don't have to use these, but they can add a level of moral complexity to the situation.

The mission write-up is your guide, not a straightjacket. If you have a question about how something works in the mission, refer to the write-up. If you can't find the answer to your question, it's okay to make something up.

> ## Mission Advice and Mission Arcs
> You'll periodically see sidebars like this one throughout this chapter that give you advice on running specific missions, or on stringing multiple missions together to create a story arc. These sidebars are just that: advice. You can use it if it's helpful, or do your own thing if you'd rather.

Endgame Missions

There are two **endgame missions** in **Uprising**: one where la Résistance stages a violent revolution to try to finally overthrow the government, and one where the government storms la Cave in force to try to stamp out la Résistance once and for all.

Players, you can trigger the mission "The Revolution" (**page 267**) by taking the Resistance advance of the same name. Likewise, GM, you can trigger the mission "The Purge" (**page 272**) by taking the government advance of the same name.

Both of these missions are very difficult, and the PCs will have to bring every resource to bear for each of them. They get a prep scene before "The Revolution," but not before "The Purge." Note, though, that these missions might not go as expected. If the PCs fail at "The Revolution," they lose the matching advance and the government earns an immediate advance. Likewise, if the GM fails at "The Purge," the opposite happens.

One significant difference between endgame missions and the other missions is the mission's goals. To succeed on an endgame mission, the PCs must complete **every** mission goal; la Résistance doesn't get advancement points for this. There are no government goals; the government's goal is simply to stop the PCs from completing Resistance goals.

Each endgame mission also has an **Aftermath** section that details what happens if la Résistance wins or the government wins.

Warehouse Raid

The warehouse belongs to Sun Systems Biotech. Somewhere in there is medicine we need, bandages, painkillers, and other medical supplies. Go in there and get it, then get out. Try not to make a mess.

Set: A Sun Systems Biotech warehouse after curfew. Security is tight, but they're not expecting company.

Mission Opposition: Fair (+2)

Running "Warehouse Raid"

"Warehouse Raid" makes an excellent introductory mission to show the players how the game works. Let them decide how they want to approach the problem. Do they want to sneak in? Go in guns blazing? Try to talk their way in or pose as Corvid security? Let them use the prep scene to make these choices and take prep actions accordingly.

When you're running the mission, look for opportunities to allow the PCs' plans to work out well. *Also* look for opportunities to throw them a curve ball; no plan survives contact with the enemy, after all.

Resistance Goals

» Get into the warehouse undetected 1 advancement point

» Bypass security systems 1 advancement point per security system bypassed

» Hack the manifest to cover your tracks 1 advancement point

» Steal the medical supplies 1 advancement point per crate (maximum 4)

» Don't kill anyone 3 advancement points

Zones

» **Undetected**

» **Spotted**

» **Amongst the Crates**

» **On the Balcony**

» **In the Offices**

» **Outside**

Cast

GUARD

Guard, Fair (+2)

Late Shift, Terrible (-2)

SECURITY SYSTEM

Security System, Fair (+2)

Design Flaw, Terrible (-2)

GUARD SEARGENT

Guard Sergeant, Good (+3)

Impatient, Poor (-1)

CONDITIONS

☐ **Staggered**

GUARD CAPTAIN RODRIGUEZ

ASPECTS

CRUEL, PETTY TYRANT; OVERCONFIDENT

STUNTS

Because **I know this warehouse**, I get +2 to gaining the advantage with Observe while in the warehouse.

MEANS

Fight: Good (+3)

Maneuver: Mediocre (+0)

Manipulate: Fair (+2)

Observe: Average (+1)

CONDITIONS

☐ STAGGERED

☐ REELING

Setup

There are twice as many guards in the warehouse as there are PCs in the mission, split evenly between **AMONGST THE CREATES, ON THE BALCONY,** and **OUTSIDE.** Also, there are two security systems present in each zone except for **UNDETECTED** and **SPOTTED,** and initially these systems only pass boosts to the guards. Guard Captain Rodriguez is **IN THE OFFICES.**

Government Goals

» Spot the PCs 3 advancement points

» Sound the alarm 3 advancement points

» Prevent the crates of medical supplies from being stolen 1 advancement point per crate (maximum 4)

» Apprehend PCs for questioning 3 advancement points per PC

Transgressions

» A PC kills someone 1 blowback, but 3 blowback if it's Guard Captain Rodriguez

» A PC allows someone who's seen them to escape 3 blowback

» A PC causes significant property damage to the warehouse or its contents 5 blowback

We Shall Die with Our Arms Unbound

Complications and Discoveries

» **Backup (5 blowback):** Bring in guards equal to the number of PCs, along with one guard sergeant.

» **Sound the Alarm (5 blowback):** Security systems can now cause physical harm, and all guards get +1 to rolls made to find PCs.

» **Alert SecSpec (10 blowback):** Write **SecSpec Alerted** on an index card and put 3 blowback tokens on it for the countdown. The countdown now has a spot in turn order. On its turn, remove a token from the card. If you can't remove a token from the card, instead add a Sun Systems SecSpec (see below) to the scene for each PC in the mission, then put 3 blowback tokens back on the index card. Continue the countdown until the end of the mission.

» **Unwelcome Information (compel):** The medical supplies are earmarked for a hospital that provides free medical care to all Citizens. Stealing them could sway public sentiment against la Résistance.

SUN SYSTEMS SECSPEC

Sun Systems SecSpec, Good (+3)

Keyed Up, Poor (-1)

CONDITIONS

☐ **Staggered**

Mariela d'Angelo, Provocateur

Mariela d'Angelo is the prodigal daughter of the Resistance. She broke away early, after a disagreement with Clare, but still publishes digital tracts on the corruption and stagnation of both the government and now the Resistance. She created a new, untraceable way to pass subversive information with wearable tech.

Her curly dark hair cut short and her refined profile disguise one of the most notorious firebrands in the city. She stops short of suggesting it all be burned down, but more than once her explosive exposés have rocked the city.

If you have G54, you can use the Intellectual card to represent Mariela.

MARIELA

ASPECTS

INSTIGATING ANARCHIST; INFORMATION NETWORK; "LA RÉSISTANCE IS JUST AS BAD AS THE GOVERNMENT!" (pick two)

MEANS

Fight: Fair (+2)

Maneuver: Average (+1)

Manipulate: Good (+3)

Observe: Mediocre (+0)

CONDITIONS

☐ STAGGERED

☐ REELING (optional)

☐ DESPERATE (optional)

ound

Convoy Ambush

Corvid Economics is sending a convoy full of high-tech weaponry to a private buyer. There'll be crates of weapons in that convoy, weapons we can use, but there's a prototype "smart gun" in one of the trucks that could give us an edge. Get those weapons for us or, failing that, destroy them so that whoever Corvid is supplying *doesn't*.

Set: The streets of Paris Nouveau during midday. Government vehicles are whizzing by, and any minute the convoy will appear.

Mission Opposition: Good (+3)

Running "Convoy Ambush"

This is an ambush, so frame the prep scene as the PCs actually making preparations for the ambush: setting up positions, wiring explosives, getting to know the layout, and so forth. They have a short lead time—maybe a day or two—to figure out what their plan is during the prep scene.

There's any number of ways the PCs can ambush the convoy, but the convoy might just take off and leave them behind. If it does, this mission could very easily transition into a chase sequence.

Resistance Goals

- » Steal the weapon shipments 3 advancement points per truck (maximum 9)
- » Destroy the weapon shipments 1 advancement point per truck (maximum 3)
- » Steal the prototype smart gun 3 advancement points
- » Destroy the prototype smart gun 1 advancement point
- » Allow no civilian casualties 3 advancement points

Zones

- » BEHIND COVER
- » AMONGST THE CONVOY
- » IN A TRUCK
- » IN TRAFFIC
- » THE ROOFTOPS

Cast

CONVOY GUARD

CONVOY GUARD, Fair (+2)

CAUGHT FLATFOOTED, Terrible (-2)

CORVID SECSPEC, Good (+3)

DISTRACTED, Poor (-1)

CONDITIONS

☐ STAGGERED

Setup

The convoy consists of five trucks: three transports containing weapons shipments, and two troop vehicles guarding the transports. The smart gun is in one of the transports. There are twice as many convoy guards as PCs, divided equally between the two troop vehicles. There's one SecSpec per PC; at least one is in each transport, with the remaining in the troop vehicles. There are five more convoy guards, each one driving one of the trucks. Finally, unless the PCs do something about it, there are numerous civilians throughout the area.

Give the PCs some control over where they start off. This is an ambush, after all. They can't start **AMONGST THE CONVOY** or **IN A TRUCK** without really good justification for doing so, but all the other zones are fair game. The PCs don't all have to start occupying the same zone.

Government Goals

» Escape the ambush 3 advancement points

» Take out PCs 3 advancement points per PC

» Prevent the PCs from taking or destroying weapons shipments 3 advancement points per shipment (maximum 9)

» Prevent the PCs from taking or destroying the smart gun 3 advancement points

Transgressions

» A PC kills an NPC combatant 1 blowback

» A PC takes down a verticopter 3 blowback

» A PC takes an action that results in civilian casualties 3 blowback

» A PC takes an action that results in massive damage to a public space 3 blowback

» A PC destroys a weapon shipment or the smart gun 5 blowback

Complications and Discoveries

» **Backup (5 blowback):** Another truck arrives carrying one convoy guard per PC, plus a Corvid SecSpec.

» **Gendarmes Arrive (7 blowback):** Gendarmes arrive equal to twice the number of PCs.

» **A Truck Escapes (8 blowback):** One of the trucks manages to break away from the fight, and the PCs must chase it down or else let it escape.

» **Air Support (10 blowback):** A military verticopter arrives and starts attacking the PCs.

» **Civilian Casualties (compel):** Whenever a PC makes an indiscriminate attack, such as with an explosive or fully automatic weapon, you can compel them, saying that they harm or kill civilians.

GENDARME

GENDARME, Fair (+2)

ANGRY AND IMPULSIVE, Terrible (-2)

MILITARY VERTICOPTER

ASPECTS

HEAVILY ARMORED AIR ATTACK VEHICLE; FAST, MANEUVERABLE, AND FAR AWAY

STUNTS

Because I have **massive firepower**, I can spend a fate point to cause harm to everyone in one physical zone.

Because I'm a **verticopter**, I occupy the IN THE AIR zone. If I'm destroyed, I crash into another physical zone; everyone in that zone must roll against the mission opposition to avoid taking harm.

MEANS

Fight: Good (+3)

Maneuver: Mediocre (+0)

Manipulate: Fair (+2)

Observe: Average (+1)

CONDITIONS

☐ STAGGERED

☐ REELING

Corporate Espionage

Sun Systems Biotech has been working on engineering a hardy form of wheat that can grow in irradiated soil. Our sources indicate that they've got a working sample, but that they're planning on sitting on it so they can sell it. We'd rather get our hands on it so we can give it to those who need it most: the people. We've got backstopped identities for you so that you can get into their facility while it's still open, before security becomes impregnable. Try to keep this one quiet.

Set: A Sun Systems Biotech facility, during the day with people everywhere. Security is almost impenetrable at night, so going into the facility in disguise is the best way to get the seed.

Mission Opposition: Good (+3)

Running "Corporate Espionage"

This mission operates a lot like Warehouse Raid, except that the PCs have to deal with the additional wrinkle of hiding in plain sight. Of particular note is the **Disguised** zone. The assumption is that the PCs are entering the facility in disguise. If they are, they can invoke that zone to their benefit, and tie boosts to it. However, you can also compel that zone whenever a disguise might be a liability, or whenever someone pays extra attention to a PC.

Ask your PCs to tell you about their disguises. How are they disguising themselves? Who do they look like? What are their false identities? How have they ensured these identities have enough history and documentation that they'll stand up to more than a casual inspection?

A fun way to ratchet up the tension in this mission is to run each security checkpoint as a conflict between the PCs and the security systems, with the security systems trying to spot the PCs with facial recognition on their turns.

Resistance Goals

» Get past security without setting off any alarms 1 advancement point per PC

» Get the wheat sample 3 advancement points

» Escape with the wheat sample 3 advancement points

» Don't blow your cover 1 advancement point per PC

» Don't kill anyone 3 advancement points

Zones

» **Disguised**

» **Revealed**

» **Security Checkpoint A**

» **The Hallways**

» **Security Checkpoint B**

» **The Labs**

» **Security Checkpoint C**

» **The Storage Rooms**

Cast

SECURITY SYSTEM

SECURITY SYSTEM, Fair (+2)

DEFECTIVE PROCESSING UNIT, Terrible (-2)

SUN SYSTEMS SECSPEC

SUN SYSTEMS SECSPEC, Good (+3)

BORED, Poor (-1)

CONDITIONS

☐ STAGGERED

Note: Security Systems can try to reveal PCs. This requires a roll to resolve an uncertain outcome against the PC. If the PC fails, she becomes REVEALED and is no longer DISGUISED.

ALFONSE DU PRIX

ASPECTS

HEAD OF SUN SYSTEMS SECURITY; CRISIS OF FAITH

STUNTS

Because I'm **head of security**, I can spend a fate point to call two SecSpec into the scene.

MEANS

Fight: Good (+3)

Maneuver: Mediocre (+0)

Manipulate: Average (+1)

Observe: Fair (+2)

CONDITIONS

☐ STAGGERED

☐ REELING

Setup

The PCs all start out **Disguised** and at **Security Checkpoint A**, in the lobby. Most of the NPCs in the building are civilian scientists and maintenance staff, but there are SecSpec present. Specifically, there are SecSpec equal to twice the number of PCs at each Security Checkpoint as well as in **The Hallways**. There are two SecSpec in **The Labs** and **The Storage Rooms**, and there are three security systems in each physical zone in the mission. Alfonse du Prix is at **Security Checkpoint C**. There are civilian scientists and maintenance staff present in all physical zones except **The Storage Rooms**.

Government Goals

- » Reveal PCs 1 advancement point per PC
- » Prevent the PCs from crossing Security Checkpoint A 3 advancement points
- » Prevent the PCs from crossing Security Checkpoint B 3 advancement points
- » Prevent the PCs from crossing Security Checkpoint C 3 advancement points
- » Sound the alarm 3 advancement points
- » Detain PCs for interrogation 3 advancement points per PC
- » Prevent the PCs from escaping with the wheat sample 3 advancement points

Transgressions

- » A PC kills someone in the facility 1 blowback
- » A PC disables a security system 1 blowback
- » A PC uses intimidation to accomplish a goal 1 blowback
- » Alfonse du Prix dies 3 blowback
- » A PC reveals their own identity 3 blowback
- » Someone sees a PC steal the wheat sample 5 blowback

Complications and Discoveries

» **Backup (5 blowback):** Bring in SecSpec equal to the number of PCs.

» **Sound the Alarm (5 blowback):** Security systems get +2 on all rolls to try to reveal PCs.

» **Mass Evacuation (10 blowback):** During a conflict, add the CIVILIAN EVACUATION situation aspect with 3 tied boosts. This aspect lasts until all of its tied boosts have been spent, at which point the aspect disappears and the facility becomes empty of anyone save for the PCs, the security systems, the SecSpec, and du Prix. All NPCs get +2 to try to reveal PCs once the evacuation is complete; if the alarm is also going off, that bonus stacks with the bonus from this complication.

» **Uncovered Motives (compel):** Sun Systems Biotech isn't actually holding the wheat back for profit. Rather, there have been some questions about its safety, and they're continuing to test and develop it. Their plan, once it's deemed ready, is to make it a low-cost supplement to APE, available to all Citizens.

Esfir, Mercenary

There are those in Paris Nouveau who swear allegiance to the almighty credit, and Esfir is one of them. She's a soldier for hire, but not simply a paid killer. She refuses to act as an assassin, but will gladly act as body-guard or hired muscle for the right price.

No one knows her last name or much about her other than her carefully cultivated reputation for being freakishly accurate with a gun and un-swervingly loyal to whoever is paying her bills. Such mercenary behavior can often cause sticky dilemmas between old and new loyalties, but so far, nothing has stuck to Esfir.

If you have G54, you can use the Mercenary card to represent Esfir.

ESFIR

ASPECTS

MYSTERIOUS MERCENARY; LOYALTY FOR HIRE; UNCANNY AIM (pick two)

MEANS

Fight: Good (+3)

Maneuver: Fair (+2)

Manipulate: Mediocre (+0)

Observe: Average (+1)

CONDITIONS

☐ STAGGERED

☐ REELING (optional)

Corporate Retaliation

One of our contacts, Sparrow, has sensitive information for us about a possible threat on la Cave. Go find out what he knows. If you can act on this information immediately, do so.

Set: The back streets of Paris Nouveau, just before curfew.

Mission Opposition: Good (+3)

Running "Corporate Retaliation"

The briefing for this mission is a lie. Sparrow has betrayed la Résistance and is luring the PCs into a trap. It's not entirely his fault; he's being black-mailed into it, which can easily lead to a future mission if you wish. The people springing the trap can be any corporation or individual that the PCs have had a run-in with who might be looking for payback. Initially, let the PCs know about the goals listed in *"Resistance Goals (Initial)"*. Once the trap is sprung, swap those goals out for the goals listed in *"Resistance Goals (Actual)"*.

Be aware that you'll get blowback for each exchange that passes. The longer the PCs take trying to escape, the harder things get.

This is a great mission to run after the PCs have started making waves. "Warehouse Raid" and "Convoy Ambush" can both make them powerful enemies, and this mission can illustrate how those enemies can come back to haunt them.

Resistance Goals (Initial)

- » Find out what Sparrow knows 3 advancement points
- » Don't get caught 1 advancement point per PC

Resistance Goals (Actual)

- » Escape the ambush 3 advancement points per PC
- » Take Sparrow prisoner for interrogation 3 advancement points
- » Take Hitomi von Krauss prisoner for interrogation 3 advancement points

Zones

- » BEHIND COVER
- » IN HIDING
- » THE ALLEYS
- » THE STREET
- » THE ROOFTOPS
- » THE SEWERS

Cast

MERCENARY SOLDIER

MERCENARY SOLDIER, Fair (+2)

RESTLESS, Terrible (-2)

MERCENARY SNIPER

MERCENARY SNIPER, Good (+3)

PRONE, Poor (-1)

CONDITIONS

☐ STAGGERED

SERGEANT HITOMI VON KRAUSS

ASPECTS

RUTHLESS CORPORATE ASSASSIN; OLD WAR INJURY

STUNTS

Because I'm **slippery**, I get +2 to avoid physical harm with Manipulate, provided I can use deception to do so.

Because I'm a **killer**, I cause an extra condition whenever I successfully cause physical harm with Fight, provided I intend to kill.

MEANS

Fight: Fair (+2)

Maneuver: Good (+3)

Manipulate: Mediocre (+0)

Observe: Average (+1)

CONDITIONS

☐ STAGGERED

☐ REELING

SPARROW, INFORMATION BROKER

ASPECTS

SOFT-SPOKEN INFORMATION BROKER; ABHORS VIOLENCE

STUNTS

Because I **never go in unprepared**, I start each scene with CAREFUL PLANNING with one tied boost.

MEANS

Fight: Mediocre (+0)

Maneuver: Average (+1)

Manipulate: Fair (+2)

Observe: Good (+3)

CONDITIONS

☐ STAGGERED

Setup

Sparrow is waiting for the PCs in **THE ALLEYS**. He waits for them to get close before he signals the ambush; if PCs are particularly paranoid or observant, give them a chance to spot the ambush before he springs it. There are mercenary snipers on the rooftops equal to the number of PCs, and there are three times as many mercenary soldiers as there are PCs, all of them **IN HIDING**, half of them **BEHIND COVER**. Hitomi von Krauss is also **IN HIDING** and **BEHIND COVER**. Sparrow runs after he springs the trap.

Government Goals

» Take the PCs by surprise 3 advancement points

» Take PCs dead or alive 3 advancement points per PC

» Hitomi von Krauss survives and avoids capture 3 advancement points

» Sparrow dies 3 advancement points

Transgressions

» A round ends 2 blowback

» The PCs don't spot the ambush 3 blowback

» A PC causes civilian casualties or significant property damage 3 blowback

» A PC kills Sparrow 3 blowback

Complications and Discoveries

» **Backup (5 blowback):** Bring in mercenary soldiers equal to twice the number of PCs, or bring in mercenary snipers equal to the number of PCs.

» **Cut Off! (5 blowback):** Cut off a PC's escape route. She'll need to find a new one.

» **Sparrow's Motive (compel):** Sparrow is being blackmailed by the ambushers' employers. They're threatening to out him as a Resistance spy, and Clare has refused to help him. Sparrow strongly suspects that Clare expected the PCs to kill him.

Missing Supplies

Someone's stealing our supplies. You've been doing a good job gathering them, but now there's a traitor to deal with. Find out what you can, but do it quietly. We don't want a witch hunt, nor do we want people to lose confidence in Resistance leadership or security. Go talk to Henri Singh, the quartermaster. He can tell you more.

Set: La Cave, the city below Paris Nouveau.

Mission Opposition: Fair (+2)

Running "Missing Supplies"

Run this mission when you want to give the PCs a break from the tension, and let them get to know the other members of la Résistance. This mission is all investigation. It *could* break out into combat, but that's unlikely.

This mission also gives the PCs a chance to prove themselves as worthy additions to la Résistance. Portray each character they interact with distinctly, and give every character a name, even the nameless NPCs. If the PCs seem to really like a particular NPC, write his or her name down. If they particularly *dislike* an NPC, write that NPC's name down too. Try to get a list of six or seven names. You'll certainly want them on-hand in later missions. Heh heh.

It's fine to decide now on the identity of the traitor—or *traitors*, if multiple people seem likely. It's also fine to defer it, and figure it out later, if the PCs are unlikely to uncover the traitor's identity. Once you decide on the traitor's identity, though, just make sure you stay consistent about it.

Resistance Goals

» Question people about the missing supplies 1 advancement point per successful questioning

» Don't arouse suspicion 3 advancement points

» Discover the identity of the traitor 3 advancement points

» Discover important information about the traitor 3 advancement points

Resistance Goals and Multiple Traitors

If you decide there's more than one traitor in this mission, then the Resistance goals that involve discovering the traitor or discovering information about the traitor can each be accomplished once *per traitor*. Yes, that means the PCs can get quite a few advancement points if they ferret out a lot of information.

Zones

- » La Cave
- » Moulin Rouge
- » The Storeroom
  - » The Louvre
- » The Canals
- » The Ruined Tower
- » Père-Lachaise Cemetery
- » Trusted
- » Distrusted

Cast

RÉSISTANCE OPERATIVE

Résistance Operative, Good (+3)

Trust No One, Poor (-1)

CONDITIONS

☐ Staggered

MARYA

ASPECTS

Savvy Arms Dealer; Hunted

STUNTS

Because I **don't back down**, I get +2 to gain the advantage with Manipulate when I'm using subtle threats.

MEANS

Fight: Mediocre (+0)

Maneuver: Good (+3)

Manipulate: Fair (+2)

Observe: Average (+1)

CONDITIONS

☐ Staggered

SIDENGE

ASPECTS

Bristling with Cyberware; Unsubtle

STUNTS

Because I'm **covered in armor**, I do not mark any conditions from the first time I take harm during a scene.

MEANS

Fight: Good (+3)

Maneuver: Mediocre (+0)

Manipulate: Fair (+2)

Observe: Average (+1)

CONDITIONS

☐ **Staggered**

☐ **Reeling**

ARIELLE

ASPECTS

SARDONIC SNIPER; ANGER MANAGEMENT ISSUES

STUNTS

Because I'm **better at a distance**, I get +2 to cause harm with Fight to targets outside my physical zone.

MEANS

Fight: Mediocre (+0)

Maneuver: Fair (+2)

Manipulate: Average (+1)

Observe: Good (+3)

CONDITIONS

☐ STAGGERED

JEAN LE ROUX, MOULIN ROUGE BARTENDER

ASPECTS

MERCENARY BARTENDER; UNSETTLING

STUNTS

Because **everyone talks to a bartender**, I get +2 to gain the advantage with Observe, provided I've had time to talk with the person I'm exploiting.

MEANS

Fight: Fair (+2)

Maneuver: Average (+1)

Manipulate: Mediocre (+0)

Observe: Good (+3)

CONDITIONS

☐ STAGGERED

☐ REELING

HENRI SINGH, RÉSISTANCE QUARTERMASTER

ASPECTS

AMIABLE QUARTERMASTER; DRINKING PROBLEM

STUNTS

Because I **keep careful stock**, I get +3 to gain the advantage with Observe when I'm in my storeroom.

MEANS

Fight: Average (+1)

Maneuver: Mediocre (+0)

Manipulate: Fair (+2)

Observe: Good (+3)

CONDITIONS

☐ STAGGERED

Setup

The PCs effectively have the run of la Cave. There aren't any government or corporate forces present, and we strongly advise you not to bring them in, even if you have government advances that would allow you to do so. This mission works best as an investigation scene. As for the locations of specific NPCs, use your best judgment. Some might be obvious, but feel free to put them wherever it seems appropriate.

Government Goals

- » Keep the identity of the traitor a secret 3 advancement points
- » Keep the fate of the supplies a secret 3 advancement points
- » Ensure that the PCs are exposed as traitor-hunters 3 advancement points
- » Ensure that violence erupts 3 advancement points

Transgressions

- » A PC reveals that they're hunting a traitor 3 blowback
- » A PC uses violence or intimidation 5 blowback
- » A PC does something that runs counter to the interests of la Résistance 5 blowback

Complications and Discoveries

- » **Tight Lips (10 blowback):** The PCs are asking too many pointed questions, and people clam up. The mission opposition increases by +1, and all NPCs get +1 to avoid giving the PCs information.
- » **Dead End (15 blowback):** The investigation dead-ends. The PCs can't get any more information on the traitor right now.
- » **Dirty Secrets (compel):** A PC finds out that Clare has traded some item they've "liberated for the people" to the White Hooks gang in exchange for an alliance.
- » **Side Business (compel):** A PC finds out that an NPC they've grown fond of is selling Resistance goods on the black market. This person *isn't* the traitor who the PCs are looking for, as this NPC's thefts have been small enough to escape notice.

Selise the Hilt, Crime Boss

Other than the Knife Sisters, there are few factions that inspire both fierce loyalty from their followers and intense fear from their targets. Knives are, of course, their weapon of choice. The entire organization is populated by women, led by women. A woman can start as the lowest rank, the Point, and progress through the Tip, the Edge, the Blade, the Heel, the Shank, and finally, the Hilt. To achieve the Hilt, the rank where the blade is in you the deepest, well... you might have to do some unpleasant things.

There has only ever been one other Hilt, and she's not discussed anymore. In fact, most Knife Sisters know better than to ask Selise any extraneous questions. Is this because of the jagged scars across her cheeks, where it looks like she's been pressed up against a cheese grater? Her salt-and-pepper hair is cut ragged and short, possibly by a knife, and she has a clay-red scorpion tattoo on her neck.

The Knife Sisters are known for their unflinching advocacy for women who need their help. Woe betide the one who draws their cuts, though. They are without mercy for those they deem undeserving of life.

Selise is an ally of the Resistance when it suits her work, but not one to be treated carelessly. She has her own agenda and will pursue it to the bitter end.

If you have G54, you can use the Crime Boss card to represent Selise.

SELISE

ASPECTS

Hilt of the Knife Sisters; Bloodthirsty; Women First (pick two)

MEANS

Fight: Good (+3)

Maneuver: Average (+1)

Manipulate: Mediocre (+0)

Observe: Fair (+2)

CONDITIONS

☐ Staggered

☐ Reeling (optional)

☐ Desperate (optional)

Peace Offering

Representatives of three gangs—the White Hooks, Sang Royal, and the Knife Sisters—are meeting you in a high-class APE dispensary after hours. Your job is to negotiate alliances with each of them, get them to agree to help our cause. We've given you cases containing gifts for the representatives of the three gangs, to be opened by them, *not* you. Get us those alliances; we need their manpower.

Set: A high-class APE dispensary after dark. The meeting is in the back room, and tensions are high. Nobody in this room likes anyone else in this room very much. The gangs have agreed to meet, but they are not predisposed to help la Résistance, and they only barely tolerate each other. The PCs have their work cut out for them.

Mission Opposition: Great (+4)

Running "Peace Offering"

In this mission, the PCs must negotiate alliances with three gangs who don't like each other, and who have no reason to help la Résistance. To help convince the gangs, La Résistance has given the PCs cases containing gifts (read: "bribes"), with instructions not to open the cases.

If the PCs decide they want to open the cases, that's fine. They'll have to bypass the security passcodes, rolling against the mission opposition, on each case. And unless the PCs succeed with style, the gang leaders will know the cases have been opened. The *"Complications and Discoveries"* section has suggestions for what could be in the cases: namely, the items that the PCs stole during "Warehouse Raid," "Convoy Ambush," and "Corporate Espionage." For this reason, this mission works best if you run it after the PCs have completed those three.

The White Hooks are a notoriously violent gang known for bloody executions, torture, and brutal, decisive action. Takeda, their negotiator, is twitchy, cheerful, and a little creepy.

The Knife Sisters are composed entirely of women. While not as gratuitously brutal as the White Hooks, they are still extremely violent, and are the White Hooks' biggest competition. Selise, their negotiator, is quiet, unnerving, and disturbingly religious.

Sang Royal style themselves as modern-day Knights of the Round Table. They are always led by a man who calls himself Arthur, and the top members of the gang name themselves after knights from Arthurian legends. They purport to be honorable, but such is not always the case. Gawain, their negotiator, is often the voice of reason in negotiations such as this.

Make it apparent that these people don't like each other, and that they don't much like the PCs either. Make the PCs work for their victory. There's a truce at the moment, but that can change.

Resistance Goals

» Secure an alliance with the White Hooks 3 advancement points

» Secure an alliance with the Knife Sisters 3 advancement points

» Secure an alliance with Sang Royal 3 advancement points

» Ensure the survival of each gang representative 1 advancement point per representative (maximum 3)

Zones

» THE DISPENSARY

» THE APE PROCESSING ROOM

» THE STREET

» THE STOREROOM

» BEHIND COVER

Cast

WHITE HOOKS ENFORCER

WHITE HOOKS ENFORCER, Fair (+2)

UNNECESSARILY CRUEL, Terrible (-2)

KNIFE SISTER

KNIFE SISTER, Fair (+2)

BLOOD FRENZY, Terrible (-2)

SANG ROYAL KNIGHT

SANG ROYAL KNIGHT, Fair (+2)

HONORABLE IN COMBAT, Terrible (-2)

TAKEDA, WHITE HOOKS NEGOTIATOR

ASPECTS

Smiling Killer; Twitchy, Wired Reflexes

STUNTS

Because I'm **unpredictable**, whenever a conflict gets physical, I gain a boost tied to one of my aspects, my choice.

MEANS

Fight: Fair (+2)

Maneuver: Good (+3)

Manipulate: Average (+1)

Observe: Mediocre (+0)

CONDITIONS

☐ Staggered

☐ Reeling

SELISE, THE HILT OF THE KNIFE SISTERS

ASPECTS

Hilt of the Knife Sisters; Bloodthirsty

STUNTS

Because my arms house **retractable blades**, I get +2 to cause harm when I'm using my blades to do so.

MEANS

Fight: Good (+3)

Maneuver: Mediocre (+0)

Manipulate: Average (+1)

Observe: Fair (+2)

CONDITIONS

☐ Staggered

☐ Reeling

GAWAIN, SANG ROYAL NEGOTIATOR

ASPECTS

WARRIOR OF HONOR; POOR TACTICIAN

STUNTS

Because I'm the **voice of reason**, I get +2 to avoid people gaining the advantage over me.

MEANS

Fight: Fair (+2)

Maneuver: Average (+1)

Manipulate: Good (+3)

Observe: Mediocre (+0)

CONDITIONS

☐ STAGGERED

☐ REELING

Setup

Everyone starts off in **THE APE PROCESSING ROOM**, around a table. Takeda, Selise, and Gawain are all present, and each has a guard contingent, with guards equal to the number of players, from their respective gang. The PCs have a **GIFTS** aspect with five tied boosts, representing the cases of equipment and supplies meant as gifts for the gangs.

Government Goals

» Cause the talks to erupt into violence 3 advancement points

» Ensure that Takeda dies 3 advancement points

» Ensure that Selise dies 3 advancement points

» Ensure that Gawain dies 3 advancement points

Transgressions

» A PC kills one of the gang members 1 blowback

» A PC opens one of the cases without succeeding with style, or is otherwise discovered doing so 2 blowback

» A PC offends one of the gang representatives 3 blowback

» A PC kills or incapacitates one of the gang representatives 5 blowback

» A PC initiates violence against one of the gangs 5 blowback

Complications and Discoveries

» **Backup (5 blowback):** One of the gangs calls in gang members equal to the number of PCs.

» **Things Go South (10 blowback):** One of the gang representatives cuts off negotiation and leaves without agreeing to an alliance.

» **Takeda's Gift (compel):** Takeda is being given the prototype smart gun stolen during "Convoy Ambush" (if the PCs got it) or a crate of guns and explosives (if they didn't).

» **Selise's Gift (compel):** Selise is being given medical supplies that can clearly be used to manufacture drugs. If the PCs stole any medical supplies during "Warehouse Raid," they recognize these supplies as the same.

» **Gawain's Gift (compel):** Gawain is being given the wheat sample from "Corporate Espionage" (whether or not the PCs got it; if they didn't, Clare simply used back channels to buy it). This will give Sang Royal a stranglehold on black-market food.

Mercy

Notre-Dame de la Merci—Our Lady of Mercy—is an old church just outside of the city limits, in a section of Old Paris called Drytop. It's also a makeshift hospital for Naturels who need medical attention. You're going to talk to Father Sebastian, Drytop's leader, and convince him—and the medical staff—to join us here in la Cave.

Set: This scene moves from location to location. It starts in Paris Nouveau after curfew, then the PCs have to get through the Wall, which encloses the city. Once through, they have to navigate Old Paris, a ruined wasteland city full of Exiles. Then they have to find their way to Drytop, a settlement in Old Paris that contains Our Lady of Mercy, a church, meeting hall, and hospital.

Mission Opposition: Good (+3)

Running "Mercy"

This mission is an opportunity to show the PCs what the world beyond the walls is like. Spoiler warning: it's not as bad as the government says it is. Paris beyond the walls is a ruin, but radiation isn't a major hazard in most places, and many people live outside the walls, grow their own food, and are otherwise healthy and relatively prosperous.

It's worth noting that, while the PCs' job is to bring Father Sebastian and the Mercy staff to la Cave, these people don't necessarily *want* to leave. They can help a lot of people where they are now, and they can do so with little government interference. Transplanting themselves to la Cave is no small thing, and they'll have to be convinced it's the right thing to do.

Resistance Goals

» Get to the Wall without alerting suspicion 1 advancement point

» Get through the Wall without alerting suspicion 3 advancement points

» Get to Drytop without alerting suspicion 3 advancement points

» Convince Father Sebastian to bring the Mercy staff to la Cave 3 advancement points

» Ensure that Father Sebastian and the staff arrive safely back at la Cave 3 advancement points

Zones

- » **Under the Radar**
- » **Pursued**
- » **The Streets**
- » **The Wall**
- » **Old Paris**
- » **Drytop**
- » **Our Lady of Mercy**

Cast

GENDARME

Gendarme, Fair (+2)

Tired and Restless, Terrible (-2)

DRYTOP NATUREL

Drytop Naturel, Fair (+2)

Scared, Terrible (-2)

GENDARME SERGEANT

Gendarme Sergeant, Good (+3)

Irritable, Poor (-1)

CONDITIONS

☐ **Staggered**

FATHER SEBASTIAN

ASPECTS

Ex-Cit Priest; Trusting

STUNTS

Because I'm a **pillar of the community**, I start every conflict in Drytop with **HELPFUL PARISHIONERS** with a tied boost.

Because I'm a **pacifist**, I get +2 to avoid physical harm with Manipulate when I'm dealing with someone who has qualms with harming an un-armed person.

MEANS

Fight: Average (+1)

Maneuver: Mediocre (+0)

Manipulate: Fair (+2)

Observe: Good (+3)

CONDITIONS

☐ **STAGGERED**

Setup

THE STREETS and THE WALL are crawling with gendarmes and gendarme sergeants. You have an effectively unlimited supply of them, but don't put the PCs up against more than twice their number in gendarmes accompanied by their number in gendarme sergeants at one time, unless you start bringing more in with blowback. Out in OLD PARIS, things are a little different. There are scattered gendarme patrols of about the same size, but they're less frequent and easier to avoid. In DRYTOP proper, gendarmes don't attack unless you use blowback. The PCs start off UNDER THE RADAR and in THE STREETS.

Government Goals

- » Spot any of the PCs 1 advancement point each time
- » Prevent the PCs from crossing the Wall 3 advancement points
- » Father Sebastian turns the PCs down 3 advancement points
- » Father Sebastian dies 3 advancement points
- » Take out a PC 1 advancement point per PC

Transgressions

- » A PC kills someone 1 blowback
- » A PC gets spotted by gendarmes 3 blowback
- » A PC kills Father Sebastian 5 blowback

Complications and Discoveries

- » **Backup (5 blowback):** Bring in gendarmes equal to twice the number of PCs, accompanied by one gendarme sergeant.
- » **The Wall Goes on Lockdown (10 blowback):** When the PCs try to cross the Wall, either on the way to Drytop or on the way back, the mission opposition increases by +2 and all gendarmes and gendarme sergeants get +2 to rolls made to find the PCs.
- » **Father Sebastian Refuses (15 blowback):** Father Sebastian refuses to leave Drytop of his own volition. The medical staff still might come.
- » **My Place Is Here (compel):** Father Sebastian makes it clear that if he and the medical staff leave Drytop, the Naturels still dwelling out in Old Paris will be without medical care.

The Honorable Winston Proctor, Judge

For those who survive the gendarmes' version of justice, they may find themselves under the beak-like gaze of the Honorable Winston Proctor. Judge Proctor's court is not a desirable terminus point, as he's famed for his malevolent temper.

Due process is discarded, and he acts as both the judge and the jury. You can be sure he'll almost always rule in favor of either the government or a beleaguered corporation. He's not all bad, though—he'll occasionally favor the accused with tales of a particularly good catch he fished out of the Seine last weekend.

If you have G54, you can use the Judge card to represent the Honorable Winston Proctor.

THE HONORABLE WINSTON PROCTOR

ASPECTS

The Ruthless Arm of the Law; Malevolent Temper; On the Payroll

(pick two)

MEANS

Fight: Good (+3)

Maneuver: Mediocre (+0)

Manipulate: Fair (+2)

Observe: Average (+1)

CONDITIONS

☐ Staggered

☐ Reeling (optional)

Recruitment Drive

We need support from as many people as we can get, and that means hijacking the signal. InfoSec-West owns the signal in Paris Nouveau; they're the largest— really the only—provider of Infosphere access in the city. If you can pirate their signal, we can start talking directly to the people. Try not to leave evidence behind.

Set: The InfoSec-West building after curfew, patrolled by mercs and watched by an AI named Helios.

Mission Opposition: Great (+4)

Resistance Goals

» Get to the uplink room 1 advancement point

» Install the backdoor 3 advancement points

» Don't kill anyone 3 advancement points

» Don't trip the alarm 3 advancement points

» Don't leave evidence behind 3 advancement points

Zones

» UNDETECTED

» SPOTTED

» THE HALLWAYS

» SERVER ROOM

» OFFICE

» THE ROOF

» THE UPLINK ROOM

Cast

MERC SECURITY GUARD

MERC SECURITY GUARD, Fair (+2)

PAID LOYALTY, Terrible (-2)

MERC SERGEANT

MERC SERGEANT, Good (+3)

TEMPER, Poor (-1)

CONDITIONS

☐ STAGGERED

HELIOS

ASPECTS

SECURITY AI; NARROW FOCUS

STUNTS

Because I have **eyes everywhere**, I get +2 to gain the advantage with Observe within the InfoSec-West building.

MEANS

Fight: Fair (+2)

Maneuver: Mediocre (+0)

Manipulate: Average (+1)

Observe: Good (+3)

CONDITIONS

☐ STAGGERED

Setup

There's a moderate human presence in the building after hours, since each physical zone has a merc sergeant as well as merc security guards equal to twice the number of players. The real threat, though, is Helios, the building's security AI. Helios is present in every physical zone except **THE ROOF**. The PCs start off **UNDETECTED**, so the mercs won't search for them without cause. Helios, however, will search constantly, looking for any individual who doesn't have clearance to be here after hours.

Government Goals

» Spot a PC 1 advancement point per PC

» Detain a PC for questioning 3 advancement points per PC

» Prevent the PCs from installing the backdoor 3 advancement points

Transgressions

» A PC gets caught by Helios or a merc 1 blowback

» A PC kills someone 2 blowback

» A PC causes damage to the building or the equipment inside 3 blowback

» A PC disables Helios 5 blowback

Complications and Discoveries

» **Backup (5 blowback):** Bring in merc security guards equal to the number of PCs.

» **Sound the Alarm (10 blowback):** Helios and all mercs get +2 to rolls made to find PCs.

» **Seal the Exits (10 blowback):** The only way out is through THE ROOF.

» **Helios pings the guards (compel):** Helios tells the guards to go search a particular physical zone containing PCs.

» **A Full Dossier (compel):** A PC discovers that InfoSec-West has a full dossier on him or her, including his or her involvement with la Résistance and details of involvement on some past missions.

Daphne Macdonald, Propaganda Director

Daphne certainly looks charming and fresh-faced with her smattering of freckles and her high auburn ponytail. But don't make the mistake of underestimating her power—hers is the brain that cranks the government propaganda machine 24-7; "and an extra day on leap years!" she always chirps.

Her poison pen has driven most of the legitimate news operations from Paris Nouveau, which is just how she likes it. The less competition she has, the easier it is to keep on message—the government's message.

If you have G54, you can use the Director card to represent Daphne Macdonald.

DAPHNE MACDONALD

ASPECTS

VOICE OF THE GOVERNMENT; SECRETS, LIES, AND INNUENDOS; "WHAT I SAY IS TRUTH." (pick two)

MEANS

Fight: Mediocre (+0)

Maneuver: Fair (+2)

Manipulate: Good (+3)

Observe: Average (+1)

CONDITIONS

☐ STAGGERED

☐ REELING (optional)

White Hats, Black Market

There's a hacker named Delacroix who runs a black-market enterprise for getting items to concerned citizens. Make contact with her. We'd like to set up a business relationship. Here's the catch: the only way to talk to Delacroix is in VR, in the Infosphere. Good luck.

Set: Virtual reality in all its endless, unreal variety.

Mission Opposition: Good (+3)

Running "White Hats, Black Market"

This mission takes place entirely in VR, where the PCs have to track down Delacroix and broker a deal with her. Delacroix spends time in a VR domain called Tír na nÓg, a gathering place for hackers from all over the world.

Delacroix isn't overtly hostile to the PCs, but she *is* mischievous, and she does like to make people prove themselves before she'll help them. She'll be pretty angry if the PCs show up with a bunch of watchdogs on their trail, though.

The government is always watching in VR, which forces the PCs to act quickly. In this mission, you'll get blowback frequently for seemingly innocuous things.

In this mission, getting "flagged by the system" means that a PC took a condition other than **ANGRY** or **WOUNDED**.

Resistance Goals

» Find Tír na nÓg 1 advancement point

» Make contact with Delacroix 3 advancement points

» Make a deal with Delacroix 3 advancement points

» Don't get flagged by the system 1 advancement point per PC

Zones

» **ANONYMOUS**

» **REVEALED**

» **MONITORED**

» **LOCKED OUT**

Cast

WATCHDOG PROGRAM

WATCHDOG PROGRAM, Fair (+2)

SINGLE-MINDED, Terrible (-2)

DELACROIX

ASPECTS

HOTSHOT HACKER; IDEALIST

STUNTS

Because I have **layers of anonymity**, I get +2 to avoid others gaining the advantage over me in VR.

Because I have **many little birds**, I get +2 to gain the advantage over others in VR.

MEANS

Fight: Mediocre (+0)

Maneuver: Good (+3)

Manipulate: Average (+1)

Observe: Fair (+2)

CONDITIONS

☐ STAGGERED

☐ REELING

Setup

All PCs start off **ANONYMOUS** and in a VR room set up by la Résistance. From there, they can travel to any number of VR zones in the Infosphere. Watchdog programs are common, and you have an effectively unlimited supply of them. However, don't send in more watchdog programs than triple the number of PCs at once, unless you spend blowback. Delacroix, too, can interact with (and test) the PCs, regardless of where they are in relation to her in the Infosphere.

Government Goals

» Take out a PC 3 advancement points per PC

» Take out Delacroix 3 advancement points

We Shall Die with Our Arms Unbound

Real Harm in Cyberspace

Because the ability to enter the Infosphere through VR requires a direct neurosensory interface, harm you experience in the Infosphere *does* translate to harm in the real world, and you *can* die if you're killed in VR. The harm may look a little different in the real world—something that looks like a gunshot in cyberspace may cause lasting mental trauma in real life—but either way, marking **WOUNDED** is appropriate.

Transgressions

» A PC does anything big, flashy, or obvious 1 blowback

» A PC moves from one zone to another 2 blowback

» A PC wastes time doing something unnecessary 2 blowback

» A PC forces another user out of VR 3 blowback

Complications and Discoveries

» **Security Patrol (5 blowback):** Bring in watchdog programs equal to the number of PCs.

» **Security Spike (5 blowback):** Choose a PC, who must roll to avoid harm against the mission opposition. If they fail, they take two conditions.

» **Identiscan (compel):** A PC gets scanned by a security checkpoint, and is no longer **ANONYMOUS**.

Black Bag

You've been caught. What now?

Set: Bound and guarded in an interrogation room.

Mission Opposition: Great (+4)

Running "Black Bag"

Run this mission after all the PCs have been captured, and don't give them a prep scene beforehand. The PCs get captured and taken to a secret internment facility for questioning. They're each confronted by a woman who identifies herself as "Etta Clatch"; each is a different woman, but they all look the same. The PCs don't know this at first, because they're kept in separate rooms.

Clatch doesn't use violence. She might threaten violence eventually, but only against other people. Keep the PCs guessing. Tell them that their lives *are* on the line, though.

Conduct the interrogation round-robin style, jumping from PC to PC. This is interrogation, though, not torture. Make them uncomfortable in an enjoyable way, the way a horror movie makes you uncomfortable, but remind them that they can say "brake" if things get too real.

The primary purpose of this mission is to sow discord in the group. If a PC survives, what does that mean? Did she give up information? And if a PC doesn't give anything up and lives anyway, what does *that* mean? Why did he get special treatment?

Resistance Goals

» Don't tell the government anything 3 advancement points per PC

» Learn something useful 3 advancement points per PC

Zones

» THE INTERROGATION ROOM (one for each PC)

» APPARENTLY COOPERATING

» HOSTILE WITNESS

» ON THE RUN

» THE HALLWAYS

We Shall Die with Our Arms Unbound

Cast

SOLDIER

SOLDIER, Fair (+2)

BEHAVIORAL CONDITIONING, Terrible (-2)

ELITE SOLDIER

ELITE SOLDIER, Good (+3)

BEHAVIORAL CONDITIONING, Poor (-1)

CONDITIONS

☐ STAGGERED

ETTA CLATCH, INTERROGATOR

ASPECTS

UNNERVING CALM; BLINKS A LOT WHEN SHE LIES

STUNTS

Because I have an **eye for weakness**, I gain another boost when I gain the advantage by exploiting someone's weakness.

MEANS

Fight: Average (+1)

Maneuver: Good (+3)

Manipulate: Mediocre (+0)

Observe: Fair (+2)

CONDITIONS

☐ STAGGERED

☐ REELING

Setup

Each PC is bound effectively, so trying to escape their bonds will prompt a roll against the mission opposition. However, escaping their bonds is only part of what they have to do. The PCs have no equipment; it's all been taken from them. There's an Etta Clatch in each Interrogation Room, as well as four soldiers and an elite soldier outside each Interrogation Room; they all enter on the second round of a conflict if a PC escapes their bonds.

Once the PCs have escaped, they'll have to find their way out of the maze-like complex, and THE HALLWAYS have an effectively unlimited number of soldiers and elite soldiers. Even so, don't attack a PC or PCs with any number of soldiers greater than triple the number of attacked PCs, plus elite soldiers equal in number, without spending blowback. If PCs decide not to escape, this is an interrogation, but it still works best if you run it as a conflict. Etta Clatch is gaining the advantage and causing harm, though she's doing it socially rather than physically.

Government Goals

- » Get a PC to give up a secret about la Résistance 3 advancement points per PC

- » Make a deal with a PC 3 advancement points per PC

Transgressions

- » A PC stonewalls Etta Clatch 1 blowback

- » A PC kills someone 1 blowback

- » A PC breaks their bonds 3 blowback

- » A PC escapes through force 5 blowback

Complications and Discoveries

- » **Backup (5 blowback):** Bring in soldiers equal to twice the number of PCs, as well as an elite soldier.

- » **Sound the Alarm (5 blowback):** Any PC trying to escape must roll against the mission opposition each turn in order to find the way out. If a PC fails, they spend the rest of the turn hiding from patrols.

- » **Leverage (5 blowback):** Etta Clatch gets +2 on her next roll to interrogate a PC.

- » **Uncomfortable Information (compel):** Etta reveals knowledge of something deeply personal to a PC; ask that player what it is.

Brandeis Bellweather, Government Revenue Officer

Brandeis doesn't like the term "stealing." Instead, he "appropriates" from the government's coffers to add to those of the more deserving citizenry. The fact that he hasn't been caught yet is a testament to his canny ability to sense which way the wind is blowing. Truly, any government system is profligate with waste, and he finds ways to enrich total strangers by making small deposits into many accounts.

Because his office handles thousands of such accounts on a daily basis, this steady channeling of credits elsewhere goes unnoticed, as it is a mere trickle. He's taking great chances, though, and the Resistance is slowly cultivating him as a potential member. To them, though, his idealism could be a liability.

If you have G54, you can use the Communist card to represent Brandeis Bellweather.

BRANDEIS BELLWEATHER

ASPECTS

> IDEALISTIC ROBIN HOOD'ER; FINGERS IN ALL THE PIES; DANGEROUS PAPER TRAIL (pick two)

MEANS

Fight: Mediocre (+0)

Maneuver: Average (+1)

Manipulate: Good (+3)

Observe: Fair (+2)

CONDITIONS

☐ STAGGERED

☐ REELING (optional)

☐ DESPERATE (optional)

Raid

You thought you had some downtime, but you were wrong. Now there's gendarmes everywhere.

Set: One of la Résistance's safehouses, or a PC's own safehouse.

Mission Opposition: Good (+3)

> ### Running "Raid"
> This mission is meant to happen during a moment of downtime, between missions. Let the PCs run through a prep scene as if you're going to run a different mission, then spring this on them in the middle of preparation. The PCs are somewhere they believe is safe.

Resistance Goals

» Escape 1 advancement point per PC

» Save incriminating evidence 3 advancement points per piece of evidence (maximum 9)

» Save innocents 1 advancement point per innocent (maximum 4)

Zones

» **DOWNSTAIRS**

» **UPSTAIRS**

» **OUT BACK**

» **THE ROOF**

» **THE BASEMENT**

» **THE STREETS**

Cast

GENDARME

GENDARME, Fair (+2)

TWITCHY, Terrible (-2)

GENDARME SERGEANT

GENDARME SERGEANT, Good (+3)

ITCHING FOR VIOLENCE, Poor (-1)

CONDITIONS

☐ STAGGERED

THE FIRE

ASPECTS

DANGEROUS AND UNPREDICTABLE; UNTHINKING HEAT

MEANS

Burn: Good (+3)

STUNTS

Because I'm **just a fire**, I can use Burn to cause harm, but not to do anything else.

Because **water douses me**, I can take harm from it.

Because I **spread quickly**, I spread to another zone each exchange on my turn, and I can cause harm to everyone in every zone I occupy.

CONDITIONS

☐ STAGGERED

Running the Fire

When the fire first shows up, pick its zone. It can cause harm to everyone in its zone with Burn, its only means. Every exchange on its turn, it spreads to another zone. It occupies every zone that it spreads to, and can cause harm to everyone in all of those zones.

Characters can cause harm to the fire, but only with water and other fire-preventive measures, and typically only while in the same zone. When the fire takes harm, it can choose to mark a condition, be taken out, or remove itself from the zone in which it took harm.

Setup

The PCs are in the safehouse with a few innocent Resistance sympathizers and some incriminating evidence. Gendarmes attack from all sides; the initial attack has gendarmes equal to four times the number of PCs, as well as one gendarme sergeant per PC.

Government Goals

» Kill or capture PCs 3 advancement points per PC

» Kill or capture innocent sympathizers 1 advancement points per innocent (maximum 4)

» Take incriminating evidence 3 advancement points per piece (maximum 9)

Transgressions

» A PC kills someone 1 blowback

» A round ends 1 blowback

Complications and Discoveries

» **Backup (5 blowback):** Bring in gendarmes equal to the number of PCs, plus one gendarme sergeant.

» **Fire! (10 blowback):** The fire enters the scene. If the fire's already in the scene, it reaches something explosive—pick a zone that the fire occupies, and cause harm to everyone there with a +4 bonus.

» **Inside Man (compel):** A PC finds out that the gendarmes were tipped off to this location. GM, you can decide who the informant is.

Demonstration

This is what we've been building up to: the first step of the revolution! We've organized a demonstration in front of the Ministry of Agriculture. We're going to make them hear us. We're going to demand they complete the terraformation and allow Citizens outside the Wall. If they don't hear us… we'll *make* them hear us. We need you there with us.

Set: In front of the Ministry of Agriculture, during a peaceful protest that goes horribly wrong.

Mission Opposition: Good (+3)

Running "Demonstration"

The plan is to run a peaceful demonstration. No plan survives contact with the enemy, though. Almost as soon as the demonstration begins, soldiers show up and start detaining people. The PCs have to hold the soldiers off long enough for the crowd to escape.

Hitomi von Krauss, the leader of the hit squad that may have ambushed the PCs in another mission, shows up in this one. If the PCs managed to kill her in "Corporate Retaliation," she now has obvious cybernetic augmentations that probably have something to do with her survival. She definitely recognizes the PCs.

Resistance Goals

» Hold off the soldiers so the protesters can escape   2 advancement points per round where the PCs hold the soldiers off (maximum 10)

Zones

» **Amongst the Crowd**

» **The Steps**

» **The Streets**

» **The Rooftops**

Cast

GOVERNMENT SOLDIERS

GOVERNMENT SOLDIER, Fair (+2)

BEHAVIORAL INHIBITORS, Terrible (-2)

VON KRAUSS'S MERC

VON KRAUSS'S MERC, Good (+3)

UNWILLING TO DIE, Poor (-1)

CONDITIONS

☐ **STAGGERED**

CAPTAIN HITOMI VON KRAUSS

ASPECTS

RUTHLESS CORPORATE ASSASSIN; OLD WAR INJURY

STUNTS

Because I'm **slippery**, I get +2 to avoid physical harm with Manipulate, provided I can use deception to do so.

Because I'm a **killer**, I cause an extra condition whenever I successfully cause physical harm with Fight, provided I intend to kill.

MEANS

Fight: Fair (+2)

Maneuver: Good (+3)

Manipulate: Mediocre (+0)

Observe: Average (+1)

CONDITIONS

☐ **STAGGERED**

☐ **REELING**

Setup

The PCs are on **THE STEPS**, in front of the Ministry of Agriculture, with the protesters. The soldiers attack from **THE STREETS**, while von Krauss and her mercs attack from **THE ROOFTOPS**, rappelling down. In the first round, there are twice as many soldiers as PCs and as many mercs as PCs. Each round, bring in more soldiers and mercs in the same numbers, until the PCs decide to retreat or are defeated. Bring von Krauss in during the third round.

Government Goals

» Kill or capture PCs 3 advancement points per PC

» Break up the protest during the first round 6 advancement points

» Break up the protest during the second round 4 advancement points

» Break up the protest during the third round 2 advancement points

» Break up the protest during the fourth round 1 advancement point

Transgressions

» A PC kills someone 1 blowback

» The first round ends 1 blowback

» A PC kills Hitomi von Krauss 3 blowback

» The second or third round ends 3 blowback

» The fourth or fifth round ends 5 blowback

Complications and Discoveries

» **Panic! (5 blowback):** The crowd panics, forcing everyone **AMONGST THE CROWD** to roll against the mission opposition to avoid taking harm.

» **Troop Surge (10 blowback):** Bring in mercs and soldiers in the same numbers as when a round ends.

» **Hostage (compel):** Someone important to a PC is taken hostage by one of the mercs or soldiers.

General Theodore Akiyama, Resistance General

Akiyama is Clare's highest ranked general in the Resistance. He has been unswervingly faithful since the early days. Rumors say that they were romantically entangled at some point, but that may be fanciful myth-making. It's hard to imagine General Akiyama as a suitor now—his eyes make even the bravest recruits quake.

He is the one entrusted with the Resistance's grueling training program, nicknamed l'Enfer by his long-suffering soldiers. Occasionally recruits have been known to die at his hands, but it's likely they wouldn't have lasted long in the Resistance anyway.

If you have G54, you can use the General card to represent General Theodore Akiyama.

GENERAL THEODORE AKIYAMA

ASPECTS

Harsh Resistance General; Living Legend; The Stare

MEANS

Fight: Good (+3)

Maneuver: Average (+1)

Manipulate: Mediocre (+0)

Observe: Fair (+2)

CONDITIONS

☐ Staggered

☐ Reeling (optional)

☐ Desperate (optional)

We Sl

The Friend

You may think of this person as a friend. You may even love them. But they're a traitor, an agent of the government, and we cannot abide that. We are not, however, unreasonable. Bring them in. Make them turn. A double agent is more valuable than a corpse.

Set: The target's house, after dark. Curfew is in effect.

Mission Opposition: Average (+1)

Running "The Friend"

This mission is a good opportunity to present the PCs with a difficult moral dilemma. Choose a friend of one or more PCs; the more PCs, the better. Is this person really a traitor? Can they be reasoned with? Will they come in willingly? If they do, will la Résistance let them survive?

Alternately, the PCs may just wish to storm the house and take the target down. They may want some good old-fashioned revenge. That works too. If this happens, play up the fact that innocents are present. Use potential collateral damage to create tough decisions.

This can be a good mission to run as a follow-up to "Missing Supplies," particularly if a friend of the PCs was implicated in that mission.

Resistance Goals

» Get the target to come to la Cave 3 advancement points

» Don't threaten the target 3 advancement points

» Don't hurt the target 3 advancement points

» Don't use violence at all 3 advancement points

» If the target won't come in, kill them 5 advancement points

Zones

» **TRUSTED**

» **UPSTAIRS**

» **DOWNSTAIRS**

» **OUTSIDE**

Cast

Special: The target is a character that the PCs consider a friend.

FAMILY MEMBER

> **FAMILY MEMBER**, Fair (+2)

> **SCARED**, Terrible (-2)

GENDARME

> **GENDARME**, Fair (+2)

> **INDISCRIMINATE**, Terrible (-2)

Setup

The target is inside the house, wherever you'd like her to be, with her family. The PCs start off **OUTSIDE**; also **OUTSIDE**, patrolling around the house, are gendarmes equal to triple the number of PCs.

Government Goals

- » Prevent the PCs from entering the house 3 advancement points
- » Kill or capture PCs 3 advancement points per PC
- » Allow the target to escape the house 3 advancement points

Transgressions

- » A PC threatens violence 1 blowback
- » A PC kills someone 2 blowback
- » A PC kills the target or one of the target's family members 5 blowback

Complications and Discoveries

- » **Backup (5 blowback):** Bring in gendarmes equal to the number of PCs.

- » **Silent Alarm (10 blowback):** Nothing happens immediately. However, a few minutes later, bring in gendarmes equal to triple the number of players, and any gendarmes still outside enter the house.

- » **The Target Escapes (15 blowback):** The target flees, escaping out into Paris Nouveau.

» **The Target's Motive (compel):** The target tells the PCs why she betrayed la Résistance. Some time ago, a good friend of hers was killed, seemingly by government agents. However, the target learned recently from hacked Resistance files that the hit was ordered by Clare, as a way to encourage the target to join.

Roland Roundtree, Farmer

Roland and his family are Naturels. They have never had neural casings implanted. Periodically, sales reps from Cryptiq, Inc. show up at the worn wooden door of Roundtree Farms. They are fed, talked round in circles, and sent packing.

Roland's profession is practically extinct, given the soil around Paris Nouveau being irradiated—or is it? He and his family are hard at work trying to restore their farmland, which makes them a distinct danger to the government's propaganda ministries. He also will occasionally shelter Resistance recruits recovering from the surgery to remove their neural casings.

If you have G54, you can use the Farmer card to represent Roland Roundtree.

ROLAND ROUNDTREE

ASPECTS

STUBBORN FARMSTEADER; RESISTANCE SYMPATHIZER; "WE'LL MAKE THESE CROPS GROW." (pick two)

MEANS

Fight: Average (+1)

Maneuver: Fair (+2)

Manipulate: Mediocre (+0)

Observe: Good (+3)

CONDITIONS

☐ **STAGGERED**

☐ **REELING** (optional)

☐ **DESPERATE** (optional)

Rendition

A high-value target will be presenting an opportunity for us very soon. You'll take that opportunity, and take the target alive. Let me be clear: we need him alive. Someone is holding the purse strings, dangling incentives in front of our operatives and getting them to defect. This target, a former acquaintance of yours, can lead us to the Paymaster.

Set: The streets of Paris Nouveau, midday in a crowded plaza.

Mission Opposition: Good (+3)

Running "Rendition"

This scene has an unexpected wrinkle: there's a second hit squad, this one with deadly intent. The PCs have to fight von Krauss's men *and* the bodyguards, while keeping the target alive for questioning.

The target here is deliberately vague; use someone the PCs have interacted with before, someone who used to work for la Résistance but has recently been revealed as a traitor. This could be a PC or an NPC; the more they hate this person, the better.

Once again, Hitomi von Krauss shows up. It doesn't matter how many times the PCs have killed her; she's back. If PCs start to really get curious about this, you can allow them to follow the thread later. Maybe she's being resurrected by cybertechnology, or maybe she's a clone. Have fun with it!

Resistance Goals

» Take the target alive 3 advancement points

» Get the target back to la Cave alive 5 advancement points

» Lose or kill anyone pursuing you 3 advancement points

Zones

» **The Rooftops**

» **The Streets**

» **The Plaza**

» **Amongst the Crowd**

» **Behind Cover**

Cast

Special: The target is a character who the PCs actively dislike, but who is technically an ally.

BODYGUARD

BODYGUARD, Fair (+2)

FLAT-FOOTED, Terrible (-2)

MERCENARY

MERCENARY, Good (+3)

OVERCONFIDENT, Poor (-1)

CONDITIONS

☐ **STAGGERED**

CAPTAIN HITOMI VON KRAUSS

ASPECTS

RUTHLESS CORPORATE ASSASSIN; OLD WAR INJURY

STUNTS

Because I'm **slippery,** I get +2 to avoid physical harm with Manipulate, provided I can use deception to do so.

Because I'm a **killer,** I cause an extra condition whenever I successfully cause physical harm with Fight, provided I intend to kill.

MEANS

Fight: Fair (+2)

Maneuver: Good (+3)

Manipulate: Mediocre (+0)

Observe: Average (+1)

CONDITIONS

☐ **STAGGERED**

☐ **REELING**

☐ **DESPERATE**

Setup

The target is walking **AMONGST THE CROWD** in **THE PLAZA**, surrounded by bodyguards, one per PC. Hitomi von Krauss and her team, composed of mercenaries equal to twice the number of PCs, are waiting in ambush; some of them are **BEHIND COVER** in **THE PLAZA**, some are **AMONGST THE CROWD** in **THE PLAZA**, and some are on **THE ROOFTOPS**. Give the PCs a few minutes to prepare an ambush, allowing them to decide where they're waiting for the target. After the first round, Hitomi and her men attack. Their goal is to kill the target, but they'll also try to kill the PCs. They're not here to take prisoners.

Government Goals

» Kill the target 5 advancement points

» Kill the PCs 3 advancement points per PC

Transgressions

» A PC kills someone other than the target 1 blowback

» A PC initiates overt violence while **AMONGST THE CROWD** 3 blowback

» A PC kills Hitomi von Krauss 5 blowback

Complications and Discoveries

» **Backup (5 blowback):** Bring in mercenaries equal to the number of PCs.

» **Panic! (5 blowback):** The crowd panics! Anyone **AMONGST THE CROWD** must roll against the mission opposition to avoid taking harm.

» **The Target Escapes (10 blowback):** The target gets away, and the PCs can't find him.

» **The Target's Motive (compel):** The target didn't really betray la Résistance; he's acting as a double agent, and has been found out. That's why von Krauss's men attacked.

Anna Mae Sun, CEO

The youngest CEO in Paris Nouveau, Anna Mae Sun leads Sun Systems Biotech with a deft touch. It was her vision that brought AR to the Citizens en masse. Her father, Alfred Sun, managed to drag Sun Systems into several shady deals and toxic amounts of debt, but Anna Mae has kept the company's balance sheets in the black and on an upward trend, ever since she took over after Alfred's alcohol-induced breakdown.

Her biggest coup was the flawlessly programmed SunLife online store. She created a seamless portal for Citizens to purchase veils and skins for their online personas and domains. Within SunLife, it takes one swipe of a finger to charge a purchase to your account, and most Citizens are millions of credits in debt.

If you have G54, you can use the Capitalist card to represent Anna Mae Sun.

ANNA MAE SUN

ASPECTS

BILLIONAIRE TECH GENIUS; SUN SYSTEMS CEO; ESCAPING HER FATHER'S SHADOW (pick two)

MEANS

Fight: Mediocre (+0)

Maneuver: Fair (+2)

Manipulate: Average (+1)

Observe: Good (+3)

CONDITIONS

☐ STAGGERED

☐ REELING (optional)

☐ DESPERATE (optional)

The Paymaster

We know now who's been turning people away from us, and it's time for him to die. His name is Emir von Krauss; he's the Vice President of Corvid Economics and attaché to the Ministry of Agriculture. He's also Hitomi von Krauss's father. He's attending a gala at l'Apogée tonight, and we've managed to procure invitations to the event, as well as backstopped identities. For those of you with obvious modifications, we've paid off people on the wait staff to allow you in through the back door. Go kill Emir.

Set: A gala up on l'Apogée, which the PCs have tickets to.

Mission Opposition: Good (+3)

Running "The Paymaster"

The PCs must play things carefully here. Maintaining their cover is a delicate thing, and they'll need to find a way to get von Krauss isolated and to take him out.

They also have the opportunity to talk to him before they kill him, either through force or finesse. If they do, they might find out that his primary goal is peace, stability, and enough resources for everyone to live comfortably. He'll admit that that's a long ways away, but also that the instability and unrest that la Résistance is fomenting is making it increasingly difficult for him to effect change from within. Then he'll make an offer: work for him, help him change the system from within, and he'll ensure they're well supplied and well rewarded.

It's up to you how truthful Emir is being.

Resistance Goals

» Isolate the Paymaster 1 advancement point

» Kill the Paymaster 3 advancement points

» Don't let anyone see you kill him 3 advancement points

» Don't kill anyone else 3 advancement points

» Don't arouse suspicion 3 advancement points

Zones

» **MINGLING**

» **STANDING OUT**

» **GAUCHE**

» **ISOLATED**

» **NEAR THE PAYMASTER**

Cast

GOVERNMENT SOLDIER

GOVERNMENT SOLDIER, Good (+3)

BORED, Poor (-1)

CONDITIONS

☐ **STAGGERED**

EMIR VON KRAUSS, THE PAYMASTER

ASPECTS

CORPORATE BUREAUCRAT; MONEY MAKES THE WORLD GO ROUND

STUNTS

Because I have **allies everywhere**, I can spend a fate point to force a PC to roll against the mission opposition to avoid taking harm from the crowd.

Because the **soldiers are on my payroll**, I can spend a fate point to bring in two government soldiers.

MEANS

Fight: Average (+1)

Maneuver: Good (+3)

Manipulate: Fair (+2)

Observe: Fair (+2)

CONDITIONS

☐ **STAGGERED**

☐ **REELING**

Setup

Emir is **Mingling**. There are guards present, twice as many as there are PCs, mostly on the periphery of the event. They're also **Mingling**, effectively, but not **Near the Paymaster**. They're not looking for infiltrators, and they won't unless PCs arouse suspicion in some way.

Government Goals

» Discover the PCs 1 advancement point per PC

» Allow the Paymaster to escape 5 advancement points

» Kill or capture PCs 3 advancement points per PC

» Start a bloodbath to blame on la Résistance 3 advancement points

Transgressions

» A PC insults or threatens someone 1 blowback

» A PC uses violence on a guest 1 blowback

» A PC kills someone other than the Paymaster 3 blowback

» A PC kills the Paymaster 5 blowback

Complications and Discoveries

» **Backup (5 blowback):** Bring in soldiers equal to twice the number of PCs.

» **Evidence Is Discovered (5 blowback):** Provided the PCs have left evidence, a soldier discovers it. Soldiers start looking for the PCs.

» **Emir Escapes (15 blowback):** Emir is now well protected, and the PCs can no longer get to him.

» **Fundraising Event (compel):** The PCs discover that the gala is a fundraising event, that the people there are trying to raise funds to provide better-quality food to Citizens, and that Emir is the host.

» **Emir Offers a Deal (compel):** Emir offers one or more PCs the deal described in the *"Running 'The Paymaster'"* sidebar.

The Revolution (Endgame Mission)

This is it. The moment we've been working toward. We have enough popular support to start a real war, a war for the fate of Paris Nouveau. You've earned the right to kindle that war. The first step is to take to the streets and get people to fight. But, once you do that, your *real* goal is to get to the top of l'Apogée and stop the signal. That's right: stop it. Permanently. No more AR, no more VR, no more Infosphere. Just people, living in the real world, starting over. Without the signal, the government and corporations lose their hold on the people. The soldiers and gendarmes lose their edge. Without the signal, *we win*.

Set: The streets of Paris Nouveau, then L'Aeriee, then l'Apogée.

Mission Opposition: Great (+4)

> ### Running "The Revolution"
> Make the PCs work for this one. To make sure of this, here's a gift: you get +10 blowback at the start of this mission. Use it well.

Now, look at the notes you've no doubt been taking throughout the campaign. Remember all the people who have betrayed la Résistance, or who you've decided were secret traitors all along. Think of all the enemies the PCs have gone up against but not defeated. Whoever they are, use them in this mission. All of them. You can insert them into any scenes you like, without spending blowback. In addition, you can kill PCs who don't have **Marked for Death** marked. As long as you take out a PC and spend 5 blowback, you can narrate that PC's death. The stakes are high. Have fun.

Resistance Goals

- » Rally the people. Arm them. Start a war.
- » Get to the base of the Tower.
- » Ascend to l'Apogée.
- » Find the signal transmitter.
- » Destroy the transmitter, once and for all.

Zones

- » THE STREETS
- » LE BAS
- » THE ELEVATOR
- » L'APOGÉE
- » THE TRANSMITTER STATION
- » HIDDEN
- » BEHIND COVER

Cast

GENDARME

GENDARME+2

BLOODLUST, Terrible (-2)

GOVERNMENT SOLDIER

GOVERNMENT SOLDIER, Good (+3)

ON EDGE, Poor (-1)

CONDITIONS

☐ STAGGERED

We Shall Die with Our Arms Unbound

GOVERNMENT MECH

ASPECTS

WALKING TANK; SUBMIT OR BE DESTROYED

STUNTS

Because I have **heavy ordnance**, I can spend a fate point to cause harm to everyone in my zone, rolling once.

Because I'm **heavily armored**, I get +2 to avoid physical harm with Fight.

MEANS

Fight: Good (+3)

Maneuver: Average (+1)

Manipulate: Fair (+2)

Observe: Fair (+2)

CONDITIONS

☐ STAGGERED

☐ REELING

MILITARY VERTICOPTER

ASPECTS

HEAVILY ARMORED AIR ATTACK VEHICLE; FAST, MANEUVERABLE, AND FAR AWAY

STUNTS

Because I have **massive firepower**, I can spend a fate point to cause harm to everyone in one physical zone.

Because I'm a **verticopter**, I occupy the IN THE AIR zone. If I'm destroyed, I crash into another physical zone; everyone in that zone must roll against the mission opposition to avoid taking harm.

MEANS

Fight: Good (+3)

Maneuver: Mediocre (+0)

Manipulate: Fair (+2)

Observe: Average (+1)

CONDITIONS

☐ STAGGERED

☐ REELING

Setup

The PCs start off on THE STREETS. While they are in THE STREETS or at LE BAS, you have an effectively unlimited number of gendarmes and soldiers to throw at the PCs. THE STREETS are crowded with Citizens fighting the gendarmes and soldiers, who might attack the PCs at any moment. Don't bother keeping track of how many are in the scene at a time. There are a lot. That said, don't attack a single PC with more than four or five enemies within one exchange; you don't want to push things too hard too fast.

Once the PCs get to THE ELEVATOR, you have a military verticopter to throw at them—no need to spend blowback to bring it in. At L'APOGÉE, there are soldiers everywhere, and the place is locked down tight. Again, you have an effectively unlimited number of soldiers, but don't attack the PCs with a group that's more than double their size without spending blowback to bring in more. THE TRANSMITTER STATION is guarded by twice as many soldiers as PCs, as well as two government mechs.

Once they're inside THE TRANSMITTER STATION, make the PCs work just a little bit more for the win. Whether they're setting up a hack, smashing things manually, or setting charges to go off, give them a few more exchanges of holding off soldiers, twice as many as PCs, before they accomplish their final goal and win.

Transgressions

- » A conflict round ends 2 blowback
- » A non-conflict scene ends 5 blowback

Complications and Discoveries

- » **Backup (5 blowback):** Bring in soldiers equal to twice the number of PCs.
- » **Air Support (10 blowback):** Bring in a military verticopter.
- » **Mech Support (10 blowback):** Bring in a government mech.

Aftermath: The PCs Win

This is it. Between the war started in the streets and the destruction of the signal, the government is ready to topple. When the signal is finally cut, all of the soldiers, gendarmes, and other people fighting for the government and corporations lose access to AR and are temporarily disoriented. Mechs and verticopters are disabled entirely, as are automated security systems. This gives the Citizens enough of an edge to push the government the rest of the way and send Paris Nouveau into total anarchy.

Let the players wrap up. Go around the table, one by one, and ask them what happens in the coming months. How do things improve? How do they get worse? How do they change? If their character is still alive, how does he or she contribute to the new order, if at all? Once every player has had a chance to contribute to the wrap-up, add something yourself. The game is over. La Résistance has achieved its goal. Congratulations.

Aftermath: The PCs Lose

The only way the PCs lose is if they all concede or get taken out during the mission. If a PC is taken out, that PC is probably dead. A PC who concedes might survive the failed revolution. In the wake of the war in the streets, the government cracks down and institutes martial law. Gendarmes are everywhere, along with heavily armed soldiers. Mechs are stationed around the city, and verticopters patrol the air. The iron fist tightens.

If the PCs wish, you can continue playing. La Résistance loses its The Revolution advance, and the government earns an immediate advance. Any players whose characters died can make new ones, triggering the betrayal or sacrifice milestone (*page 147*), as appropriate. If the PCs take The Revolution again, you can run this mission again as-is, modify it, or make a new version.

The Purge (Endgame Mission)

The wolves are at our door. The government and the corporations that control it have amassed their forces, and are minutes from attacking la Cave and wiping us out. We need to fight. We need to drive them off! We cannot let them end our revolution here!

Set: La Cave, as it is being assaulted by government soldiers.

Mission Opposition: Great (+4)

Running "The Purge"

Don't run a prep scene before this mission.

Make the PCs work for this one. To make sure they have to, here's a gift: you get +10 blowback at the start of this mission. Use it well.

Now, look at the notes you've no doubt been taking throughout the campaign. Remember all the people who have betrayed la Résistance, or who you've decided were secret traitors all along. Think of all the enemies the PCs have gone up against but not defeated. Whoever they are, use them in this mission. All of them. You can insert them into any scenes you like, without spending blowback. In addition, a PC does not need to have **MARKED FOR DEATH** marked in order for you to kill them during this mission. As long as you take out a PC and spend 5 blowback, you can narrate that PC's death. The stakes are high. Have fun.

Resistance Goals

» Hold the government off while our people escape.

» Kill whoever is in command.

» Escape la Cave.

Zones

» **LA CAVE**

» **MOULIN ROUGE**

» **THE STOREROOM**

» **THE LOUVRE**

» **THE CANALS**

» **THE RUINED TOWER**

» **PÈRE-LACHAISE CEMETERY**

» **HIDDEN**

» **BEHIND COVER**

Cast

GENDARME

GENDARME, Fair (+2)

BLOODLUST, Terrible (-2)

GOVERNMENT SOLDIER

GOVERNMENT SOLDIER, Good (+3)

ON EDGE, Poor (-1)

CONDITIONS

☐ STAGGERED

GOVERNMENT MECH

ASPECTS

WALKING TANK; SUBMIT OR BE DESTROYED

STUNTS

Because I have **heavy ordnance**, I can spend a fate point to cause harm to everyone in my zone, rolling once.

Because I'm **heavily armored**, I get +2 to avoid physical harm with Fight.

MEANS

Fight: Good (+3)

Maneuver: Average (+1)

Manipulate: Fair (+2)

Observe: Fair (+2)

CONDITIONS

☐ STAGGERED

☐ REELING

Setup

Allow the PCs to start in whichever zones they'd like; they're on home turf, and they get to prepare. Resistance agents and Citizens taking shelter in la Cave are everywhere, and la Résistance's chief goal here is stalling the government while Citizens and key members of la Résistance escape to somewhere safe. To model this, set a round goal, after which the PCs have held out long enough to allow those who need to escape to do so; three full rounds per PC (minimum 10 rounds) should work.

Choose someone to command the army, someone the PCs have had a run-in with before. Hitomi von Krauss is a good choice, but if someone (whether an NPC or PC) has betrayed la Résistance dramatically, they're a better choice. Decide where that character is, but make the PCs figure it out; don't tell them outright.

Finally, you have as many gendarmes and soldiers as you need in this scene. They're attacking in force, and they keep pouring in. There are many soldiers on la Résistance's side too, so not every government soldier or gendarme is focused on the PCs; to model this, don't attack a single PC with more than four or five enemies during one exchange.

In addition to your hordes of soldiers and gendarmes, you have three government mechs to start. If you want more, you'll have to spend blowback.

Transgressions

» A conflict round ends 2 blowback

» A non-conflict scene ends 5 blowback

Complications and Discoveries

» **Mech Support (10 blowback):** Bring in a government mech.

» **A Devastating Blow (10 blowback):** The government kills an important Resistance agent, corners some Citizens, cuts off an escape route, or does something else that makes things look bad. Add a round to the round goal.

Aftermath: The PCs Win

The PCs have managed to fight the government off long enough for the bulk of la Résistance to escape and regroup somewhere else, a new base of operations, probably out in Old Paris. If the players wish, you can continue playing. The government loses its The Purge advance, and la Résistance earns an immediate advance. Any players whose characters died can make new ones, triggering the sacrifice or betrayal milestone (***page 147***), as appropriate. Describe to the PCs the location of la Résistance's new headquarters.

Aftermath: The PCs Lose

La Résistance has been crushed. The PCs are likely dead, in hiding, or employed by the government. In the days immediately following the Purge, the government institutes martial law. Gendarmes and soldiers are everywhere, mechs are stationed in important locations, and verticopters patrol the skies. Ask each player to describe one thing that happens in the coming months. When they're all done, add your own narration. The game is now over.

Appendices

Pronunciation: Easier Than You Think

In this game, we use a lot of potentially unfamiliar French terms. This is meant to give you the flavor of cyberpunk Paris, not to quiz you on your skills in another language. We have provided this handy pronunciation guide to help you at your table.

The goal is not to have perfect French, but to prevent it from being a roadblock in your game. Instead of standard phonetic pronunciations, we've provided a way to sound it out so your Paris Nouveau sounds more authentic. This guide will hopefully raise your comfort with a beautiful and challenging language, so you don't stumble over unfamiliar words in your own campaigns.

Note that in plurals formed with an ending "s," the "s" is silent unless the following noun starts with a vowel.

- » **Arrondissement:** Ah-ron-dees-mahn
- » **Ascenseur:** Ass-ahn-sur
- » **Élite:** Ay-leet
- » **Jardin des Tuileries:** Zhar-dahn day Tweel-ree
- » **Jean le Roux:** Zhan luh Roo
- » **L'Aerie:** Lair-ee
- » **L'Apogée:** Lah-poh-zhay
- » **La Cave:** Lah Cahve
- » **Le Chat Noir:** Luh Sha Nwar
- » **La Gendarmerie:** Lah Zhen-dar-muh-ree
- » **La Résistance:** Lah Ray-zis-tonce
- » **La Seine:** Lah Sen
- » **La Societé:** Lah So-see-ay-tay
- » **Le Bas:** Luh Bah
- » **Les Citoyens:** Lay Sit-why-en
- » **Les Élites:** Lays Ay-leet
- » **Les Gendarmes:** Lay Zhen-darm
- » **Le Silence:** Luh See-lonce
- » **Les Naturels:** Lay Nat-ur-els
- » **La Tour Eiffel:** Lah Tour Eff-ell
- » **Le Treillis:** Luh Tray-yee
- » **L'Ombre:** Lom-bruh
- » **Moulin Rouge:** Moo-lan Rouge
- » **Paris Nouveau:** Pah-ree Noo-voh
- » **Père-Lachaise:** Pear La-shez
- » **Pont Alexandre III:** Pon Ah-lex-ahn-druh
- » **Pont des Arts:** Pon daysars (combine into one word)
- » **Pont des Invalides:** Pon days-on-va-leed (combine into one word)
- » **Pont-Marie:** Pon Mah-ree
- » **Terraformation:** Tare-ah-for-mah-see-on

THE CLEANER
La Société

CONDITIONS

When successfully attacked, mark one. When successfully attacked with style, mark two.

◇ ANGRY
The person who made you Angry gets a boost against you.

◇ WOUNDED
The GM's Budget increases by 1.

◇ DEPLETED
Your refresh drops to zero. Lose half your current fate points, rounded up.

◇ COMPROMISED
Whenever you buy equipment, the GM gains blowback equal to the cost of the equipment.

◇ MARKED FOR DEATH
If the GM takes you out, she can pay 5 blowback to remove you from play permanently. If a PC takes you out, they can spend a fate point to do the same.

ASPECTS

Answer each with a single word or a short phrase.

WHAT MAKES YOU THE BEST CLEANER IN PARIS NOUVEAU?

WHY DO YOU KILL SO OFTEN?

WHO IS THE ONE PERSON YOU TRUST?

WHO DO YOU WISH YOU COULD REMOVE FROM PLAY, BUT CAN'T?

WHY DID YOU JOIN LA RÉSISTANCE?

MEANS

FIGHT **MANIPULATE** **MANEUVER** **OBSERVE**

REFRESH

2

1

0

STUNTS

*You start with **great wealth**. Pick two more.*
Reduce your refresh by one to pick one more.

- *Because I have **great wealth**, equipment that I buy costs 1 point less, to a minimum of 1.*

- *Because I have **stealth augmentations**, I can spend a fate point to disappear from a scene. I can show up during a later exchange in a different zone.*

- *Because I have an **information network**, when I create a prep advantage with Manipulate, I tie another boost to it as long as I can access my network of spies.*

- *Because **I serve my masters**, I can call upon my corporate sponsor to get me out of trouble, once per mission. Their help, however, is never free.*

- *Because I **kill without hesitation**, when I successfully cause physical harm, I can give the GM 1 blowback to force my opponent to mark an extra condition, provided my intent is to kill.*

- *Because I'm **slippery**, I get +2 to avoid detection with Maneuver.*

ADVANCEMENT

***During a mission**, if my advancement track becomes full, I can immediately clear it to gain 5 fate points.*

***At the end of a mission**, I earn one advancement point per true statement:*

- ➤ *I killed someone without being detected.*

- ➤ *I disposed of evidence of wrongdoing.*

- ➤ *I struck from a position of advantage or hiding.*

***During a debrief**, if my advancement track is full, I can clear it to advance.*

EQUIPMENT & NOTES

THE BLUEBLOOD
La Société

ALIASES

CONDITIONS

When successfully attacked, mark one. When successfully attacked with style, mark two.

◆ ANGRY
The person who made you Angry gets a boost against you.

◆ WOUNDED
The GM's Budget increases by 1.

◆ DEPLETED
Your refresh drops to zero. Lose half your current fate points, rounded up.

◆ COMPROMISED
Whenever you buy equipment, the GM gains blowback equal to the cost of the equipment.

◆ MARKED FOR DEATH
If the GM takes you out, she can pay 5 blowback to remove you from play permanently. If a PC takes you out, they can spend a fate point to do the same.

ASPECTS

Answer each with a single word or a short phrase.

WHERE DOES YOUR WEALTH AND PRIVILEGE COME FROM?

WHAT DO YOU WANT, BUT CAN'T BUY?

WHO DO YOU RELY UPON TO GET YOU THE THINGS YOU WANT?

WHO'S LOOKING TO USURP YOURRIGHTFUL PLACE?

WHY DID YOU JOIN LA RÉSISTANCE?

MEANS

FIGHT MANIPULATE MANEUVER OBSERVE

REFRESH

2

1

0

STUNTS

You start with **great wealth**. Pick two more.
Reduce your refresh by one to pick one more.

- Because I have **great wealth**, equipment that I buy costs 1 point less, to a minimum of 1.

- Because **money talks**, whenever I buy equipment, I can reduce the cost by 1, to a minimum of 1. If I do, the GM gets 2 blowback.

- Because I **deal in favors**, when I gain the advantage in a social situation, I gain another boost.

- Because **the camera loves me**, I can make a Manipulate or Maneuver prep advantage without spending a prep action, but only if I tell the press something juicy, giving 5 blowback to the GM.

- Because I have **bodyguards**, I can bring them into any conflict, once per mission. If I do, they're an aspect with a tied boost. I'll work with the GM to make sure their inclusion makes sense in the scene.

- Because **words cut**, when I successfully cause harm in a social situation, I can give the GM 1 blowback to force my opponent to mark an extra condition.

ADVANCEMENT

During a mission, if my advancement track becomes full, I can immediately clear it to gain 5 fate points.

At the end of a mission, I earn one advancement point per true statement:

- ➤ I convinced someone to agree with my way of doing things.

- ➤ I used money or influence to solve a problem.

- ➤ I used other people to do my dirty work.

During a debrief, if my advancement track is full, I can clear it to advance.

EQUIPMENT & NOTES

THE OFFICER
La Société

CONDITIONS

When successfully attacked, mark one. When successfully attacked with style, mark two.

◇ ANGRY

The person who made you Angry gets a boost against you.

◇ WOUNDED

The GM's Budget increases by 1.

◇ DEPLETED

Your refresh drops to zero. Lose half your current fate points, rounded up.

◇ COMPROMISED

Whenever you buy equipment, the GM gains blowback equal to the cost of the equipment.

◇ MARKED FOR DEATH

If the GM takes you out, she can pay 5 blowback to remove you from play permanently. If a PC takes you out, they can spend a fate point to do the same.

ASPECTS

Answer each with a single word or a short phrase.

WHAT MILITANT ORGANIZATION ARE YOU IN CHARGE OF?

WHY DO YOU DESERVE THAT POSITION?

WHAT DO YOU HIDE FROM YOUR SUBORDINATES?

WHO IS YOUR GREATEST ENEMY?

WHY DID YOU JOIN LA RÉSISTANCE?

MEANS

CHOOSE ONE:
*FIGHT +3 MANIPULATE +2, MANEUVER +2, OBSERVE +1 OR
FIGHT +2, MANIPULATE +3, MANEUVER +1, OBSERVE +2 OR
FIGHT +1, MANIPULATE +2, MANEUVER +2, OBSERVE +3*

FIGHT

MANIPULATE

MANEUVER

OBSERVE

REFRESH

2

1

0

STUNTS

You start with **great wealth**. Pick two more. Reduce your refresh by one to pick one more.

- Because I have **great wealth**, equipment that I buy costs 1 point less, to a minimum of 1.

- Because I have **authority**, I can have my men accomplish one action for me, without rolling, once per mission. The GM will tell me what consequences I face as a result.

- Because I have **clearance**, I can enter a secure area openly, with little trouble. The GM will tell me what consequences I face as a result.

- Because I'm a **warrior**, I get +2 to cause harm with Fight in close-quarters combat.

- Because I have a **war chest**, I can become <aspect>Depleted</aspect> in order to get equipment with a total cost of 4, without spending fate points. I can do this during a prep scene or even during a mission, provided it makes sense to do so.

- Because I **command**, I get +2 to gain the advantage with Fight when I'm engaged in combat with allies or subordinates present.

ADVANCEMENT

During a mission, if my advancement track becomes full, I can immediately clear it to gain 5 fate points.

At the end of a mission, I earn one advancement point per true statement:

➤ I issued an order, and it was obeyed without question.

➤ I helped create a plan that our group executed.

➤ I used violence to solve a problem.

During a debrief, if my advancement track is full, I can clear it to advance.

EQUIPMENT & NOTES

THE HACKER
Les Citoyens

ALIASES

CONDITIONS

When successfully attacked, mark one. When successfully attacked with style, mark two.

◇ ANGRY
The person who made you Angry gets a boost against you.

◇ WOUNDED
The GM's Budget increases by 1.

◇ COMPROMISED
Whenever you buy equipment, the GM gains blowback equal to the cost of the equipment.

◇ BLACKLISTED
Equipment you buy or requisition costs another fate point.

◇ MARKED FOR DEATH
If the GM takes you out, she can pay 5 blowback to remove you from play permanently. If a PC takes you out, they can spend a fate point to do the same.

ASPECTS

Answer each with a single word or a short phrase.

WHAT'S YOUR REPUTATION IN THE DATASPHERE?

WHAT HACK DO YOU REALLY WISH YOU HADN'T PULLED?

WHO DO YOU OFTEN RELY UPON FOR MEATSPACE HELP?

WHO DO YOU WANT TO TAKE DOWN A PEG OR TWO?

WHY DID YOU JOIN LA RÉSISTANCE?

MEANS

CHOOSE ONE:
FIGHT +1, MANIPULATE +3, MANEUVER +2, OBSERVE +2 OR
FIGHT +2, MANIPULATE +1, MANEUVER +2, OBSERVE +3 OR
FIGHT +1, MANIPULATE +2, MANEUVER +2, OBSERVE +3

FIGHT
MANIPULATE
MANEUVER
OBSERVE

REFRESH

2
1
0

STUNTS

You start with **just another citizen**. Pick two more. Reduce your refresh by one to pick one more.

- Because I'm **just another citizen**, I can ignore the effects of either Compromised or Blacklisted until the end of the scene, once per mission. If I do so, the next time I attempt to clear the condition I ignored, my opposition increases by 2.

- Because I can **spoof my markers**, once per mission I can immediately clear my Compromised condition by giving the GM 2 blowback.

- Because I have **eyes everywhere**, I get +2 to gain the advantage with Observe, provided I can access security cameras & the like.

- Because I can **spike the A/R**, I can spend a fate point to take out all blanks and agents in one zone without rolling, provided they have active neural casings. The GM gets blowback for each one I take out, though.

- Because I can **spoof the A/R**, I can enter any scene disguised as someone else. My disguise is an aspect with a tied boost.

- Because I post **screeds on the boards**, whenever I gain the advantage in a way related to mobilizing the hacker underground of Paris Nouveau, I gain another boost. After I roll, I can gain more boosts by giving the GM 2 blowback per extra boost.

ADVANCEMENT

During a mission, if my advancement track becomes full, I can immediately clear it to gain 5 fate points.

At the end of a mission, I earn one advancement point per true statement:

▶ I obtained valuable or illicit information.

▶ I caused havoc within a computerized system.

▶ I solved a problem by clever application of my hacking skills.

During a debrief, if my advancement track is full, I can clear it to advance.

EQUIPMENT & NOTES

THE SOLDIER
Les Citoyens

CONDITIONS

When successfully attacked, mark one. When successfully attacked with style, mark two.

⬦ ANGRY

The person who made you Angry gets a boost against you.

⬦ WOUNDED

The GM's Budget increases by 1.

⬦ COMPROMISED

Whenever you buy equipment, the GM gains blowback equal to the cost of the equipment.

⬦ BLACKLISTED

Equipment you buy or requisition costs another fate point.

⬦ MARKED FOR DEATH

If the GM takes you out, she can pay 5 blowback to remove you from play permanently. If a PC takes you out, they can spend a fate point to do the same.

ASPECTS

Answer each with a single word or a short phrase.

WHAT FORM OF VIOLENCE OR BULLYING ARE YOU AN EXPERT AT?

WHOSE POSITION DO YOU COVET?

WHY DON'T YOU RESPECT YOURSUPERIORS?

WHAT CAUSES YOU TO EMPLOY VIOLENCE THE MOST OFTEN?

WHY DID YOU JOIN LA RÉSISTANCE?

MEANS

CHOOSE ONE:

FIGHT +3, MANIPULATE +2, MANEUVER +1, OBSERVE +2 OR
FIGHT +2, MANIPULATE +3, MANEUVER +1, OBSERVE +2 OR
FIGHT +1, MANIPULATE +3, MANEUVER +2, OBSERVE +2

FIGHT   MANIPULATE   MANEUVER   OBSERVE

REFRESH

2

1

0

STUNTS

You start with **just another citizen**. Pick two more. Reduce your refresh by one to pick one more.

- Because I'm **just another citizen**, I can ignore the effects of either **Compromised** or **Blacklisted** until the end of the scene, once per mission. If I do so, the next time I attempt to clear the condition I ignored, my opposition increases by 2.

- Because I have **combat training**, I get +2 to cause harm with Fight if I intend to kill my target.

- Because I have been subjected to **behavioral conditioning**, I get +2 to avoid attempts to gain social or psychological advantages against me.

- Because I have **friends on the force**, I can call upon them to gain access to a restricted location without too much trouble. The GM will tell me what it costs me.

- Because I have **implanted meta-data readers**, I get +2 to gain the advantage with Observe, provided I'm using the metadata of a person I can see.

- Because I have **tactical training**, when I cause harm with Fight and spend boosts, I get +3 instead of +2 for each boost spent.

ADVANCEMENT

During a mission, if my advancement track becomes full, I can immediately clear it to gain 5 fate points.

At the end of a mission, I earn one advancement point per true statement:

➤ I obeyed an order without question.

➤ I used intimidation or force to solve a problem.

➤ I maintained my composure during a chaotic or stressful situation.

During a debrief, if my advancement track is full, I can clear it to advance.

EQUIPMENT & NOTES

THE MALCONTENT
Les Citoyens

- - - - - - - - - - - - - - - - - -

CONDITIONS

When successfully attacked, mark one. When successfully attacked with style, mark two.

- - - - - - - - - - - - - - - - -

◇ ANGRY
The person who made you Angry gets a boost against you.

◇ WOUNDED
The GM's Budget increases by 1.

◇ COMPROMISED
Whenever you buy equipment, the GM gains blowback equal to the cost of the equipment.

◇ BLACKLISTED
Equipment you buy or requisition costs another fate point.

◇ MARKED FOR DEATH
If the GM takes you out, she can pay 5 blowback to remove you from play permanently. If a PC takes you out, they can spend a fate point to do the same.

ASPECTS

Answer each with a single word or a short phrase.

WHAT MADE YOU BELIEVE THAT ANARCHY WAS THE ONLY SOLUTION?

WHAT CORPORATION OR ORGANIZATION DO YOU WANT TO TEAR DOWN MORE THAN ANY OTHER?

WHAT'S THE WORST THING YOU'VE EVER DONE IN SERVICE OF YOUR CAUSE?

WHO IS YOUR MOST RELIABLE ALLY?

WHY DID YOU JOIN LA RÉSISTANCE?

MEANS

CHOOSE ONE:
FIGHT +3, MANIPULATE +2, MANEUVER +1, OBSERVE +2 OR
FIGHT +2, MANIPULATE +3, MANEUVER +1, OBSERVE +2 OR
FIGHT +1, MANIPULATE +3, MANEUVER +2, OBSERVE +2

FIGHT   MANIPULATE   MANEUVER   OBSERVE

REFRESH

2

1

0

STUNTS

You start with **just another citizen**. Pick two more. Reduce your refresh by one to pick one more.

⬡ Because I'm **just another citizen**, I can ignore the effects of either COMPROMISED or BLACKLISTED until the end of the scene, once per mission. If I do so, the next time I attempt to clear the condition I ignored, my opposition increases by 2.

⬡ Because **fortune favors the bold**, I gain a boost whenever I succeed at a reckless or impulsive action.

⬡ Because **I'm a charismatic leader**, I gain another boost whenever I gain the advantage with Manipulate, but I must give the boost to someone else.

⬡ Because **violence can be used for good**, I get +2 to cause harm with Fight when I firmly believe I'm doing the right thing.

⬡ Because I have a **reputation**, when I meet an NPC, I can declare that the NPC has heard of me and respects me, once per mission. This respect is an aspect with three tied boosts.

⬡ Because I'm **fighting for a better world**, I can spend a fate point to cause Citizens and Exiles around me to rise up and fight, once per scene. This gives me +2 to cause harm with Manipulate until the end of the scene, but the GM gets 5 blowback.

ADVANCEMENT

During a mission, if my advancement track becomes full, I can immediately clear it to gain 5 fate points.

At the end of a mission, I earn one advancement point per true statement:

➤ I killed an agent of the government.

➤ I convinced others to rise up and break their shackles.

➤ I gave an impassioned speech about overthrowing our corporate overlords.

During a debrief, if my advancement track is full, I can clear it to advance.

EQUIPMENT & NOTES

THE EX-CIT
Les Exilés

CONDITIONS

When successfully attacked, mark one. When successfully attacked with style, mark two.

⬦ **ANGRY**
The person who made you Angry gets a boost against you.

⬦ **WOUNDED**
The GM's Budget increases by 1.

⬦ **PERSON OF INTEREST**
At the start of every scene, except prep scenes and debriefs, the GM gets 1 blowback.

⬦ **BLACKLISTED**
When you buy or requisition equipment, its cost is 1 point higher.

⬦ **MARKED FOR DEATH**
If the GM takes you out, she can pay 5 blowback to remove you from play permanently. If a PC takes you out, they can spend a fate point to do the same.

ASPECTS

Answer each with a single word or a short phrase.

WHY WERE YOU STRIPPED OF YOUR CITIZENSHIP?

WHO WERE YOU IN YOUR OLD LIFE?

WHAT DO YOU DO, NOW THAT YOU LIVE IN EXILE?

WHO HELPED YOU FIND SHELTER AFTER YOU WERE EXILED?

WHY DID YOU JOIN LA RÉSISTANCE?

MEANS

CHOOSE ONE:
FIGHT +3, MANIPULATE +1, MANEUVER +2, OBSERVE +2 OR
FIGHT +2, MANIPULATE +1, MANEUVER +3, OBSERVE +2 OR
FIGHT +1, MANIPULATE +3, MANEUVER +2, OBSERVE +2

FIGHT **MANIPULATE** **MANEUVER** **OBSERVE**

REFRESH

2
1
0

STUNTS

You start with **friend of La Résistance**. Pick two more. Reduce your refresh by one to pick one more.

◆ Because I'm a **friend of La Résistance**, when I requisition equipment from la Résistance, I pay 1 point less, to a minimum of 1. I can also requisition equipment with a cost 1 higher than more.

◆ Because I have **nothing left to lose**, I can mark **ANGRY** or **WOUNDED** to get +2 or +4 to a roll, respectively.

◆ Because I'm **self-sufficient**, I get +1 to any rolls I make when I'm handling something alone.

◆ Because sometimes you have to **live to fight another day**, whenever I concede a conflict, I get another fate point at the end of the scene.

◆ Because **I always settle my debts**, whenever I mark a condition because I took harm, I get +2 to cause harm to whoever caused me harm, until the end of the scene.

◆ Because I'm **used to adversity**, I get +2 to gain the advantage with Fight when I'm going up against superior enemies.

ADVANCEMENT

During a mission, if my advancement track becomes full, I can immediately clear it to gain 5 fate points.

At the end of a mission, I earn one advancement point per true statement:

➤ I faced down adversity on my own.

➤ I won when the odds were against me.

➤ I paid kindness back in kind.

During a debrief, if my advancement track is full, I can clear it to advance.

EQUIPMENT & NOTES

THE NATUREL
Les Exilés

ALIASES

CONDITIONS

When successfully attacked, mark one. When successfully attacked with style, mark two.

⬢ ANGRY
The person who made you Angry gets a boost against you.

⬢ WOUNDED
The GM's Budget increases by 1.

⬢ PERSON OF INTEREST
At the start of every scene, except prep scenes and debriefs, the GM gets 1 blowback.

⬢ BLACKLISTED
When you buy or requisition equipment, its cost is 1 point higher.

⬢ MARKED FOR DEATH
If the GM takes you out, she can pay 5 blowback to remove you from play permanently. If a PC takes you out, they can spend a fate point to do the same.

ASPECTS

Answer each with a single word or a short phrase.

WHY DOESN'T YOUR COMMUNITY USE IMPLANTS OF ANY KIND?

HOW HAVE YOU LEARNED TO BE SELFSUFFICIENT?

WHO TAUGHT YOU THE SKILLS YOU USE TO SURVIVE?

WHO HAS DECIDED YOU'RE A THREAT?

WHY DID YOU JOIN LA RÉSISTANCE?

MEANS

FIGHT **MANIPULATE** **MANEUVER** **OBSERVE**

REFRESH

2

1

0

STUNTS

You start with **friend of La Résistance**. Pick two more. Reduce your refresh by one to pick one more.

- Because I'm a **friend of La Résistance**, when I requisition equipment from la Résistance, I pay 1 point less, to a minimum of 1. I can also requisition equipment with a cost 1 higher than normal.

- Because I **move unseen**, I get +2 to avoid detection with Maneuver.

- Because I'm **off the grid**, get +2 to avoid attempts to gain the advantage over me when that advantage would be gained by metadata or biometric scanning.

- Because I **know my environment**, whenever I invoke a situation aspect representing an environmental feature, I get +3 instead of +2.

- Because **blood is thicker than water**, whenever I enter a scene in which I can call upon my community, I can choose to gain an aspect with a tied boost. The aspect must represent something I could gain from my community.

- Because **people underestimate me**, I get +2 to cause harm with Fight against an opponent who believes himself to be my superior.

ADVANCEMENT

During a mission, if my advancement track becomes full, I can immediately clear it to gain 5 fate points.

At the end of a mission, I earn one advancement point per true statement:

- ➤ I used the environment to my advantage.

- ➤ I supported and cooperated with my allies.

- ➤ I made strides to help my community.

During a debrief, if my advancement track is full, I can clear it to advance.

EQUIPMENT & NOTES

THE ARMIGER
Les Exilés

ALIASES

CONDITIONS

When successfully attacked, mark one. When successfully attacked with style, mark two.

◆ ANGRY

The person who made you Angry gets a boost against you.

◇ WOUNDED

The GM's Budget increases by 1.

◇ PERSON OF INTEREST

At the start of every scene, except prep scenes and debriefs, the GM gets 1 blowback.

◇ BLACKLISTED

When you buy or requisition equipment, its cost is 1 point higher.

◇ MARKED FOR DEATH

If the GM takes you out, she can pay 5 blowback to remove you from play permanently. If a PC takes you out, they can spend a fate point to do the same.

ASPECTS

Answer each with a single word or a short phrase.

WHY DO YOU RELY SO HEAVILY UPON AUGMENTATIONS?

WHAT IS YOUR MOST DISTURBING PHYSICAL FEATURE?

WHICH AUGMENTATION IS YOUR FAVORITE?

WHO ACCEPTS YOU DESPITE YOUR INTIMIDATING PRESENCE?

WHY DID YOU JOIN LA RÉSISTANCE?

MEANS

CHOOSE ONE:
FIGHT +3, MANIPULATE +1, MANEUVER +2, OBSERVE +2 OR
FIGHT +2, MANIPULATE +1, MANEUVER +3, OBSERVE +2 OR
FIGHT +1, MANIPULATE +3, MANEUVER +2, OBSERVE +2

FIGHT   MANIPULATE   MANEUVER   OBSERVE

REFRESH

2
1
0

STUNTS

You start with **friend of La Résistance**. Pick two more. Reduce your refresh by one to pick one more.

Because I'm a **friend of La Résistance**, when I requisition equipment from la Résistance, I pay 1 point less, to a minimum of 1. I can also requisition equipment with a cost 1 higher than normal.

Because I'm covered in **armor plating**, I can spend a fate point to avoid marking a condition caused by physical harm.

Because I'm an **engine of destruction**, I can give the GM 1 blowback to get +2 to a Fight roll. I can do this up to three times on a given roll.

Because I'm **enormous**, I get +2 to cause harm with Fight when my size is a factor.

Because I'm **scary**, I get +2 to gain the advantage with Fight when I'm intimidating someone.

Because I'm a **pariah**, I can spend a fate point to draw the attention of any NPCs in my zone. When I do this, each of my allies gains a boost.

ADVANCEMENT

During a mission, if my advancement track becomes full, I can immediately clear it to gain 5 fate points.

At the end of a mission, I earn one advancement point per true statement:

➤ I made someone uncomfortable or afraid.

➤ I caused significant property damage.

➤ I solved a problem by using my implants.

During a debrief, if my advancement track is full, I can clear it to advance.

EQUIPMENT & NOTES

LA RÉSISTANCE

MANIFESTO

WEAKNESS

INTEL

TRAINING ARCHIVE ACCESS
Once per mission, before roll, discover passive opposition or means ratings of opposition.

WEB OF INFORMANTS
Tie +2 boosts to Observe prep advantages.

INTERROGATION TECHNIQUES
Tie +2 boosts to Fight prep advantages.

INSIDE MAN
At start of prep, GM must reveal one upcoming transgression.

GOVERNMENT CONTACTS
At start of prep, GM must reveal another upcoming transgression.

FAVOR: THE AMBASSADOR
La Résistance can call in one free favor from the Ambassador.

FAVOR: THE CONTESSA
La Résistance can call in one free favor from the Contessa.

DIRTY SECRETS
Can invoke government's scandal, and invoking for bonus adds +3.
Critical advance.

RESOURCES

HIJACKED SHIPMENTS
Can requisition equipment with cost of 0–1 per piece.

ARMORY
Can requisition equipment with cost of 0–2 per piece.

BLACK MARKET CONTACTS
Can requisition equipment with cost of 0–3 per piece.

FAVOR: THE ASSASSIN
La Résistance can call in one free favor from the Assassin.

MEANS TO AN END
At start of prep, add a fate point to Cache. Can requisition equipment with +1 cost.
Critical advance.

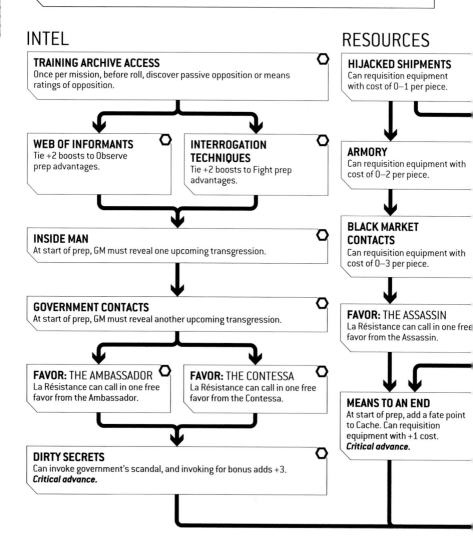

CACHE

ADVANCEMENT ⬡⬡⬡⬡⬡⬡⬡⬡⬡⬡

SUPPORT

HEARTS & MINDS
Tie +2 boosts to Maneuver prep advantages.

PROMISES & BRIBES
Tie +2 boosts to Manipulate prep advantages.

ESOURCES

REMOTE SUPPLY CACHES
Can access the Cache outside of a Cave.

GRASSROOTS
Gain +1 to rolls made to deal with Citoyens without using violence.

GENDARME CONTACS
GM must spend +2 blowback to bring gendarmes into a scene.

MEDICAL EQUIPMENT
At start of prep, clear all Wounded conditions.

CITIZEN SABOTEUR
Cross out one taken government advance, canceling its effect.

FAVOR: THE DUKE
La Résistance can call in one free favor from the Duke.

FAVOR: THE CONTESSA
La Résistance can call in one free favor from the Contessa.

FAVOR: THE CAPTAIN
La Résistance can call in one free favor from the Captain.

THE WILL OF THE PEOPLE
At start of scenes with nonmilitarized Citizens, gain CITIZEN SOLDIERS with two tied boosts. *Critical advance.*

REVOLUTION!

THE GOVERNMENT

CORPORATE

TAXATION
At start of prep, add a fate point to Bank.

WAGE NEGOTIATIONS
At start of prep, add a fate point to Bank.

ANTI-PIRACY MEASURES
Add a fate point to Bank whenever PC requisitions a piece of equipment.

SHELL COMPANIES
During debrief, put up to 4 leftover fate points back into Bank.

MANDATORY CHARITABLE DONATIONS
Add a fate point to Bank whenever PC buys a piece of equipment.

INFRASTRUCTURE INVESTMENT
During debrief, put up to 2 leftover fate points back into Bank.

CLEVER ACCOUNTING
During debrief, put all leftover fate points back into Bank.

ELITE KICKBACKS
Whenever a PC gets favor from Élite during prep, add 2 fate points to Bank. *Critical advance.*

MILITARY

GENDARME RECRUITMENT
During mission, spend 5 blowback to get gendarmes equal to double the player count, plus gendarme sergeant.

SECURITY ALLOCATION
During mission, spend 5 blow to get SecSpec equal to doub player count, plus SecSpec commander.

GENDARME TRAINING
Gendarmes and gendarme sergeants get +1 to all rolls.

SECSPEC TRAINING
SecSpec and SecSpec sergea get +1 to all rolls.

MERCENARY RECRUITMENT
Can spend 2 blowback as 1 fate point when using Gendarme Recruitment, Security Allocation, or Mandatory Military Service.

INCREASED VOLUNTEERISM
Costs -2 blowback to bring NPCs into a scene. *Critical advance.*

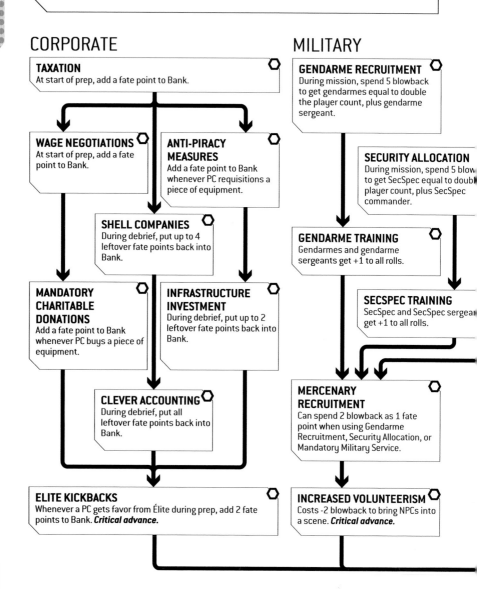

BANK

ADVANCEMENT

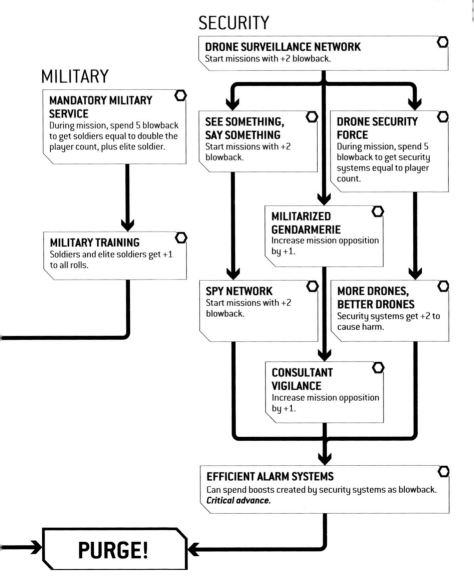

SECURITY

DRONE SURVEILLANCE NETWORK
Start missions with +2 blowback.

MILITARY

MANDATORY MILITARY SERVICE
During mission, spend 5 blowback to get soldiers equal to double the player count, plus elite soldier.

SEE SOMETHING, SAY SOMETHING
Start missions with +2 blowback.

DRONE SECURITY FORCE
During mission, spend 5 blowback to get security systems equal to player count.

MILITARIZED GENDARMERIE
Increase mission opposition by +1.

MILITARY TRAINING
Soldiers and elite soldiers get +1 to all rolls.

SPY NETWORK
Start missions with +2 blowback.

MORE DRONES, BETTER DRONES
Security systems get +2 to cause harm.

CONSULTANT VIGILANCE
Increase mission opposition by +1.

EFFICIENT ALARM SYSTEMS
Can spend boosts created by security systems as blowback.
Critical advance.

PURGE!

Secrets

Keep your secret hidden from the rest of the group.

You earn an advancement point every time your +1 advancement point text is triggered. Triggers with other numbers work the same way.

If you immediately advance, reveal your secret to the group, then give your secret back to the GM. She'll tell you what consequences you face. You'll get a new secret during the next debrief, if you survive.

If you have questions about your secret, ask the GM, or pass her a note.

Blackmail

You were a Citizen in good standing until la Résistance blackmailed you into helping them. What do they have on you? What would happen to you if it got out? How far are you willing to go to keep it covered up?

+1 advancement point whenever a Resistance goal is completed.

Immediately advance when you reveal your blackmail to the group, the general public, or both.

Mole Hunter

La Résistance has tasked you with rooting out traitors. How do you feel about that? Why did they choose you?

+1 advancement point whenever you pass la Résistance secret information about your teammates (by passing a note to the GM).

Immediately advance when you correctly accuse someone of being a spy during a debrief. Note: you'll get your new secret during *this* debrief.

Hostage

Your loyalty to la Résistance is constantly tested by the fact that it puts someone close to you—someone who's still a loyal Citizen—in danger. Who is it? Do they know that the government is watching them? What will happen to them if you step out of line? Has the government made threats to that effect?

+1 advancement point when you take someone out without generating blowback for the GM.

Immediately advance when you either convince the hostage to defect to la Résistance, or they turn against you or die.

Secret Attraction

You're drawn to someone else on the team. Who is it? Why can't you let them know? What would you do for them?

+1 advancement point whenever you give the object of your affection a boost, defend them, attack someone who's attacking them, or back them up on a decision.

Immediately advance when you declare your attraction to them, consequences be damned.

⊶Troublemaker ✊

You just want to tear things down and mess things up. Why? Are you following an ideology, or do you just like chaos? What's the worst thing you've ever done? What thing do you most want to do?

+1 advancement point whenever you take an action that gives the GM blowback.

Immediately advance when you do something incredibly stupid and destructive, regardless of the consequences.

⊶Rival ✊

You have an intense rivalry with someone else on the team. Why do you have it in for them? What real or imagined slight are you avenging? What would you do to them, given the chance?

+1 advancement point when you hinder your rival, or call them out publicly.

Immediately advance When you declare your rivalry publicly.

⊶Killer ✊

You have a taste for killing, though it troubles you deeply. What made you this way? How many people have you killed? How many of them didn't deserve it? How does killing make you feel?

+1 advancement point when you kill a named NPC.

Immediately advance when you confess your sins to someone and ask them to help you stop.

⊶Agitator

You are a spy. Your job is to sow chaos within la Résistance. Why are you loyal to the government? What have they promised you? What would you do to pursue their goals?

+3 advancement points whenever you falsely accuse someone else of being a spy.

+1 advancement point whenever the government earns any number of advancement points at once.

Immediately advance when you reveal yourself as a traitor. At the next debrief (if you survive), you'll have the choice of committing to la Résistance or remaining a traitor (and becoming an NPC).

Sleeper

You are a spy. Your job is to lie low, make la Résistance trust you, and strike at an opportune moment. Why are you loyal to the government? What have they promised you? What would you do to pursue their goals?

+1 advancement point whenever a member of la Résistance asks for your help or gives you information in confidence.

+1 advancement point whenever the government earns any number of advancement points at once.

Immediately advance when you reveal yourself as a traitor. At the next debrief (if you survive), you'll have the choice of committing to la Résistance or remaining a traitor (and becoming an NPC).

Informant

You are a spy. You've been tasked with feeding information back to the government. Why are you loyal to the government? What have they promised you? What would you do to pursue their goals?

+1 advancement point when you pass sensitive information to the government (by passing a note to the GM).

+1 advancement point whenever the government earns any number of advancement points at once.

Immediately advance when you reveal yourself as a traitor. At the next debrief (if you survive), you'll have the choice of committing to la Résistance or remaining a traitor (and becoming an NPC).

Saboteur

You are a spy. You've been told to undermine la Résistance's efforts whenever possible. Why are you loyal to the government? What have they promised you? What would you do to pursue their goals?

+1 advancement point whenever you take an action that gives the GM blowback, or convince someone else to.

+1 advancement point whenever the government earns any number of advancement points at once.

Immediately advance when you reveal yourself as a traitor. At the next debrief (if you survive), you'll have the choice of committing to la Résistance or remaining a traitor (and becoming an NPC).

Embezzler

You are a spy. The government would like you to waste la Résistance's resources and funnel money to the corporations. Why are you loyal to the government? What have they promised you? What would you do to pursue their goals?

+1 advancement point whenever you spend a fate point from the Cache, or whenever a fate point goes to the Bank.

+1 advancement point whenever the government earns any number of advancement points at once.

Immediately advance when you reveal yourself as a traitor. At the next debrief (if you survive), you'll have the choice of committing to la Résistance or remaining a traitor (and becoming an NPC).

Index

A

Abstract zone, 140
Accusations, 151-52
Action(s), 123
    narrating, 133-34
rolling for, 123-24
Active opposition, 124
Advance(s), 11
    for government, 29, 161-63
    for resistance, 26, 159-61
    immediate, 96, 150
Advancement, 150
    for player characters, 150
    government, 151
    resistance, 151
Advancement points, 11
    from secrets, 96
    from Resistance goals, 120
    track for, 11
Advice
    for player, 13-14
    for game master, 195-96
Aftermath, 202
    when PCs lose, 271, 275
    when PCs win, 271, 274
Agent(s), 184, 185
Agitator (spy), 100
Akiyama, General Theodore, 256
Allard, Raoul, 179
Ambassador, The, 112-13
Angry (condition), 143
Arielle, 158, 224
Armiger, The, 20
    example of, 85
    playsheet for, 84-85
Aspects, 10, 21-22
    boost and, 141-42
    categories of, 93
    changing character and, 94
    character, 93-94
    compelling, 92
    destroying, 95
    fate points and, 178
    invoking, 89-91, 124
    workings of, 94
    writing, 88-89

Assassin, The, 113
Augmentations, 153-54
    powering down, 37
Augmented reality (AR), 31, 35, 51-52
Avoid (end), 131

B

Bank, 29, 178
Bartender, 158
Bas, Le, 42
Bellweather, Brandeis, 249
Benefits, of equipment, 108
Betrayal milestone, 147
Biotech, 153-54
Black Bag (mission), 246-29
Black market dealer, 158
Blacklisted (condition), 144-45
Blackmail (secret), 97
Blank non-player characters, 184
Blood scrubbers, 153
Blowback, 120, 180
    spending, 182
Blueblood, The, 20
    example of, 65
    playsheet for, 64-65
Bonaparte, Napoléon, 44
Bone reinforcement, 153
Boosts, 89, 90, 141
Bouret, Elisabeth, 197
Brake, 13
Briefing, 200
Budget, 120, 178

C

Cache, 26
Captain, The, 114-15
Cast, 200
Cause harm (end), 131
Cave, La, 40, 42, 43
Character creation, 18-25
    aspects in, 21-22, 93, 94
    means and, 23-24
    playsheets for, 18-21
    of secret, 22-23
    stunts in, 24
Chase situations, 137

Citoyens/Citizens, 3, 19, 20
    civic duties of, 58
    privileges of, 31
    role of, 34-42
    gendarmes and, 58
    laws for, 27
    leaving city and, 58
Naturels and, 58
Paris Below and, 58
    in play, 69
Clare, Leader of the Resistance, 191
Clatch, Etta, 247
Cleaner, The, 20
    example of, 63
    playsheet for, 62-63
Collaboration, 14
Compel, 11, 198
    aspects and, 92
    fate points and, 178
Complications, 120, 180, 195, 201
Compromised (condition), 144
Concessions, 122
Condition(s), 11, 19
    Angry, 143
    Blacklisted, 144-45
    clearing, 142
    Compromised, 144
    Depleted, 144
    Marked for Death, 145-46
    marking, 142
    of non-player characters, 187
    Person of Interest, 144
    Wounded, 143
    Conflict(s), 121-22
    framing, 121
    running, 122
    sides in, 121
    winning, 122
Contacts, 158-59
Contessa, The, 115-16
Convoy Ambush (mission), 207-10
Corporations, 168-76
    creating, 167
Corporate Espionage (mission), 210-15
Corporate Retaliation (mission), 216-19
Corvid Economics, 168-69
Costs
    of equipment, 108
    of favors, 110
    major and minor, 124, 127
Coup, character cards from, 111
Critical advance, 159, 160, 161, 162
Cryptiq, Inc., 170
Cyber eye, 153
Cybertech, 153-54

D
d'Angelo, Mariela, 206
d'Orsay, Jules, 103-4
Daily environmental alerts, 37
Damien the Pious, 188
Debrief scene, 7, 150
    steps in, 150
Decision compel, 93
Delacroix, 244
Demonstration (mission), 253-56
Depleted (condition), 144
Description, leading with, 134
Discoveries, 120, 195, 201
Double agent, 152
Downcycling, 40
Drawbacks, of equipment, 108
Du Prix, Alfonse, 212
Duke, The, 117-18

Effort, 9, 124
    ladder of, 9
Élites, The, 109
    favors from, 109-11
    portraying, 110
    reneging on debt to, 111
Embezzler (spy), 102
EMP cluster, 153
End(s), 123
    leading with, 135
    types of, 131-32
Equipment, 108
    benefits of, 108
    buying, 109
    cost of, 108
    drawbacks of, 108
    examples of, 108
    requisitioning, 109
Esfir, 215
Event compel, 93
Exchange, 122-23
Ex-Cit, The, 20
    example of, 81
    playsheet for, 80-81
Ex-citizens, 76
Exilés, les, 19, 20, 76-78
    in play, 79

F
Fail, 124, 125
Fall, The, 47, 52-54
Fate Core, differences from, 6
Fate Dice, 5, 9
Fate point(s), 10, 11
    aspects and, 89
Bank and, 29, 178
Budget and, 29, 178
    stunts and, 24-25
Father Sebastian, 236

Favor(s), 109-11
    from Ambassador, 112-13
    from Assassin, 113
    from Captain, 114-15
    from Contessa, 116
    from Duke, 118
Field receiver, 154
Fight (means), 23, 128
    in chase situations, 137
    in hacking situations, 138
    in physical situations, 136
    in social situations, 136
    in stealth situations, 137
Fire, 252
Flaw
    in agent NPCs, 185
    in blank NPCs, 184
Food, 38
French, 21
    pronunciation guide, 276
Friend, The (mission), 257-59

G

Gain the advantage (end), 132
Game
    creation, 18
    length, 30
Game master, 195-98
    advice, 195-96
    invokes and compels, 198
Gawain, 232
Gendarme(s), 49-50, 58
Gendarmerie, 41-42
Gladwell, Peter, 183
Glorious death, 147
Government, The, 18
    Bank and, 29, 178
    Budget and, 120, 178
    building of, 29-30
    goals, 120, 194, 201
    scandal of, 29
    slogan of, 29
Government advances/advancement, 29, 151, 161
    corporate, 161-62
    military, 162
    Purge, The, 163
    security, 162
Government mech, 269, 273

H

Hacker, The, 20
    example of, 71
    playsheet for, 70-71
Hacking situations, 138
Helios, 241
Helping, 124, 126

Hidden blades, 154
High concept, named NPC, 186
Hindering, 124, 126
Hostage (secret), 98

I

Immediate advance, 96, 150
Informant (spy), 101
Information broker, 218
InfoSec-West, 170-71
Interrogator, 247
Invoke, 198
    aspect, 10, 89-90
    fate points and, 178

K

Killer (secret), 100
Knife Sisters, 158-59, 228, 229, 231

L

L'Aerie, 39-40, 42
L'Apogée, 39, 42, 47, 51
L'Ombre, 157
Ladder, of effort, 10
Lafleur Digital Media, 172
Laws, citoyens, 58
Lemarque, Grégoire, 193
London, 57
Louvre headquarters, 44
Lu, Loreena, 181

M

Macdonald, Daphne, 242
Major costs, 127
Malcontent, The, 20
    example of, 75
    playsheet for, 74-75
Maneuver (means), 23, 130
    in chase situations, 137
    in hacking situations, 138
    in physical situations, 136
    in social situations, 136
    in stealth situations, 137
Manifesto 26
Manipulate (means), 23, 129
    in chase situations, 137
    in hacking situations, 138
    in physical situations, 136
    in social situations, 136
    in stealth situations, 137
Marked for Death (condition), 14, 111, 116, 142, 145-46
Marya, 158, 222

Means, 9, 123
   leading with, 135
   rating, 23
   selection of, 23
   suited and risky, 125
   types of, 128
Mercy (mission), 234-38
Milestones, 147
Military verticopter, 270
Minor costs, 127
Missing Supplies (mission), 220-28
Mission(s), 7, 120, 200-201
   advice for, 201
   arcs of, 201
   briefing for, 200
   Clare in, 191
   endgame, 201
   making, 194-95
   opposition during, 124, 194, 200
   running, 189-90
   set, 200
   setup, 200
   tips, tricks for, 192
Missions, premade
   Black Bag, 246-49
   Convoy Ambush, 207-10
   Corporate Espionage, 210-15
   Corporate Retaliation, 216-19
   Demonstration, 253-56
   Friend, The, 257-59
   Mercy, 234-38
   Missing Supplies, 220-28
   Paymaster, The, 264-66
   Peace Offering, 229-32
   Purge, The, 272-75
   Raid, 250-52
   Recruitment Drive, 239-42
   Rendition, 260-63
   Revolution, The, 267-71
   Warehouse Raid, 202-6
   White Hats, Black Market, 243-45
Mission opposition, 124
   in destroying aspects, 95
   in gaining the advantage, 132
   in moving through zones, 139
Mole Hunter (secret), 97
Moulin Rouge
   bar, 43
   bartender, 225
Muscle enhancers, 154

N

Named non-player characters, 184, 186-87
Nameless non-player characters, 184
Nanotech, 154

Narration
   in different situations, 135-36
   use of, 133-34
Naturel, The, 20
   example of, 83
   playsheet for, 82-83
Naturels, Les, 36, 76-77
   citoyens and, 58
   salvage operations and, 44
Neese, 55
Neural casing, 34-35, 36, 51-52
   buzzing in, 42-43
Non-player characters (NPCs)
   acting, opposing with, 189
   agents and, 184, 185
   conditions and, 187
   mobs and, 195
   named, 184, 186-67
   nameless, 184
   risky, suited means of, 126
Non-player characters (NPCs), ready-made, 178
   APE Dispensary Technician, 193
   Clare, Leader of the Resistance, 191
   CEO, 263
   Crime Boss, 228
   Farmer, 259
   Foreign Consular, 183
   General, 256
   Government Revenue Director, 249
   Guerilla, 179
   Judge, 238
   Mercenary, 215
   Peacekeeper, 197
   Politician, 181
   Priest, 188
   Propaganda Director, 242
   Provocateur, 206
Nu Berlin, 56

O

Observe (means), 23, 130
   in chase situations, 137
   in hacking situations, 138
   in physical situations, 136
   in social situations, 136
   in stealth situations, 137
Officer, The, 20
   example of, 67
   playsheet for, 66-67
Opposition, 10, 124
   active, 124
   by invoking aspects, 90
   by non-player characters, 189
   mission, 124
   passive, 124

P

Paragon Gyromatics, 172-73
Paris Below, 39, 40
Paris Nouveau, 3, 18
    citizen's role in, 34-42
    structure of, 42-45
    traveling in, 45-50
Passive opposition, 124
Patches, 45, 49
Paymaster, The (mission), 264-66
Peace Offering (mission), 229-32
Père-Lachaise cemetery, 45
Person of Interest (condition), 144
Pheromone enhancement, 154
Physical zone, 140
Play, 2-5
    basics of, 9-13
    necessities of, 5
Player character (PC), 18
    advancement of, 150
    death of, 3
Player character creation, 18-25
    aspects in, 21-22, 93-94
    means and, 23-24
    playsheets for, 18-21
    of secret, 22-23
    stunts in, 24
Playsheets, 9-11, 18-21
Pont-Neuf ruins, 44
Prague, 57
Prep action, 106
Prep advantage(s), 106-7
    types of, 107
Prep scene, 7, 106
Problem solver, 159
Proctor, Judge Winston, 238
Purge, The
    advance, 163
    mission, 201, 272

Q

Quartermaster, 158, 226
Quesada Méchaniques Élite, 173

R

Raid (mission), 250-52
Rathburn Chemical Laboratories, 174
Recruitment Drive (mission), 239-42
Refresh, 11, 24
Rendition (mission), 260-63

Resistance advances/advancement, 26, 151, 159-61
    intel, 159
    resources, 160
    Revolution, The, 161
    support, 160-61
Résistance, la, 18
    building of, 26-28
    Cache of, 26
    goals of, 120, 194, 200
    leader of, 191
    manifesto of, 26
    weakness of, 26
Resolve an uncertain outcome (end), 132
Respectful play, 195
Revolution, The
    advance, 161
    mission, 201, 267-71
Risky means, 125
    for non-player characters, 126
Rival (secret), 99
Rodriquez, warehouse guard captain, 204
Roundtree, Roland, 259
Roux, Jean le, 43, 158, 225

S

Saboteur (spy), 102
Sacrifice milestone, 147
Salvage operations, 44
Sang Royal, 229, 232
Scandal, 29
Scenes, 120
Secret(s), 11, 22-23, 95-96
    immediate advances and, 96
    information, 107
    parts of, 96
    picking, 22-23
    receiving, 96
    selecting new, 97
    table consensus and, 96
Secret Attraction (secret), 98
Selise, 158-59, 228, 231
Set, 200
Setting aspects, 93
Shade, 156-57
Sidenge, 159, 223
Silence, Le, 27-28, 54, 156
Singh, Henri, 158, 226
Situation(s)
    aspects and, 93, 95
    chase, 137
    hacking, 138
    physical, 136
    social, 136
    stealth, 137
Sleeper (spy), 101
Slogan, 29

Sniper, 158
Social classes, 18-19
Social situations, 136
Société, La, 19-20, 42, 60
   in play, 61
Soldier, The, 20
      example of, 73
      playsheet for, 72-73
Sparrow, 218
Spy secrets, 100-102
St. Petersburg, 57
Staggered (condition), 185
Stealth field, 154
Stealth situations, 137
Stunt(s), 10, 19
      named non-player characters and, 186-87
Succeed, 124, 125
Succeed with style, 124, 125
Suited means, 125
      for non-player characters, 126
Sun, Anna Mae, 263
Sun Systems Biotech, 174

T

Table consensus, 27, 96
      concessions and, 122
Takeda, 231
Taken out, 11, 142, 146
Terraformation, 38, 46-47, 54
Tie, 124, 125
      boost and, 141-42
Tokyo, 57
Transgressions, 120, 180, 195, 201
Traveling, 45-46, 176
Treillis, Le, 41, 55, 155
Trouble, named non-player character and, 186
Troublemaker (secret), 99
Turns, 122, 123
Type
      agents and, 185
      blanks and, 184

U

Upfrancisco, 56, 176

V

Veils, 31, 36, 155
Verdi Transportation, 175
Versailles, 57
Virtual reality (VR), 35, 47, 52, 155-56
Von Krauss, Emir, 265
Von Krauss, Sergeant Hitomi, 218, 254, 261

W

Warehouse Raid (mission), 202-6
White Hats, Black Markets (mission), 243-45
White Hooks, 229, 231
Wounded (condition), 143

Y

York and the Boroughs, 56

Z

Zones, 139, 200
      movement and, 123
      number of, 194
      types of, 140